THE
STRUGGLE
FOR TAIWAN

Also by Sulmaan Wasif Khan

*Haunted by Chaos: China's Grand Strategy
from Mao Zedong to Xi Jinping*

*Muslim, Trader, Nomad, Spy: China's Cold War
and the People of the Tibetan Borderlands*

THE STRUGGLE FOR TAIWAN

A HISTORY OF AMERICA, CHINA, AND THE ISLAND CAUGHT BETWEEN

SULMAAN WASIF KHAN

BASIC BOOKS
NEW YORK

Basic Books
Hachette Book Group
1290 Avenue of the Americas, New York, NY 10104
www.basicbooks.com

Printed in the United States of America

First Edition: May 2024

Published by Basic Books, an imprint of Hachette Book Group, Inc. The Basic
Books name and logo is a trademark of the Hachette Book Group.

The Hachette Speakers Bureau provides a wide range of authors for speaking
events. To find out more, go to hachettespeakersbureau.com or email
HachetteSpeakers@hbgusa.com.

Basic books may be purchased in bulk for business, educational, or promotional use.
For more information, please contact your local bookseller or the Hachette Book Group
Special Markets Department at special.markets@hbgusa.com.

The publisher is not responsible for websites (or their content) that are not
owned by the publisher.

Maps by Kelly Sandefer, Beehive Mapping

Print book interior design by Sheryl Kober

Library of Congress Cataloging-in-Publication Data

Names: Khan, Sulmaan Wasif, author.
Title: The struggle for Taiwan : a history of America, China, and the island caught
    between / Sulmaan Wasif Khan.
Description: First edition. | New York : Basic Books, 2024. | Includes
    bibliographical references and index.
Identifiers: LCCN 2023044326 | ISBN 9781541605046 (hardcover) | ISBN
    9781541605053 (ebook)
Subjects: LCSH: Taiwan—History—1945– | Taiwan—Foreign relations—1945– |
    Taiwan—Foreign relations—China. | China—Foreign relations—Taiwan. |
    United States—Foreign relations—China. | China—Foreign relations—United
    States. | United States—Foreign relations—Taiwan. | Taiwan—Foreign
    relations—United States.
Classification: LCC DS799.818 .K49 2024 | DDC 951.24905—dc23/eng/20240109
LC record available at https://lccn.loc.gov/2023044326

ISBNs: 9781541605046 (hardcover), 9781541605053 (ebook)
LSC-C

Printing 1, 2024

For Odd Arne Westad and Ingunn Bjornson

CONTENTS

RUSSIAN FEDERATION

Sea of
Okhotsk

Kuril Islands

Beijing

NORTH
KOREA

Sea of
Japan

Seoul

SOUTH
KOREA

Tokyo JAPAN

CHINA

Shanghai

East
China
Sea

Fuzhou

Ryukyu Islands

Taipei

Hong
Kong

TAIWAN

South
China
Sea

Philippine
Sea

Northern
Mariana
Islands
(US)

Manila

Guam
(US)

PHILIPPINES

INDONESIA

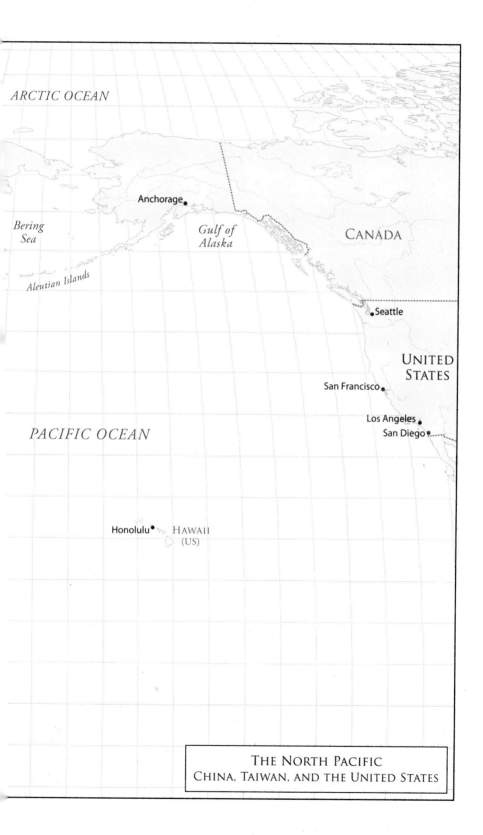

ARCTIC OCEAN

Anchorage

*Bering
Sea*

*Gulf of
Alaska*

CANADA

Aleutian Islands

Seattle

UNITED
STATES

San Francisco

PACIFIC OCEAN

Los Angeles
San Diego

Honolulu • HAWAII
(US)

THE NORTH PACIFIC
CHINA, TAIWAN, AND THE UNITED STATES

Introduction

In the spring and summer of 2022, a new trend swept American policymakers: visits to Taiwan. Strictly speaking, it was a once and possibly future policymaker who started it; news broke that Mike Pompeo, who had served as Trump's secretary of state, would arrive in Taipei in March and meet with Taiwan's president, Tsai Ing-wen. The Biden administration suddenly announced that a team of former defense officials—headed by no less a figure than the former chairman of the Joint Chiefs of Staff Mike Mullen—would be heading to Taiwan too. The delegation arrived just before Pompeo. Mullen, characteristically prudent, spoke of how his delegation, with its mix of Democrat and Republican officials, showcased "the bipartisan nature of support for the United States' strong partnership with Taiwan." As statements of support for Taiwan went, this was quite significant, not least because of the figure delivering it. But it would pale in comparison to the Pompeo show three days later. Newly slimmed down, Pompeo wore a mask in deference to Taiwan's Covid-19 regulations—and his mask sported the flags of the United States and the Republic of China (ROC, which remains, to this day, Taiwan's official name). "The moment," he declared in an interview

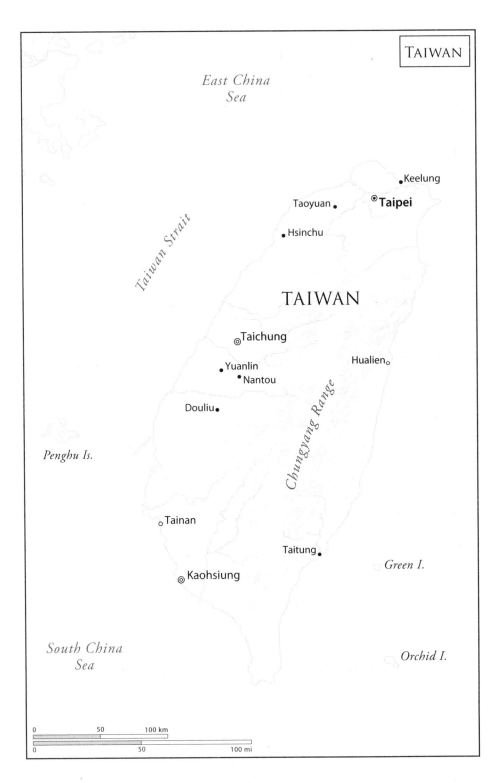

with the *Taipei Times*, "calls for clarity, transparency and a deep recognition of the central idea that we've all known: that Taiwan is not a part of China."[1]

The People's Republic of China (PRC), which had long held that Taiwan was a part of China, was predictably annoyed. But it was with the announcement that Nancy Pelosi had decided to visit Taiwan that Chinese ire came to the boiling point. Pelosi had a long and distinguished track record as a China hawk. She had reveled in unfurling a banner at Tiananmen Square to honor the protesters Beijing had mowed down there in 1989, and now she was set on going to Taiwan to show her support. And to make matters all the more galling, Pelosi was Speaker of the House, third in line for the American presidency. The status mattered. Threats of retaliation burst forth. Hu Xijin, the editor of the nationalistic Chinese tabloid *Global Times*, called for Pelosi's plane to be shot down. (This was unusual: In general, Beijing has been fairly good at keeping propaganda under control. One could threaten, but only within limits; the notion of taking a plane down was taking things too far. It suggested that somehow, somewhere, the governance machine in China was not working quite as it should.) The Biden administration announced that the American military was opposed to the Pelosi trip. None of this stopped Pelosi. She landed in Taipei to rapturous applause and Taiwanese hailing her as the "Celestial Mother of the Western Skies." One enterprising Taiwanese politician celebrated her arrival by treating citizens to "Democracy Fried Chicken."[2]

The PRC did what it always does when most annoyed with Taiwan: it started off another round of military exercises and launched missiles across the Taiwan Strait. And the missiles had the same effect they always have on Taiwan's behavior: they sharpened its resolve. Taiwan's authorities announced that they would hold drills of their own and that they were prepared to weather the storm. Nor did the missiles (which landed in the waters surrounding the island) prove effective at stemming the tide of American officials who suddenly decided that they, too, had to visit Taipei. South Carolina senator Lindsey Graham had already led a delegation of senators; now came the energetic Ed Markey of Massachusetts. Eric Holcomb of Indiana made sure that state governors were represented. Pompeo returned.[3] One began to wonder how President Tsai could possibly find time to govern while catering to the endless flood of visitors.

A historian watching the situation from afar could not help being struck by the odd mix of mendacity, amnesia, and half-truths on display. There was Beijing insisting falsely, if consistently, that Taiwan—about a hundred miles off China's coast—had always been part of China. The Americans, for their part, talked of how democracy was a common bond between the United States and Taiwan. This was true as far as it went, but it glided over the bit where America had propped up a dictator in Taiwan, whose legacy of oppression and torture haunts Taiwanese to this day. Even the name Pompeo used for Taiwan—"Republic of China"—missed the fact that many of the Taiwanese he claimed to be supporting had deeply ambivalent feelings about that name. The ROC, after all, had been a Chinese regime that had imposed rule on Taiwan by force, and had laid claim to all of China, including the large chunk of it across the strait. Taiwan, with its flourishing democracy, was different, its own entity; many Taiwanese thought it was time to change their country's name. Tsai, meanwhile, whose almost painfully bland demeanor concealed the sharpest brain among the leadership of the three countries, did not bother to offer corrections. She simply thanked America for its

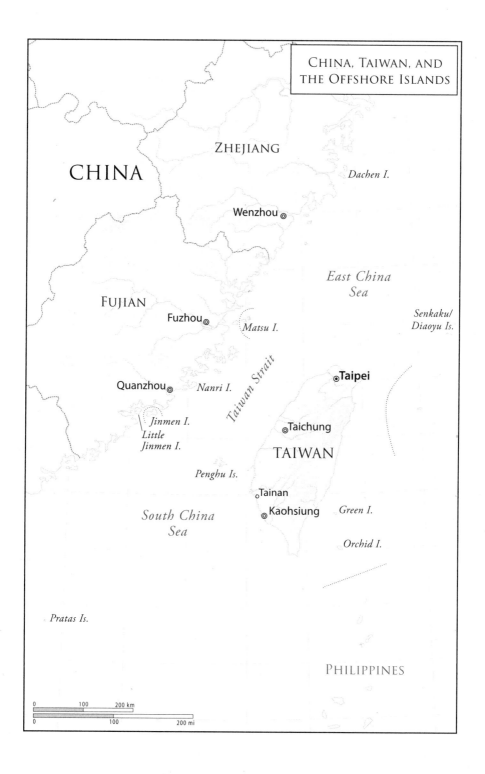

ZHEJIANG

CHINA

Dachen I.

Wenzhou

East China
Sea

FUJIAN

Fuzhou

Matsu I.

Senkaku/
Diaoyu Is.

Taiwan Strait

Taipei

Quanzhou   Nanri I.

Jinmen I.
Little
Jinmen I.

Taichung

TAIWAN

Penghu Is.

Tainan

South China
Sea

Kaohsiung   Green I.

Orchid I.

Pratas Is.

PHILIPPINES

0   100   200 km

0   100   200 mi

support in suitably flattering terms and proceeded with her attempts to get her country on a more secure footing.

Getting the past right matters. Without understanding a country's past experiences—its traumas, the precepts it forged in victory and in suffering, the deep convictions that life has left it with—one cannot understand its present. A failure to understand the American role in Chiang Kai-shek's survival, to take a simple example, means that one will fail to grasp the resentment Taiwanese feel toward the United States to this day. Absent a knowledge of US-China negotiations in the seventies, one cannot grasp the full depth of Beijing's conviction that America's current policy is a betrayal. Our predicament did not emerge in a vacuum. It needs to be set in context if we are to address it properly.

To understand how dangerous this predicament has become, consider an incident that occurred on June 3, 2023. An American destroyer was conducting a transit through the Taiwan Strait. The United States sends ships there to make clear that it considers these to be international waters; China, by contrast, claims the area belongs to the PRC. The American destroyer was on its course when a Chinese warship crossed its bow. The crossing was dangerously close. A collision was avoided only because the American ship decelerated in time.[4] Had the vessels collided, tempers would have frayed and shots might have been fired—at which point, the situation could have escalated to general conflict.

In another time, Washington and Beijing would have been able to dial the tension down. But June 2023 belongs to a different age—one in which anger and distrust have built up to the point where even the shrewdest diplomats would have had a hard time calming tempers after an initial military engagement. The United States has come to see China as an almost mortal foe, the power that, in the words of US secretary of state Antony Blinken, poses the "most serious long-term challenge to the international order." American president Joe Biden has repeatedly vowed that the United States will defend Taiwan against China if it has to. China's president Xi Jinping, meanwhile, sees the United States as leading the West in an attempt to hem China in. Taiwan, to Xi, is indisputably part of China—and like Chinese leaders before him, he has made clear that he reserves the right to use force to take it.[5] Had the Chinese and American ships collided, the full weight of all that accumulated mutual suspicion would have compelled both Biden and Xi to accuse one another of reckless aggression. Demands for compensation and retaliation would have surged in both countries. With a few bad decisions, this would have been the opening salvo in a Sino-American war.

It did not happen in June. But it could have happened then—and with more warships and aircraft in the area, it could happen in the future. Both sides have backed their rhetoric with increased military activity. Chinese aircraft regularly breach Taiwan's air defense identification zone. American ships have continued their passages through the Taiwan Strait. Even absent an accident at sea, China's determination to take Taiwan, Taiwan's determination to maintain its de facto independence, and America's determination to stand up to China have consigned us to perpetual danger.

It is tempting to believe that the path out of that danger is deterrence. Deterrence worked for decades, the story goes, in keeping China and America at peace and Taiwan blissfully independent. Both the US Defense Department and Taiwan's vice president, Lai Ching-te, have espoused their belief in peace through deterrence.[6] A closer look at the past, however, shows that deterrence did not work in isolation. At key moments—notably in 1954–1955 and 1958—luck, more than deterrence, prevented a conflict that could have gone nuclear. In 1995–1996, luck again played a larger role, and then it was strengthened by the genuine belief in Washington and Beijing that the two countries had an interest in getting along with one another, an interest larger than Taiwan's fate. That belief is absent now. And yet deterrence continues to be invoked as a panacea, with little attention paid to the context in which it is being pursued. The leader who places faith in deterrence based on a past incompletely remembered is not unlike the speeding driver who believes that skill guaranteed a safe journey, when it might have had little to do with the drive's safe conclusion. If our driver were to decide that speed can be maintained or even upped for the next trip, all might be well. But throw in a pothole at the wrong moment, or brakes that have been worn and are slow to respond, or another driver drifting suddenly into the speedster's lane, and what should have been a triumph of speed ends in conflagration. A full understanding of the triangular relationship between America, China, and Taiwan is needed if we are to avoid catastrophe.

This book, therefore, seeks to provide a comprehensive account of that relationship over the last eight decades. The story begins in 1943, when the Cairo Declaration first held forth the idea that Taiwan would be part of a Chinese state; it ends with the elections in a democratic, practically independent Taiwan in 2024. I could not have attempted such a survey without the excellent work that others have done on various aspects of those relations, though I have also benefited from primary sources from all three sides.[7] There are, to be sure, inevitable gaps in the record. But there is enough material around to guide us along the paths that brought the three countries to their present moment—and thereby, perhaps, to show where they might go in the future.

Remarkably, confusion has played the starring role in this tale so far. Grand strategy or even planning has had astonishingly little to do with PRC and US policies toward Taiwan. Much has been made of China's plan to break past the first island chain (stretching from Japan to the South China Sea, blocking China's access to the wider Pacific) or of America's plan to maintain primacy in the world. In China, the policy—such as it has been—seems to have been born of a paroxysm of wounded pride, the kind of hurt insistence that has dragged on so long, so loudly, that its original cause and any purpose it might serve have been utterly forgotten. American decisions, taken in the heat of the moment, have accreted over time into commitments that leaders had once sought to avoid. The United States now seems to see Taiwan as a means of "getting tough" on China. What it hopes to accomplish by getting tough, never mind the cost toughness might entail, remains undefined. For two countries that regularly accuse one another of Machiavellian cunning, the great powers have, on this point, proven singularly devoid of purpose. Only in Taiwan can one see careful, consistent, if sometimes risky, planning—particularly after 1971, when Chiang Kai-shek's fantasy of taking back mainland China gave way to the delicate dance of surviving with the PRC off one coast and a distant, temperamental United States off the other. Great powers can afford a pique, a strategic drift, that a small island clawing for survival cannot.

Striking, too, is the absence of inevitability in the whole tale. There was nothing inevitable about Taiwan being turned over to Chiang Kai-shek's Republic of China; indeed, there were several points where the possibility of independence for the island glimmered temptingly. Nor was it inevitable that the United States would support Chiang once he lost the Chinese Civil War to the Communists and fled to Taiwan; American policy, until the Korean War came along, had been to let events take their course. And but for the eccentricities of American politics, the Sino-American rapprochement in 1971 might well have led to Taiwan becoming part of the PRC. That Taiwan would then democratize, that Beijing would invariably alienate Taipei, that Taiwanese democracy would take the stance toward the PRC it took: all these developments were the product of decisions that could have gone several different ways—just as the choices we make today could lead us to several different futures. Even as it charts what happened, therefore, this book lingers over paths untaken. And those paths begin in Cairo.

1

The Making of the Taiwan Problem

1943 to 1953

They sat before a phalanx of cameras. Center stage was US president Franklin Delano Roosevelt, eyes hollow, face shifting from grave purpose to sudden levity, turning, every now and then, to exchange a word with his staff. To FDR's left, Winston Churchill displayed the wry resignation of a man who would rather be anywhere else but who would make the best of the situation fate had forced upon him. The British prime minister did not share FDR's obsession with the importance of China, but Britain's hopes for victory in World War II rested on American money—and both men knew it. So Churchill removed his hat, chatted with Madame Chiang Kai-shek, and finally puffed on the inevitable cigar.[1]

It was the man to FDR's right who caught the eye. Of all three men, it was he who most forcefully conveyed the image of a warrior. Trim, ramrod straight, impeccable in his uniform, every inch a soldier. Only two things marred Generalissimo Chiang Kai-shek's stern martial bearing: the fly that kept landing on his right cheek and the slight smile that every now and then forced its way across his lips.

Chiang had reason to smile. Here in Cairo, he was meeting FDR and Churchill for the first time. At least ostensibly, he was their equal. As leader of the Republic of China, he had been admitted as one of the "three great allies" doing battle against Germany and Japan in World War II. Best of all, the Cairo Declaration of November 26, 1943, that emerged from this meeting promised Chiang the return of territories that Japan had wrested from China:

> The three great Allies are fighting this war to restrain and punish the aggression of Japan. They covet no gain for themselves and have no thought of territorial expansion. It is their purpose that Japan, shall be stripped of all the islands in the Pacific which she has seized or occupied since the beginning of the first World War in 1914, and that all the territories Japan has stolen from the Chinese, such as Manchuria, Formosa, and the Pescadores, shall be restored to the Republic of China. Japan will also be expelled from all other territories which she has taken by violence and greed.[2]

This was quite a list of territories that the ROC was to get back. The losses dated not just to World War I, as the declaration mentioned, but to 1895, when China, defeated in war, was forced to cede

Taiwan (Formosa) and the Pescadores to Japan. To be promised all this at the end of the war was a coup for the generalissimo.

It would not quite work out that way. America never fully understood what it was getting into when it allied with Chiang; the US government would find itself shocked by the commitments it was dragged into. Chiang, for his part, was triumphant in World War II, only to lose China to the Chinese Communist Party (CCP). He was left with the consolation of having reclaimed Taiwan even as the Taiwanese populace turned against him. He would be able to hold on to it only because of the Korean War and the confusion about China that would remain the hallmark of American policy.

There was one crucial point the Cairo Declaration fudged: the entity that had lost Taiwan to Japan was not Chiang's China. From 1644 to 1911, China had been ruled by the Qing Empire. The empire had been formed by Manchus who had come pouring down from Manchuria (which also had not been part of China; it took the Qing to weave the region into the empire), defeated the Ming dynasty, and, bit by bit, conquered not just the former Ming territories but vast swaths of Central Asia. It was only in 1683 that the Qing seized Taiwan. Until the Qing era, it is worth emphasizing, the island had not belonged to China; indeed, its very existence did not register with most Chinese. It was populated mostly by aboriginals of Austronesian descent, and the few eccentrics from China who did take note of it seem to have been struck most of all by how different it was from China. The Ming-era traveler Chen Di, who made it to Taiwan in 1603, called the islanders "Eastern barbarians" and went so far as to mourn their interaction with Chinese traders: "Since they have come into communication with China they have developed some desires. . . . I am afraid their pure simplicity is becoming more and more corrupted."[3]

To the outside world, the island was a way station along the maritime corridors connecting East and Southeast Asia, a place where pirates, fishermen, and traders would stop before sailing on. There had been a small population of Chinese there, but they were far outnumbered by the aboriginals. Only with the arrival of the Dutch and their need for labor would the Chinese population grow. In 1661, after engaging in a series of pitched battles with Qing forces, Zheng Chenggong—pirate, dreamer, warlord, and self-proclaimed Ming loyalist—decamped to Taiwan, where he defeated the Dutch forces and ousted them from the island. Zheng died in 1662, but his successors kept harassing the Chinese coast. When the Three Feudatories rebellion challenged Qing rule in China between 1673 and 1681, the forces on Taiwan gave it their support. The Qing took this enemy seriously and—aided by an erstwhile rival, Shi Lang, who had switched sides to join them—finally conquered the island in 1683.[4]

Conquering the forces on the island did not necessitate keeping it. The object of this campaign had been to defeat an enemy; with that accomplished, it was not clear that the expense of fortifying the island was necessary. The question caused considerable debate in the Qing court. Only the argument that someone else would take it if the Qing did not moved the emperor, Kangxi, to keep Taiwan. Kangxi was wary of the European maritime presence in the region. The idea of a potentially hostile power offshore was not one he would countenance. Taiwan, therefore, was incorporated into the Qing Empire. But the Qing were motivated by maritime geopolitics, not sacred history.[5]

Two key points emerge from this narrative. First, Taiwan had not been part of China before 1683. Second, it became—and this was by no means a given—part of the Qing Empire, not China. At its peak, that empire stretched from Taiwan to Central Asia. It included, among other possessions, present-day Mongolia and large tracts of Russia. Taiwan and China were not one state but parts of an empire forged by conquest. And the Qing were wary of letting Han Chinese migrate to Taiwan; they did not want the Chinese to have a chance of plotting rebellion. Not that migration was stopped entirely—enterprising coastal itinerants from Fujian and Guangdong made up the bulk of the Han who moved to Taiwan—but it was restricted.[6] As the empire saw it, Taiwan and China were different, and it was best that they stayed that way.

The decline and fall of an imperial dynasty can be a long, convoluted process, the product of a confluence of different forces. Like other rulers, the Qing were susceptible to "imperial overstretch": the costs of holding on to those far-flung territories began to outweigh the benefits. Meanwhile, the outside world had changed. Kangxi had been wary of Western naval power—he had judged it a major threat—but his successors had not devised a plan to deal with it. The importance of sea power would become apparent in 1842, when British forces defeated the Qing in the First Opium War. The Qing were then compelled to sign the Treaty of Nanjing, the first of a series of "unequal treaties" in which a foreign power would barge in with gunboats, demand trade, and carve off part of China as a special enclave where its citizens could enjoy freedom from Chinese law. Americans, Germans, French, and Russians all followed suit. Rebellion broke out across the empire. The Taiping uprising, notably, would see rebels take the southern part of China before the Qing finally managed to put the rebellion down.[7] The empire's power was clearly on the wane.

But the unkindest cut came in 1894, when Japan went to war with the Qing dynasty. At the time, few observers rated Japan's chances against the Qing highly. But the Meiji restoration had seen Japan undertake serious military reform; its armed forces, particularly the navy, had become exemplars of modern professionalism. The defeat of the Qing forces was bewilderingly swift and devastating. The war marked Japan's emergence as a serious military power. And like the Western powers, Japan would impose an unequal treaty on China. The Treaty of Shimonoseki concluded the war in 1895. But peace came at a cost. The treaty forced the Qing to cede Taiwan to Japan in perpetuity.[8]

Taiwan's loss was just the beginning of the empire's dismemberment. The Qing had been moving toward constitutional reform, but the very act of political change encouraged unrest. The Boxers United in Righteousness stormed the capital in 1900, seeking to oust the foreigners in what they saw as patriotic support for the government. Foreigners and the Qing government alike would turn against them and put them down. But the Qing Empire was running out of time. Revolution came in 1911. It owed its success, in part, to the broad spectrum of society it encompassed: political idealists agitating for a republican government, generals discontented with their power, local powerbrokers who felt they could do better without the Qing. But that very breadth meant that keeping China together would prove difficult. The decisive blow against the Qing had been struck not by Sun Yat-sen—who founded the Kuomintang (KMT), a political party calling for democratic governance, in 1912 and had been raising funds for revolution—but by Yuan Shikai. Yuan had been a general in the Qing forces before defecting and demanding that the emperor abdicate. In 1912, the Qing submitted to that demand and Yuan would become president of the newly founded Republic of China.[9]

The republic was surprisingly swift to win international recognition. The United States, touched by Yuan's appeals that America pray for his country, led the way in 1913. Britain and Japan followed suit. But Yuan's dictatorial ways failed to keep the loose alliance of revolutionaries together. He would declare the Kuomintang a seditious organization; he sought to terminate the republic and found his own dynasty. In this latter attempt, he failed, but he did catalyze China's balkanization. Provinces seceded and came under the sway of warlords, although the term "warlord" obscures the functions of sovereignty these men exercised. They could tax citizens, sign treaties with foreign powers, and summon up armed forces to do their will. Not all the territories that had made up the vast empire agreed that they owed allegiance to the Republic of China. Tibet became functionally independent; Mongolia became a Soviet satellite, as, in a different way, did Xinjiang. These were all states, just as much as the republic was.[10] There was not one China at this time, but several.

Unification was far from foreordained. It would be pursued most vigorously by two actors: the Kuomintang and the Chinese Communist Party, which was founded in 1921. The KMT was the first to start integrating bits of China together. After being branded seditionist by Yuan, the party had managed to regroup in Guangdong. Its success in taking back much of China—limited success, for even at its peak the KMT never controlled as much territory as the Qing had or as the CCP later would—owed much to Chiang Kai-shek, who emerged as Sun Yat-sen's successor. Sun had been a skilled fundraiser, but he was ineffectual at unifying territory. Chiang's triumph was due to several factors. First, there was his sheer ruthlessness. He understood, in a way Sun had not, the importance of using force, and he did not mind being an authoritarian. The Chinese race, as he saw it, was superior, but this did not make the Chinese fit for democracy. Chiang believed in Confucianism, in Christianity, and, above all, in his own destined rule. To this ruthlessness, he added the right connections. His marriage to Soong Mei-ling, Sun Yat-sen's sister-in-law, brought him political capital at home and abroad. The marriage strengthened Chiang's position within the KMT. Soong Mei-ling was a shrewd diplomat herself, popular in America. So, too, was Chiang's new brother-in-law, T. V. Soong, who would prove adept at convincing foreigners to fund the Kuomintang's military adventures.[11]

But perhaps the key source of Chiang's success in unifying territory was the willingness of others to cooperate with him. Tired of the infighting among various armed groups, several warlords agreed to cooperate with Chiang in getting rid of their rivals to form an integrated polity. In 1926, Chiang launched the Northern Expedition, which would bring territorial integrity to much of China. The expedition drew strength from Chiang's military prowess, but it also owed much to the fact that he was working in concert with other forces in China. That cooperation extended, temporarily, to the Chinese Communist Party. The Soviet Union—after much internal debate between Leon Trotsky and Joseph Stalin—encouraged a united front between the KMT and the fledgling CCP. (An idealistic young man named Mao Zedong held official KMT positions under this united front.) But when the alliance of convenience had served its purpose, Chiang launched a savage assault upon the Communists. He was suspicious of left-wing elements, as were many of the financiers, industrial magnates, and mafia members who had helped him along on the path to power. The Shanghai massacre of 1927 saw the Communist rank and file, not to mention ordinary citizens, butchered by Chiang's forces. A handful of the CCP's members would escape, but for the time being, Chiang's government seemed secure.[12]

The twisting, turning emergence of the Republic of China would make China's claim to Taiwan a little less certain than the Cairo Declaration made it sound. A state emerging from the ruins of empire by no means has automatic claim to all the territory the empire once possessed. But what made matters all the more complicated was that even after the Northern Expedition, much of China remained out of Chiang's control. A rival claimant to China and its territories could emerge. There were warlords to the west and north. Tibet remained out of reach. And above all, the Communists still survived. They maintained that their Jiangxi soviet—the patch of territory they controlled—was a state. Chiang would squander his strength on a series of "bandit extermination" campaigns aimed at finishing the Communists once and for all. These were almost successful; he dislodged the CCP from the Jiangxi soviet in 1934. The defeated CCP survived only by undertaking the storied Long March, trudging some six thousand miles to establish a new foothold in Yan'an.[13] The Communists' state had been dislodged from its original territory, and they had gone scurrying across China. But they still had significant power and were learning all the time.

That Communist forces were left alive would come back to haunt Chiang later. But there was a more immediate problem. In focusing so heavily on the Communists, Chiang was expending strength better directed toward the larger, more sinister threat to his regime: Japan.

Seizing Taiwan in 1895 had by no means sated Japan's appetite for control of East Asia. It had gone to war with Russia in 1904, winning the southern portion of Sakhalin Island. It had annexed Korea formally in 1910. It had worked with local Chinese warlords to exert power in the remains of the Qing Empire. In 1931, it invaded Manchuria and, by 1932, set up a puppet regime there, trotting out the deposed Qing ruler, Henry Puyi, as the Xuantong emperor of Manchukuo.[14] No one was any under illusions, however, that Manchuria was anything but a Japanese colony.

In China, many were wary of where Japan would strike next. There were those in Chiang's forces who believed that this was no time to be fighting the CCP; it was time for China to unite against Japan. Chiang's was a rule that had always relied on strongmen agreeing to cooperate with him. The warlords who were part of the ROC government worked with Chiang because they felt it was in their interests, but they understood force and were willing to use it against the generalissimo if they calculated it was necessary. That was what happened in 1936. Two of Chiang's generals, Zhang Xueliang and Yang Hucheng, finally decided to kidnap Chiang to force him to come to terms with the Communists. The generalissimo was irate, but he was compelled to agree to hold off on further bandit extermination campaigns for the time being. (Not that he would forgive or forget: Zhang was later placed under house arrest and Yang would be executed.) The CCP was willing to cooperate. By 1937, the CCP (now under Mao's leadership) and the KMT were, ostensibly, united against Japan. But the Communists—who had suffered at

Chiang's hands before—were under no illusions that peace could be guaranteed forever.[15]

The coming of full-fledged war with Japan in July 1937 put this fragile unity to the test. Chiang's China, by virtue of its geographic position, bore the full brunt of the Japanese assault. Mao's China—though it would launch guerrilla operations against the Japanese and refrain from attacking Chiang's forces—was given time and space to regroup. Neither the CCP nor the KMT was above considering the possibility of coming to terms with Japan, the better to secure its own regime against the other. And the ease with which Japan conquered large parts of China had allowed it to set up a collaborationist government in 1940. Wang Jingwei's regime in Nanjing governed by Japanese sufferance, but it did purport to represent China.[16] Chiang's claim to sovereignty was far from impregnable.

There were, in sum, multiple states in the territory that had once belonged to the Qing—and the full extent of their claims was yet to be determined. China's civil wars might have paused temporarily, overshadowed by World War II, but there was nothing to stop their resumption in due course. Chiang stood at Cairo as the proud claimant of lost Chinese territory. There were Chinese who would contest that claim.

The messy politics and civil wars of contemporary China mattered not a jot to Franklin Delano Roosevelt. Nor did the checkered past that marked his own country's dealings with China weigh on him. American traders had come thronging to the China market since 1784, when a ship called *Empress of China* sailed from New York to

Guangdong. The trade grew, and with it came missionaries, eager to save Chinese souls. Profit and religion bound the United States to China.

The American government would use both diplomacy and force to protect its interests in China. The British imposition of the Treaty of Nanjing inspired the United States to follow up with the Treaty of Wangxia with the Qing in 1844, which would grant the Americans most-favored-nation status in trade with China. When the Taiping rebels waged war against the Qing from 1850 to 1864, the Americans would decide that Qing survival was in their interests. Like other foreigners, American soldiers would fight the Taiping, and guns from the American Civil War wound up circulating in China. In the scramble to exploit China, the United States was not to be left behind. It made a point of insisting on the "territorial integrity of China" when it advocated an Open Door policy in 1899 and 1900—which was a polite way of asking that the great powers who had carved China up not close their particular enclaves to traders from other great powers. When Chinese peasants, incensed by the foreigners lording over their land, marched into Beijing in 1900, the United States was one of the countries that would send troops to suppress them. In the ruthlessness with which it sought to protect its position in China, the United States was akin to other Western empires.

With that ruthlessness, there was a streak of idealism—though this would often lead to disappointment. The indemnity the Qing court would pay for the damage from the Boxer uprising was used to bring Chinese students to the United States. But the presence of Chinese in the country fueled racism, as Americans worried endlessly about the Yellow Peril. During World War I, Washington had suggested it would support China's demands for the restoration of its territories, only for those demands to go unmet at the Treaty of Versailles. It was a betrayal that China never forgot.

The illusion persists that the United States was isolationist in the interwar years; its decision to walk away from the League of Nations that its own president had called for is cited as evidence. But withdrawal from the League did not signal a retreat from world affairs or from the Asia-Pacific. In 1921–1922, the United States had convened the Washington Conference to discuss naval reduction with the other great powers, so as to maintain peace in East Asia. At this conference, the United States once again asked that all parties affirm the "territorial integrity of China."[17] As with the Open Door policy, this was not a stance meant to protect Chinese sovereignty; rather, it was meant to make sure that all the great powers—the United States, Japan, and Britain, principally—had equal opportunities to trade with and invest in China. Since its beginnings, US conduct toward China was an odd mix of exploitation, occasional flashes of altruism, and willful blindness.

FDR's China policy was very much in this tradition. There was a massive gap between the China FDR wanted and the China America got. To the president, China was an ally in the war against Japan and one of the regional policemen he thought would ensure peace and security after the war. Reality was more complicated.

The United States had been suspicious of Japanese activity since Japan annexed Manchuria. Secretary of State Henry Stimson had declared that the United States would not recognize any arrangement between China and Japan that violated American rights in the region or agreements to which the United States was party. When Japan attacked Shanghai in 1932 (a cease-fire was eventually reached, with Shanghai demilitarized), Stimson held that the United States would no longer be bound by the agreements reached at the Washington Conference. American suspicion of Japan deepened, and the United States eventually moved to counter Japanese power. In 1940, Washington placed sanctions on Japan, choking its supply of materials that could be used in war. Rather than deterring further adventures in Asia, the sanctions fueled Japanese resentment toward the United States. And the hardening line on Japan came with an attempt to back China's efforts against that country. Pilot Claire Chennault was training American volunteers to serve as part of Chiang's fledgling air force. American aid to China meant that, from 1940 on, China's war effort against Japan was drawing material support from the United States. At this point, for all its official neutrality, the United States was already a participant in World War II. The Japanese attack on Pearl Harbor on December 7, 1941, meant that Japan and America were officially at war. That attack gave China a new lease on life, as Chiang's resistance to Japan in China—crumbling and ineffectual as it was—became something important for America to buttress. Chennault's Flying Tigers were finally able to move beyond their informal role and take to the skies in combat. General Joseph Stilwell was dispatched to China to lead Chiang's forces against Japan in 1942.[18] America and China were allies.

It was here that the curious gulf between Americans on the ground and official Washington first became apparent. FDR saw a potential ally in China and Chiang. Americans serving in China, by contrast, saw a country that was divided and a leader who was incompetent. Stilwell was not shy about sharing his opinion on Chiang—"Peanut," as he called the generalissimo—peppering Washington with messages on how unwilling Chiang was to fight. Chiang was quick to demand American supplies to maintain the war effort, but he was somehow unwilling to commit those supplies to offensive maneuvers against the Japanese. The survival of his own regime was paramount. American foreign service officers in the country at the time—people like John Paton Davies and Jack Service—were the best the United States would have there: experienced, hard-headed individuals, born and raised in China, with as extensive a knowledge of that country as any American had. Like Stilwell, they were skeptical of how far Chiang was willing to go. "We recognized before December 7, 1941 that China was endeavoring to get us to fight its battle against Japan," Davies would note. "China's policy, now that we are fighting the Japanese, is to remain technically in the war so as to be able to sit at the peace table as a 'fighting' ally, to expend as little as possible of its strength and to rely upon other members of the United Nations—primarily the United States—to defeat Japan." Praise of Chiang Kai-shek's army, Davies believed, was "intemperate," perpetuated by clever China lobbyists. (He would observe, too, that the Communist forces were unusual among Chinese for being high on morale.) Davies was by no means alone in voicing concerns about Chiang's competence and dependability. As late as May 10, 1944, an American foreign service officer would report that the KMT was hoarding some of its best divisions to "blockade" the CCP, rather than directing them against Japanese.[19] There might be a united front in name, but the generalissimo was still as intent on waging war against the CCP as against Japan. Americans on the ground saw a very different China and Chiang than FDR did.

None of these concerns shifted FDR's policy. He would, on occasion, politely ask Chiang to be more cooperative, and he would go so far as to direct Stilwell to find someone else to work with, but the threat that would have been effective—cutting off Chiang's money supply—was one that the American president was unwilling to carry out. A threat has to be followed through on to be any good, and FDR felt that he could not afford to do without Chiang. The American president had a grander picture in mind. The war had come, so he believed, because of an old imperial order where there was no effective collective security mechanism. FDR was going to create a new postwar order, with regional policemen in charge of security—the "United Nations," as he had already dubbed them. China was to be one of those policemen. Its case was helped by the popularity it was winning in Washington. Chiang's wife, Soong Mei-ling, spoke first-rate English, had a Wellesley education, and, to top it all off, was a devout Protestant; she was, in short, the perfect DC lobbyist, even if she alienated some people. She was adored by the influential founder of *Time* magazine, Henry Luce, which gave her access to the rich and powerful in the capital. And when all was said and done, it was Chiang's China that was on the front lines of the war with Japan.[20] China was fighting. America had to keep it in the fight. The rest would just have to take care of itself.

There were two broad problems with FDR's policy. The first was that however anti-imperial the president might perceive himself to be, his Chinese partner was seeking to reconstitute an empire. Chiang's demands were not confined to Taiwan and the Pescadores. He wanted Manchuria, which had not been a part of China but was the springboard from which the Qing launched their invasion of China. He would insist that Outer Mongolia was part of China too. He had had some idea of claiming the Ryukyu Islands but eventually settled for suggesting that they be administered by China and the United States in tandem. He even seems to have wanted to retain some influence in Korea, though the record does not allow an exact reconstruction of his exchanges with Roosevelt on the matter. He would continue to claim Tibet and Xinjiang. He was, in short, reclaiming territories that had not been administered by China but by the Qing Empire, which had conquered China and held it along with those other territories. If Roosevelt indeed wished to put an end to empire, this was not quite the way to do it. But none of this stopped the American president. Cairo was his chance to meet his Chinese ally, and it was where he would agree that Taiwan would become a part of China. (Remarkably, American records of much of the discussion in Cairo remain unavailable; FDR appears to have carefully avoided keeping records of sensitive meetings there.) Whatever his faults, there was a certain sincerity to Roosevelt's anti-imperialism. His advisors had thought it worth considering military bases on Taiwan in the postwar world; the president, however, made it clear that any future military presence on the island would have to be a cooperative venture, with due deference to Chiang's sovereignty. Permanent base rights were out of the question because Chiang would not agree.[21] Insisting on bases unilaterally just because one was in a position to do so was what imperial powers did, and America was adamantly not an imperial power. That there was something imperialistic about distributing territory in this casual manner—a handshake at Cairo, without any thought of what the people whose future was being decided might want—did not register with the president.

This was not a course that Roosevelt had to take. If he had chosen to insist on self-determination for Taiwan in the postwar future, Chiang would have had little choice but to yield. The generalissimo's claim to Mongolia was squashed at Yalta by the one person who had greater leverage than FDR at the time: Joseph Stalin. Mongolia would stay independent, Stalin said, and though T. V. Soong, Chiang's representative, tried to explain that this was unfeasible, there was no getting away from it. What a great power wanted, a great power got. (Chiang was not above revisiting the matter. In 1955, when he and the Soviet Union had long fallen out with one another, Chiang would have his ambassador at the United Nations veto Mongolia's application for membership in that organization. Mongolia was not a sovereign state, the ambassador argued, but just Outer Mongolia, a part of the Republic of China. The move was in defiance of American wishes, but Chiang was willing to undertake it nonetheless.) Stalin was openly contemptuous of the Chinese; he thought the Cairo Declaration was fine but the Chinese needed to be "made to fight," which, according to him, they had not done. That they had fought badly Stalin held to be the fault of their leaders. He could not understand why Roosevelt wanted the Chinese in this international organization he was obsessed with; they were weak, and the Europeans would not like it. Roosevelt explained that "he was thinking farther into the future and that after all China was a nation of 400 million people, and it was better to have them as friends rather than as a potential source of trouble."[22] It made a certain amount of sense—but it missed the bit where those four hundred million people fighting with one another would make them difficult to fit in an international organization. Herein lay the second problem with FDR's China policy. It was premised on a cohesive, unified, reasonably well-governed China. This was a China that, as he was being told, he simply did not have.

It was not that Roosevelt was altogether unaware of the problem of Chinese infighting. It was just that he understood it poorly enough to send the worst possible person to deal with it. Patrick Hurley had served as secretary of war, risen to the rank of major general in the

US Army, and, Republican roots notwithstanding, inveigled his way into sundry diplomatic missions for FDR. These attributes seem to have outweighed his brashness for the president, who appointed Hurley his personal envoy to China. Hurley was utterly confident in his ability to make peace between the CCP and the KMT. Entranced by the generalissimo, he was the opposite of an even-handed interlocutor; he would help Chiang get Stilwell removed. To Chiang, Stilwell was an insult. It was unbefitting the dignity of a Chinese leader to be told how to dispose of his troops by a foreigner, and Stilwell's insistence that Chiang work with the Communists was simply unbearable. Hurley was far more congenial. When Hurley obtained a commitment from the CCP to cooperate with the KMT, Chiang insisted that the CCP's forces would have to be subsumed by his. Another representative might have seen the impossibility of this. But Hurley was willing to do Chiang's bidding: his eagerness to go back to Mao with Chiang's demands would cost America a great deal of credibility with a party that shrewd observers were already seeing as China's future. The failure did not harm Hurley's career; he would be appointed ambassador to China.[23] FDR's was the sunny confidence of a great power coming of age, adamant that it could and should remake the world. If the warnings of his own officials gave him pause, the president's policy never showed it.

Neither FDR nor Chiang knew much about Taiwan. How could they? Taiwan had been Japanese for almost as long as either of them could remember, and they had little understanding of how complex the feelings of a colony can be. The Japanese colonial adventure in Taiwan had got off to a rocky start. Taiwanese, angered at not being consulted in their cession, launched a guerrilla war, which claimed more Japanese soldiers than the Sino-Japanese War of 1894-1895 had. But by World War II, the empire had had time to learn how to govern. The governance was never free of racial supremacism; in Taiwan, people had known the pain that comes from being second-class citizens. But though they spoke Japanese only because their imperial rulers had demanded it, decades later, many older Taiwanese would remain more comfortable, more themselves in that language. For some, at least, Japanese rule had meant advancement, opportunity, and greater life expectancy than they would have had in China. Some would fight as members of the Japanese armed forces; some would fight to overthrow the Japanese Empire.[24] Being the model colony, Taiwan had been spared some of the contempt that Korea would receive—a legacy that marks Japan's relations with both its erstwhile possessions to this day.

The sense of identity that emerged on Taiwan, therefore, was odd and fractured. There were those who would consider themselves Japanese, those who would consider themselves Taiwanese, those who hearkened to their Chinese roots, those who identified as Hakka, those who belonged to specific aboriginal tribes, and those whose attachment was purely to the square patch where they farmed, marketed, and lived. At its core, identity is about experience—and experience can be complex, multifaceted, disorienting. Su Beng, for example, who would become a prominent activist for Taiwanese independence, recalled growing up in the Japanese colonial era and watching the activities of groups like the Taiwanese Cultural Association and the Taiwan Autonomy Alliance. These were groups opposed to Japanese rule, and their names reflected a sense of Taiwanese identity. His mother would instill in him a fear of the Japanese police. But Su Beng would also recall the evenhandedness with which his Japanese teacher at school treated both the Japanese and

Taiwanese students there and, later, his joy at enrolling in Waseda University in Tokyo. When, after the political awakening that Waseda provided, he ran away to join the Chinese Communist Party in Zhangjiakou, he was accompanied by a Japanese girlfriend. (Joining the CCP was by no means incompatible with a stand for Taiwanese independence: Mao, as Su Beng would note, had suggested that both Taiwan and Korea could be independent when talking with Edgar Snow.)[25]

Peng Ming-min, who would also become a Taiwanese independence activist and later a presidential candidate, recalled a "complex feeling" upon hearing of the Sino-Japanese War: schoolteachers denouncing the ungrateful Chinese for refusing Japan's selfless offer to modernize their country, parents celebrating the valor China had shown in resisting. If Japanese officialdom was discriminatory, there were also Japanese who felt that discrimination against Taiwanese was unacceptable. (Japan had tried and failed to get a clause on racial equality written into the Treaty of Versailles of 1919. The failure had rankled, and Japan's colonial subjects had not been shy in persisting with that demand on their own behalf.)[26] You could assert independence from the Japanese Empire and still fall in love with the country and with individuals from it. Where all this would go was uncertain. It was likely that Taiwanese would welcome the end of the war, but what destiny they would choose for themselves in that postwar world was incalculable.

This was a level of complexity for which the KMT was entirely unprepared. There had been some discussion of how to administer Taiwan when victory came. Was it to be run as a special administrative region, along the lines of Xinjiang, Tibet, or Mongolia? Should it be treated like any other district? Or was it something in between? To many of the discussants, it was simple. True, there were a handful of foreigners and Japanese on the island, but the overwhelming majority of the population was Taiwanese. And Taiwanese, in essence, were transplants from Fujian and Guangdong. Years of Japanese colonial rule might have made a slight difference, but with proper education, there was no reason they could not be trained to think correctly within, say, a couple of years. The Soviets, after all, had absorbed people from Belarus, west Ukraine, and the Baltic states. Why could China not do the same?[27] It was a view as astonishingly arrogant as it was totalitarian: people could simply be educated into being like everyone else. And it boded ill for that day FDR and Chiang had anticipated, when Taiwan would be reunited with China.

The United States hit Hiroshima with the first nuclear bomb on August 6, 1945. On August 8, Stalin declared war on Japan. On August 9, Soviet troops were on their way to Manchuria and Korea; that same day, the United States dropped a second nuclear bomb, this time on Nagasaki. By August 15, 1945, the Japanese emperor announced that Japan had surrendered.[28]

Now began the difficult process of redistributing the defeated empire's holdings. A broad range of fates awaited those territories. Zones of occupation could carve a territory up. This was Korea's fate: it was divided between American and Soviet forces, with the understanding that it would, in due course, be reunified, held as a trusteeship (administered by the United Nations until it was judged ready for independence), and then become sovereign. A victorious power could hold on to territory before ceding it to another country:

the Soviets still occupied Manchuria but were supposed to withdraw their troops and return it to China. And a country could simply reclaim the territory it had once lost. Moscow would keep the Kuril Islands, which Russia had lost to Japan. In China itself, exhausted Japanese officials surrendered to their Chinese counterparts. American soldiers—there were about sixty thousand in China around the time of the Japanese surrender—helped oversee the process. Across the strait, ROC soldiers and officials started arriving on Taiwan to accept the Japanese surrender and commence their administration of the island. Fifty years of Japanese rule were at an end. The Japanese on the island numbered over three hundred thousand. Most were repatriated. Overwhelmingly, they surrendered without resistance.[29]

The Japanese repatriation was only one of the population shifts Taiwan was experiencing. By 1949, there would be over 6 million native born Taiwanese—*benshengren*, as they came to be called—whose ancestors had settled on the island in centuries past. The KMT's takeover of Taiwan would bring between one and two million immigrants from mainland China; these were dubbed the *waishengren*, people from outside districts. (Some two hundred thousand aboriginals still lived in Taiwan, but as a political factor, they were considered irrelevant by both *benshengren* and *waishengren*.) It was the relationship between these two groups that would set the tenor for Taiwan's politics.[30]

But all that lay in the future. What is surprising, looking back at 1945, is how peaceful the initial transfer of power was. The Taiwanese lined up to welcome their Chinese compatriots. There was a touch of condescension as they registered the bedraggled looks and uncouth manners of the soldiers—not least because the KMT troops were accompanied by American advisors. There were jokes about how, even now, they did not dare face the Japanese without American protection. But it would take time and grievance for condescension to give way to hostility. Chen Yi, Chiang's new administrator, would make a speech, celebrating the recovery of the island and holding out a vision of how it would become a new Taiwan, based on Sun Yat-sen's Three Principles. There was an opportunity here for the ROC to win Taiwanese over to the idea that China was something worth belonging to. But the soldiers looting whatever they could, the officials squeezing every last drop of profit they could, and Chen's stacking his office with mainlanders rather than Taiwanese—these were things that the Taiwanese would find hard to forgive.[31]

Back in China, it looked as though the end of one war would mean the resumption of another. Chiang's truce with the Communists had always been a precarious one; talks in Chongqing in 1945 did little to stabilize it. Now, as Chiang basked in the official recognition of the United States and Mao sought to hold on to the territory he had gained, there were signs that the truce might break down. The curious thing is that United States, rather than clinging to its official recognition of Chiang's KMT government as the sole legitimate ruler of China, made a good-faith effort to broker a new peace between the two sides. The emergence of the Cold War—American diplomat George Kennan would sound the alarm in his "Long Telegram" on February 22, 1946—would soon see a knee-jerk anti-Communism coming to define American foreign policy.[32] Congressional hearings about the losses to Communism, invasions, proxy wars, coups successful and unsuccessful—all these lay in the not too distant future. But throughout 1946, the story of American policy toward China was one of a great power willing to accept its limitations. Perhaps this was because the envoy the United States dispatched to China was General George Marshall. Marshall had the pragmatism to realize that he could not solve China's problems for the Chinese, and his standing at home meant that there would be acceptance (though imperfect) of his decisions.

The Marshall mission is often remembered as a failure, an American attempt to settle a peace between two sides that were never going to reach one. But seen in another light, it was as successful a mission as one could hope for. Marshall went and tried; domestic politics and mere goodwill demanded at least the effort. But it was a fruitless task. Chiang kept demanding, as he had with Hurley, that the Communist forces be integrated into his. This would have been tantamount to Mao giving up sovereignty altogether, which he had no intention of doing and which Marshall never expected him to do absent a truly democratic China. Interestingly enough, Mao seems to have entertained the possibility of reaching a modus vivendi with Chiang. As long as Mao kept control of the territory he had won, the final settlement of the differences between the two leaders was something that could await the future. Two Chinas—each with their own capital, their own troops, occasionally engaged in armed conflict but resigned to one another's existence—would have been a feasible outcome in early 1946.[33] But Chiang was having none of it, and he let Marshall know as much.

Marshall tried for thirteen months but failed to broker a lasting deal between the KMT and CCP. His acceptance of that failure came with a desire to drop Chiang as a military ally. Rather than fighting for a partner who showed no interest in being reasonable, it was time to cut America's losses and let events in China take their course. It seems perfectly logical in retrospect—and yet, Marshall could have recommended committing troops to support Chiang. Had he done so, the United States would have probably spent the early Cold War in a quagmire that made Vietnam look like a picnic. Given where American policy on such choices would wind up during the Cold War (the commitment to South Vietnam comes to mind), Marshall's decision was a shining exemplar of what policy should look like. There were limits to his accomplishment. He was unable to turn off the spigot of economic aid flowing from America to Chiang. But he kept American troops out of the Chinese Civil War, despite demands from both Chiang and voices within the American establishment.[34] He went; he investigated what could be done; he decided to live with what he could not change.

Chiang fired the opening shots in the Chinese Civil War in 1946, while Marshall was still shuttling haplessly between the CCP and KMT. The Soviet Union had been occupying Manchuria since it joined the war against Japan in August 1945. In March 1946, Stalin decided to withdraw his troops. To Chiang, this was an excellent opportunity to seize territory. KMT forces attacked their CCP counterparts on March 31. There was nothing foreordained about Chiang's defeat in the civil war. As late as 1948, the struggle could have gone his way. There were many reasons for his loss—the tactical brilliance of some of the CCP generals, the desertion of some of the KMT troops, luck—but one in particular stood out: his government's capacity to alienate the people it governed.[35] Its heavy-handedness and corruption fueled rebellion. Perhaps the clearest demonstration of that dynamic came not in the main theater of the Chinese Civil War but in Taiwan, on February 28, 1947.

The 228 incident, as it came to be known, started off simply enough. Mismanagement and corruption meant that Taiwan's

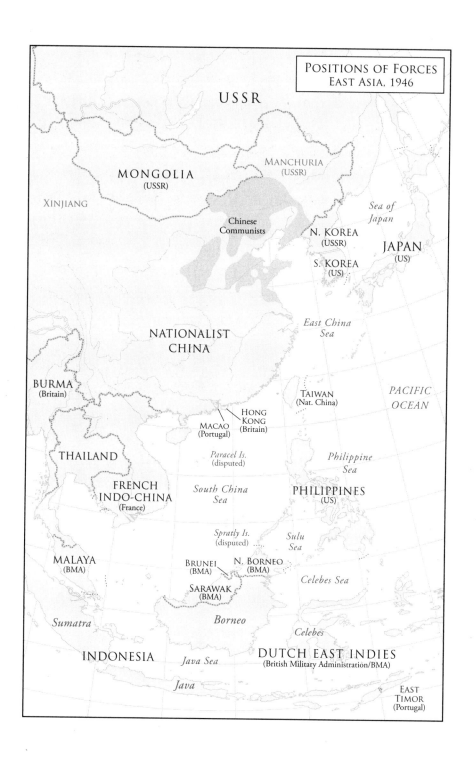

POSITIONS OF FORCES
EAST ASIA, 1946

USSR

MONGOLIA
(USSR)

MANCHURIA
(USSR)

XINJIANG

Chinese
Communists

N. KOREA
(USSR)

Sea of
Japan

JAPAN
(US)

S. KOREA
(US)

East China
Sea

NATIONALIST
CHINA

TAIWAN
(Nat. China)

PACIFIC
OCEAN

BURMA
(Britain)

HONG
KONG
(Britain)

MACAO
(Portugal)

Paracel Is.
(disputed)

Philippine
Sea

THAILAND

FRENCH
INDO-CHINA
(France)

South China
Sea

PHILIPPINES
(US)

Spratly Is.
(disputed)

Sulu
Sea

MALAYA
(BMA)

BRUNEI
(BMA)

N. BORNEO
(BMA)

Celebes Sea

SARAWAK
(BMA)

Sumatra

Borneo

Celebes

INDONESIA

Java Sea

DUTCH EAST INDIES
(British Military Administration/BMA)

Java

EAST
TIMOR
(Portugal)

economy had not done well since being turned over to the KMT; there was general discontent among the populace. On February 27, a woman selling cigarettes was approached by agents of the KMT monopoly bureau. Cigarette sales were taxable, and the woman, so the agents claimed, was dodging taxes. She protested. The agents pistol-whipped her, leaving her unconscious. The crowd that had gathered rumbled angrily toward the agents. The agents fired their way to safety. In its general outlines, it was a story you could find anywhere on the globe: the impoverished trying to scrape out a living, the petty functionaries of an unsympathetic government denying them the capacity to do so, the swelling anger—all the more intense for the knowledge that the government officials were corrupt smugglers themselves. The sequel was predictable too. Crowds marched in protest against the KMT on February 28. Police shot wildly and martial law was declared. A gulf had opened up between the government and the governed. The hapless KMT governor Chen Yi took two tacks. First, he promised reform; a settlement committee would meet with government representatives, so that local grievances could be channeled to the governor. Second, he called for military reinforcements, despite having promised that troops would not be summoned. Armed resistance broke out. A militia called the 27th Brigade would take to the hills of Nantou County in an attempt to launch guerrilla war against the KMT. The KMT forces, far better armed, were able to suppress these groups, but it was a long, arduous task. It was an indiscriminate one too. Chiang's understanding of the situation was simple. The Taiwanese were recalcitrant because of long years of Japanese rule, and the agitation was driven by Communists. Protest was treachery. Protesters had to be killed or incarcerated. Thus began the long era of totalitarian rule over Taiwan, which Taiwanese called the White Terror.[36]

There were several problems with this approach. In denouncing all opposition as treacherous, Chiang was missing a chance to recognize and thus address the very real grievances among Taiwanese. There *were* Communists agitating against the ROC—Xie Xuehong, for example, was a Taiwanese Communist who would help organize the 27th Brigade before returning to China—but much of the anger stemmed from the corruption and brutality Taiwanese were experiencing at the hands of their purported compatriots. If anything, Chiang was creating an environment where Communism would thrive: it was an ideology that did well in poverty and despair. The policy also gave ROC officials—soldiers, bureaucrats—an easy pretext for oppression. They could seize whatever they wanted from those they governed simply by threatening to accuse their target of "anti-government sentiment." This only deepened the distrust and tension. The ROC could round up those fighting and kill them, but it could not quench the smoldering resentment. Rebellion would emerge, suddenly and unexpectedly, in years to come. In 1950, for example, Su Beng, now back in Taiwan, would organize a few youths to launch a revolution for the island.[37] It was in reaction to 228 that the Taiwan independence movement was born. Its origins lay in a desire for independence not from the People's Republic of China—the outcome of the Chinese Civil War was still undecided—but from the Republic of China, which claimed sovereignty over the island. Calls for self-determination, for Taiwan's future to be decided by the Taiwanese, would come from the island as well as from those driven into hiding in Japan, America, or elsewhere.

There were American officials who were sympathetic to such calls. Those stationed on Taiwan were not oblivious to the White Terror, and some wondered whether their policy on Taiwan needed to change. One option was UN trusteeship: the island would be placed under the UN Trusteeship Council (the boots on the ground, presumably, would have been American) as it made the transition from colony to self-government. This meant reneging on the commitment made at Cairo, but there were at least three instances of American officials considering the option seriously. The first came from George Kerr, the American vice-consul in Taipei. Kerr had advocated trusteeship status for Taiwan as early as 1942. Disgusted by the violence the KMT had unleashed, he and his colleagues in the consulate called for American intervention. Taiwanese, they believed, were well-disposed to the United States; the United States should show that it would support people who wanted to determine their own futures. The swiftness with which the ROC put down the uprising caused the Americans to abandon the plan, but the idea of trusteeship would be raised once again, when General Albert Wedemeyer was sent on a fact-finding mission to China in 1947.[38]

Wedemeyer was not impressed with what he saw. He found the KMT "spiritually insolvent"; they were eager to foist responsibility for addressing China's woes onto the American delegation, while corruption and mismanagement remained rampant. (The Communists, Wedemeyer would note, were enjoying "excellent spirit.") His visit to Taiwan highlighted the gulf between rulers and ruled:

Our experience in Formosa is most enlightening. The administration of the former Governor Chen Yi has alienated the people from the Central Government. . . . They cannot attribute their failure to the activities of the Communists or of dissident elements. The people anticipated sincerely and enthusiastically deliverance from the Japanese yoke. However, Chen Yi and his henchmen ruthlessly, corruptly and avariciously imposed their regime upon a happy and amenable population. The Army conducted themselves as conquerors. Secret police operated freely to intimidate and to facilitate exploitation by Central Government officials. . . .

The island is extremely productive in coal, rice, sugar, cement, fruits and tea. Both hydro and thermal power are abundant. The Japanese had efficiently electrified even remote areas and also established excellent railroad lines and highways. Eighty percent of the people can read and write, the exact antithesis of conditions prevailing in the mainland of China. There were indications that Formosans would be receptive toward United States guardianship and United Nations trusteeship. They fear that the Central Government contemplates bleeding their island to support the tottering and corrupt Nanking machine and I think their fears well founded.[39]

This was as crisp and shrewd an assessment of the situation on Taiwan as the United States could get. The cause for discontent had been analyzed clearly. A course of action that promised a better future was being gestured at: trusteeship for Taiwan, with independence, presumably, to follow. (It was not just a matter of being decent to the Taiwanese; if discontent remained inflamed, the area would be vulnerable to Communism. Tellingly, Wedemeyer recommended trusteeship for Manchuria.) It was a difficult course of action but, theoretically at least, a feasible one. Had it been pursued, the world might well have had a sovereign Taiwan.

The problem was that the US government was far from unanimous on what to do about China. Wedemeyer was right in pointing out the flaws of the ROC, but dragging the United Nations in was surely a bit too much. It would undermine the strength of the very regime America was supporting—indeed, Wedemeyer had ultimately endorsed that support, recommending further military aid to the KMT, its spiritual insolvency notwithstanding.[40] It was surprising how often American officials would recognize irredeemable incompetence in a leader and still recommend military support. It was as though once in a bad relationship, they were unable to see a way out. America was still supplying weaponry to the generalissimo; seizing his territory while doing that was just too much of a stretch. Having made the commitment at Cairo, the United States might question it, but it never had the courage to undo it altogether.

One person who did have that courage was George Kennan. The civil war had not been kind to Chiang; he resigned the presidency to Li Zongren (though he would soon be back in the role). The KMT's defeat in the Chinese Civil War was imminent. On July 6, 1949, with that possibility weighing heavily on his mind, Kennan drew up a document perhaps even more remarkable than the Long Telegram for which he is famed. The goal was to keep Formosa and the Pescadores out of the Communists' hands. This, in turn, required the ejection of KMT forces on the island and "the establishment of a provisional international or U.S. regime which would invoke the principle of self-determination for the islanders and would eventually, prior to a Japanese peace settlement, conduct a plebiscite to determine the ultimate disposition of Formosa and the Pescadores.

Formosan separatism is the only concept which has sufficient grass-roots appeal to resist communism."[41]

This was a profound reading of the situation. Chiang, Kennan was arguing, would be powerless against Communism. Communism thrived where there was oppression. Give people the hope that oppression could be lifted, however, and Communism could be defeated. In Taiwan's case, that meant encouraging those who were calling for self-determination. Following this course would require either multilateral cooperation—Kennan was willing to canvas the views of Australia, India, and the Philippines to see if they were amenable—or a unilateral declaration from the United States that it was taking over because "events had invalidated all the assumptions underlying the Cairo Declaration and that U.S. intervention was required by the interests of stability in the Pacific area as well as by the interests of the inhabitants of the islands." The obvious problem was that this would require the use of force to eject the three hundred thousand KMT soldiers already on Taiwan, which Kennan was willing to do if necessary. Chiang could, if he wished, remain on the island as a political refugee. The Taiwanese, in due course, could be asked what form of government they desired. The whole proposition was ambitious. Going unilaterally, Kennan acknowledged, "would offend the sensibilities of many people in the Department on legal and procedural grounds, and we would probably have to cut some legal corners to justify it." But the alternative was resigning oneself to Communist control of Taiwan, precariously close to vital American interests in Okinawa and the Philippines.[42]

Here, once again, was a glimmer of the possibility of an independent Taiwan. If the United States was serious about independence, this was precisely the form of policy that was required. The task might well have been easier than anticipated: there were KMT officials—such as Chen Yi's successor, Wei Daoming, and General Sun Liren—who might have contemplated a declaration of autonomy. Had they persuaded, as they were certainly capable of doing, the three hundred thousand troops to go along with them, the American military might not have had to expend a terrible amount of effort in moving Taiwan to independence.[43] Having evicted the KMT troops, the United States could have gone ahead and organized a plebiscite. At the time, the United States was inclined to establish diplomatic relations with the eventual government in China. When the Communists came to power, they might have objected to the withdrawal of the Cairo commitments. But they were so desperate for capital and recognition at the time that they might well have dropped their objections, not least since the Americans would no longer be tied to the despised Chiang.

The problem was that the requirements Kennan was spelling out were too onerous; he himself would withdraw the memo the very same day. (His reasons for withdrawing it remain uncertain.) Invoking Theodore Roosevelt, he noted that the policy required "resolution, speed, ruthlessness and self-assurance." The United States had been known to show speed and ruthlessness, perhaps, but combining them with resolution and self-assurance was a harder ask. Government is a curious beast—Kennan would later compare it to a primeval dinosaur—and the confidence to rethink old assumptions quickly and act anew does not come easily to it. It did not help that the Joint Chiefs of Staff had no wish to get involved in Taiwan; there was, they felt, enough around the globe to keep them occupied.[44] So much for resolution and self-assurance.

There was a desire for a referendum in Taiwan and American officialdom knew it. It knew, too, what was needed to make it happen. But it lacked the appetite to accept the costs the requisite policy would entail. It was an understandable decision, but a decision nonetheless—and one that could have been different. With the benefit of hindsight, this was perhaps the moment when the United States had the greatest room for action that would deny Taiwan to China. But it did not. Taiwan remained under ROC control.

Back in China, the civil war was raging to its conclusion. KMT forces lost battle after battle, and Chiang was driven south. His generals were defecting. Fu Zuoyi, for example, had given up Beijing and gone over to the CCP's side. The KMT had entertained the notion that it might have to decamp to Taiwan as a last retreat for a while; gold and treasure had been shipped there, as had historical curios and documents. It was not a scenario Chiang was happy about, but he found himself driven to it. By the summer of 1949, he was back in Guangdong, where the KMT had been confined before that Northern Expedition of 1926. But this time, there would be no triumphant march north ending in unification. His generals were not in a mood to follow his orders. Lu Han, the general he had hoped would lead the campaign against the Communists in Yunnan and Guizhou, wanted none of Chiang's authority; he sought support from other generals to kidnap Chiang. The desperate generalissimo fled for Taiwan at the end of 1949.[45]

For Chiang, this was but a temporary retreat to a bastion from which he would someday reconquer the mainland. In and of itself, the withdrawal to Taiwan did not assure Chiang's security as head of the KMT regime. His had always been a fragile authoritarianism: a shifting coalition of warlords on whose consent and support he relied for authority. That support had waxed and waned over the years, and so, too, had Chiang's power. He had managed to remain—barely—primus inter pares through a blend of political machination and foreign support. Now, as he scrapped to remain at the top of the political pyramid, he would need both. American support was by no means certain. There were US officials who thought the generalissimo had run his course and that the only way of saving Taiwan was to be rid of him. There were other candidates for leadership in the KMT: the general Sun Liren, for example, or K. C. Wu, the governor of Taiwan. Neither of these men was above indicating that he could accept American support and rule Taiwan instead of Chiang. The KMT based on Taiwan was not the only option either. There were still Nationalist forces holding on to Hainan island (they would be defeated only in 1950), and they could have become the main recipients of American aid instead. And there were still Taiwanese independence activists—people like Thomas Liao—scattered across East Asia who were reaching out to interested American agents and asking for Taiwan to be placed under UN trusteeship.[46] There were alternatives to Chiang's rule, and those alternatives meant that he faced formidable challenges in staying in power.

Two things helped him. The first was the fact that the United States was, as it always had been, deeply divided on the question of ditching him. And division in a government generally allows a status-quo policy to drag interminably on. Madame Chiang was still able to rouse the China lobby to denounce the abandonment of the generalissimo. Douglas MacArthur, whose star was at its zenith, was adamant that this was the moment to support Chiang, not cut him loose. Having backed Chiang thus far, the United States was unable to let him go.[47]

The second thing that assured Chiang's survival was an old play from the dictator's handbook: he made sure that a loyalist was in charge of internal security. If one wishes to survive as an authoritarian, it is absolutely crucial that the police—with all the secret intelligence and paramilitary functions that they might have—be kept under one's control. Chiang entrusted the police to his son Chiang Ching-kuo. Chiang Ching-kuo had lived in Moscow, and he had learned all there was to learn about surveillance, terror, infiltration, and arrest from the Communists there. He had returned to serve his father's regime, and now his skills as a spy chief would ensure that Chiang remained in power.[48]

Chiang Ching-kuo's police would penetrate almost every pocket of life on Taiwan. Officially, they were out to arrest enemies of the state. The CCP had shown a knack for peeling off Chiang's political supporters, so that danger would have to be guarded against. In practice, this meant rooting out every source of potential dissent. It made a coup against Chiang impossible, but it also perpetuated the brutal authoritarianism of the White Terror. It is difficult, even now, to know just how many were rounded up and executed; the regime was almost as enthusiastic in its erasure of records as it was in its cruelty. But tens of thousands of Taiwan's residents were imprisoned and thousands were executed. Some were sent to Green Island: a gorgeous volcanic island on the Pacific that would serve as a desolate prison camp. Being imprisoned for decades was not uncommon.[49] There was no space that was wholly free from inspection, no relationship so sacred that betrayal was an impossibility.

From the very first, then, "Free China" was founded on a base of authoritarianism and terror. Chiang genuinely believed that his rule was crucial to China's well-being and to the struggle against Communism; if it took ruthless imprisonment and executions to assure his rule, then that was just a price that would have to be paid. His rival, Li Zongren, had disappeared to the United States for medical treatment, and Chiang, who had not given up his post as party chairman or his supervision of the military, would return to the presidency in 1950. It was one of Li's abiding gripes: Chiang might give up the presidency, but he would never give up power. Martial law was reimposed on Taiwan in 1949. The constitution, which took effect in 1947, was left unchanged; the KMT was purporting, still, to govern all of China. Theoretically, that constitution called for elections to fill three branches of government. Candidates would run for election to the Legislative Yuan and the National Assembly. (Some of these seats were to be filled by elections from certain groups, such as Tibetans or Chinese living abroad.) The office of president was to be up for election every six years, with a limit of two terms. But Chiang was not the man to let a crisis go unexploited. He had adjusted the constitution to grant himself temporary powers in April 1948. The purpose was to allow the president to take emergency measures to suppress Communist rebellion; the judiciary would eventually suspend elections until the rebellion was over. Those temporary provisions would remain in effect until 1991.[50]

These measures did arouse US concern. Chiang was creating a situation where an alienated populace might well turn to Communism. "It is my feeling," wrote the American chargé d'affaires in China, "that arrests and trial are continuation of KMT intolerant police state methods which have consistently served to alienate population."[51] But beyond earnest representations, there was little leverage the United States was willing to use. Only Kennan's idea of going in and evicting the KMT by force would have been effective, and that was something no one was willing to countenance.

On October 1, 1949, Mao Zedong's Communists had declared the foundation of the People's Republic of China. Mao's mental map of China had, until around this point, been shifting at the edges. He had come of age in a China broken; he was by no means adamant on how far the territorial extent of his China could or should go. Had Taiwan been denied to the KMT and moved from trusteeship to eventual independence, it is perfectly possible that the CCP would have abandoned all thoughts of taking it. Mao did not start out thinking that the vast peripheral regions the Qing had conquered had to be part of his China. In 1933, the CCP had suggested that the borderlands—Tibet, Xinjiang, Inner Mongolia, Guizhou—could opt for self-determination. This might, of course, have been a manipulative ploy, but it might also have been a genuinely sincere declaration, one made in the youthful idealism that withers with power. In 1936, Mao had granted an interview to Edgar Snow in which he said that the CCP would support Taiwan's struggle for independence.[52] Snow was gullible where China was concerned, but he was an honest reporter: there would have been no tampering with Mao's words. At least in the 1930s, Mao (like many Chinese) seems to have thought of Taiwan as something apart from China proper. His concept of a state was, at the time, a patch of territory where he exerted power, and it was something moveable. The Jiangxi soviet had been a state; he had lost the territory he held there and withdrawn to other territory, taking the state with him. Yan'an had been the base of a state; the loss of it had hurt, but it had not terminated the sovereignty of the CCP. Excluding Taiwan from the state the CCP ruled, therefore, was not a stretch—particularly when one considered that the CCP was, when all was said and done, a land-based gang of peasants. There was little reason a small island across the waters would feature much in their thinking.

Mao's attitude changed not so much toward Taiwan as toward Chiang. Had Chiang opted for a truce when Marshall was pleading with him for one, Mao might have been content with two Chinas. In 1945, at the fruitless peace talks with the KMT, he had been willing to accept some form of partition. Even after the Chinese Civil War started in 1946, the Communists seemed—at least initially—to be open to a truce. Unity, after all, was not China's default condition; a divided China was something normal to Mao and something that could be lived with. Only when Chiang's forces took his beloved Yan'an in 1947 did the war goal shift from survival to the complete defeat of the KMT regime. Chiang, for his part, remained unprepared to countenance anything other than the complete destruction of the CCP.[53] Wherever he was, if he retained armed forces and American support, Chiang would be a threat.

So when Taiwan became the KMT's last foothold in the civil war, it was inevitable that the Communists would turn their attention to it. Chiang was not content to sit quietly on the island and lick his wounds. Chiang was using Taiwan as a base from which to wage naval war against the CCP. For the Communists, as for the Qing Empire before them, the problem was not Taiwan itself but the hostile enemy that held it. Something had to be done. In the official mind of the PRC, there was a fusion of concerns: the geostrategic need to deny an enemy a base from which the PRC could be attacked and the refusal to let a reviled foe hold territory so close. This fusion applied to other regions too. Zhou Enlai would note that while China had indeed promised self-determination to places like Xinjiang and Tibet, this was not an opportune moment for it to be exercised; imperialists (for the United States seemed intent on helping Chiang) were too intent on tearing China apart. The CCP's mental map of China had altered. It would now take in Xinjiang and Tibet, and it was only the fortunes of war that would thwart its quest for Taiwan.[54]

The first check the Communists faced in the quest to do something about Taiwan came at the Battle of Guningtou. In a fierce battle for the island of Kinmen, which lay just off the coast of Fujian, in late October 1949, the Communist forces lost. It was a consequential battle; it meant that the Kinmen and other offshore islands, not to mention Taiwan, would remain under KMT control. But at the time, the check seemed only temporary. The CCP had been unfamiliar with naval warfare and with the locals. It was willing and able to learn from its mistakes. The Communist People's Liberation Army (PLA) managed to defeat the Nationalists on Hainan Island in part because it had learned those lessons. Better preparation in the future would make for victory. So Mao focused on consolidating his victories and planned for an assault on Taiwan by some point in 1951. He would, he knew, require air and sea power, so in his talks with Joseph Stalin in December 1949, he asked if the Soviets were willing to send pilots or military detachments to assist the PRC. This, Stalin would not commit to. He did not, he explained, wish to give the Americans a pretext for intervening. He did, however, offer staff and instructors. He also suggested sending a landing unit to Taiwan, which would then conduct propaganda operations and inspire a revolution there.[55] Just how well such a unit would have fared is debatable. Chiang's intelligence apparatus was formidable; a propaganda unit would likely have been butchered. But in due course, once its naval strength had grown to the point where it could land forces on Taiwan and engage Chiang in full battle, the PRC had every reason to expect to conquer Taiwan and incorporate it into new China.

The official mind of the US government is one in which ideas—especially those having to do with what must be defended—rarely die. Instead, they burrow deep, only to reassert themselves at the least opportune moments. A president, a secretary of state, the National Security Council (NSC) might make decisions about what will guide the country, only for those decisions to be revisited and undone in the heat of a crisis. Interests that are peripheral at best become vital. The result is a government that shifts between two gears—strategic drift and sudden energetic action—while constantly revisiting its options. That tendency would be the hallmark of American conduct in the Korean War, and it would leave a far longer lasting stamp on Taiwan's status than Washington had ever intended.

At the beginning of 1950, American policy on China and Formosa was a shining exemplar of confusion. Moscow had provided ample evidence of what George Kennan had described as "efforts . . . to advance official limits of Soviet power," whether through the Berlin blockade or the coup in Czechoslovakia. Given that evidence, Washington was not going to be sanguine about Soviet influence in China. Kennan and John Paton Davies had had hopes that the CCP, like Josip Broz Tito's Yugoslavia, would defy Soviet authority. Mao's announcement on June 30, 1949, that China would "lean to one side" and partner with the Soviet Union seemed to dash those hopes. But Mao had never intended for his relationship with the Soviets to exclude the possibility of decent relations with the United States. As far as he was concerned, the key obstacle to a modus vivendi was American support for the despised Chiang. The CCP had refused to accord diplomatic status to American officials in China as its armies took over Beijing and Nanjing—but then, American officials had yet to recognize the CCP government. Claiming diplomatic privilege without diplomatic relations was a dubious proposition. The absence of those privileges did not stop CCP officials from trying to reach out to the US officials on their soil. Victory in the civil war did not change the CCP's America policy. Even as he concluded a Treaty of Friendship, Alliance, and Mutual Assistance with the Soviet Union on February 14, 1950, Mao was investigating the possibility of trade relations with the United States.[56] He had no intention of reducing his China to the status of Soviet satellite. Balancing the United States against the USSR made sound strategic sense.

Washington was still trying desperately to figure out what its stance on China was. It was hamstrung by its own fervent anti-Communism. There had been a suspicion of Communism even before the Cold War in the United States; with the Cold War underway, it spiraled to giddying heights. Being soft on Communism was the new death blow to a political career. By February 1950, Senator Joseph McCarthy would find that hunting Communists purportedly hiding in government was a path to political power. But even before McCarthy became a destructive force, Washington was being accused of losing countries to Communism. Politically, that accusation was deadly—and its deadliness was undiminished by its inanity. That countries had their own trajectories, their own choices, that Washington was far from omnipotent, was something the body politic was simply unprepared to fathom. The Truman administration (Harry Truman had succeeded FDR as American president) would have to issue a massive China white paper just to show that there had been little it could have done to save Chiang's regime. The paper was an exhaustive account of American dealings with China (it would insist that the Open Door policy showed friendship toward China, forgetting that the policy had been aimed at forcing the country open to all comers). It left members of the KMT incensed: "Unfair and unjust," in the words of one KMT official. And if it seemed to close off the possibility of working with the KMT, it offered no advice on how to deal with the CCP other than to wait for regime change. Secretary of State Dean Acheson's letter transmitting the report to the president noted:

> It has been urged that relatively small amounts of aid—military and economic—to the National Government would have enabled it to destroy communism in China. The most trustworthy military, economic, and political information available to our Government does not bear out this view. . . .
>
> And now it is abundantly clear that we must face the situation as it exists in fact. We will not help the Chinese or ourselves by basing our policy on wishful thinking. We continue to believe that, however tragic may be the immediate future of China and however ruthlessly a major portion of this great people may be exploited by a party in the interest of a foreign imperialism, ultimately the profound civilization and democratic individualism of China will reassert themselves and she will throw off the foreign yoke. I consider that we should encourage all developments in China which now and in the future work toward this end.
>
> In the immediate future, however, the implementation of our historic policy of friendship for China must be profoundly affected by current developments. It will necessarily be influenced by the degree to which the Chinese people come to realize that the Communist regime serves not their interests but those of Soviet Russia and the manner in which,

having become aware of the facts, they react to this foreign domination.[57]

Theoretically, at least, the policy sketched here had the United States washing its hands of Chiang Kai-shek, though money and weapons would continue to pour into his coffers. There was no immediate plan to unseat the CCP. If a Chinese movement against it developed, Acheson was saying, the United States would support it. But beyond that, Washington could and would do nothing. It was an odd mix of policies: no help for Chiang except that which he was already getting by default; no resistance to the PRC except the threat of regime change if it ever became feasible.

All of this raised a practical question: What did America want to do about Taiwan? On this, policymakers had a panoply of opinions. Short of engineering a coup that somehow deposed Chiang and led to self-determination for the island, the only option for keeping Taiwan from the Communists was the one Kennan had suggested—and that meant using force. To deny Taiwan to the Communists, the United States would have to deny it to the Nationalists already on the island. The only way of doing that was to take up arms to evict the KMT troops. This was precisely the point Acheson tried to bring home to members of the Senate. But where Kennan had called for a Theodore Roosevelt–style assault to remove KMT forces from Taiwan and thereby deny the island to China, Acheson was counseling resignation to the inevitable. He began by informing the senators that there was no way of retaking continental China. Other countries, notably Britain, were flocking to recognize the PRC. To Acheson, Formosa had been a Chinese territory, and remained so. Therefore, the United States had two options: it could seize the island—which

Acheson thought the American public was unprepared to do—or it could let it fall. While the Joint Chiefs of Staff were unhappy about a prospective Communist regime on Formosa, the island was not something they had deemed vital to American national security. The senators, however, thought differently. Surely the government could be doing more to arm the KMT. And General Douglas MacArthur and Admiral Arthur Radford, celebrated heroes, men of valor and geostrategic wisdom, had said that Taiwan had to be kept out of Communist hands. Military personnel always had differing opinions, countered Acheson, which was why one had to go with what the Joint Chiefs deemed essential.[58] Those differences underscored a key point: official American opinion on the China-Taiwan conundrum was still deeply conflicted.

Those differences were not confined to the military or the Senate; they ran through the fabric of the executive branch. President Truman, on January 5, 1950, would reiterate his country's commitment to the Cairo Declaration, but he would make clear that he had no intention of getting involved in China's civil war. He added that "at the present time"—and that was crucial—the United States had no intention of setting up bases on Taiwan. The United States would not give Chiang military aid, though money would continue to come in. Acheson was on the same page. But whatever the secretary of state's preferences, his own department had not given up on the possibility of trusteeship. The assistant secretary, Dean Rusk, would write about the perils Communism posed to America's standing in the world. Rusk wanted a stance that showed "resolution." Such a stand could be taken on Taiwan. "If the United States were to announce that it would neutralize Formosa, not permitting it either to be taken by Communists or to be used as a base of military operations against the mainland," Rusk declared in May 1950, "that is a decision which we could certainly maintain, short of open war by the Soviet Union." It would, he admitted, raise the risk of war, but this was a risk worth taking. Once neutralized, the island could begin the move toward trusteeship.[59] It was, in Rusk's thinking, not the geostrategic significance of Taiwan that mattered but its political significance. America had to show it was tough on Communism. Sifting through such memoranda, one has the odd feeling of having stumbled into a scene from *Waiting for Godot*, in all its endlessly repetitive futility. It was another echo of what Wedemeyer had hinted at in 1947, of what Kennan had devised a plan for in 1949. This was where the United States government was, still lost in an unending conversation about what to do about Taiwan, still churning its wheels in the deepening mud, and still getting absolutely nowhere.

In thinking through the strategic points that it had to defend in the Cold War, then, Washington was divided. For Truman, Acheson, and the Joint Chiefs, Taiwan was not a vital interest. Japan and the Philippines needed to be defended. Taiwan did not.[60] But there were powerful voices within the institutions those people were in charge of that were calling, in no uncertain terms, for the defense of Taiwan. It was a finely poised debate. A slight shift of weight could tip the balance one way or another.

The shift began with a speech. The question of which points were worth defending and which were not was one that the American public needed clarity on, in part so that it could understand why the Truman administration had washed its hands of China. So Acheson decided to clarify the matter at the National Press Club on January 12, 1950. In words that would become infamous, he sketched the "defensive perimeter" that the United States had to defend:

This defensive perimeter runs along the Aleutians to Japan and then goes to the Ryukyus....

The defensive perimeter runs from the Ryukyus to the Philippine islands....

So far as the military security of other areas in the Pacific is concerned, it must be clear that no person can guarantee these areas against military attack. But it must also be clear that such a guarantee is hardly sensible or within the realm of practical relationship. Should such an attack occur—one hesitates to say where such an armed attack should come from—the initial reliance must be on the people attacked to resist it and then <u>upon the commitments of the entire civilized world under the Charter of the United Nations</u> which so far has not proved a weak reed to lean on by any people who are determined to protect their independence against outside aggression.[61]

Left out of that perimeter were the Korean Peninsula and Taiwan. Acheson was quite clearly stating that the United States was not committed to defending them. Which meant that if there were people who wanted to invade those places, they could do so secure in the knowledge that the United States would not intervene.

Kim Il-sung, the Communist leader of North Korea, had long wanted to unify the divided peninsula under his rule. The division at the end of World War II had been meant to be temporary. There was no love lost between Kim and his counterpart in South Korea, Syngman Rhee. Kim wanted to attack and conquer. What had hitherto stopped him was Moscow. Stalin had been far from convinced that Kim could win a war of unification, and he had no wish to be dragged into a war with the United States. Kim had requested Stalin's approval for an invasion before and had been turned down. But in 1950, the Soviet leader changed his mind. Mao's victory in China helped shift the needle a bit because the Chinese could now take responsibility for encouraging the war. Acheson's speech shifted it further. In April, Stalin gave Kim the now storied green light for an attack on South Korea, provided he could get Mao's commitment to support it. This Mao was willing to give, though the full extent of that support was left uncalculated and he suspected the war might be tougher than Kim anticipated. Kim attacked on June 25, 1950.[62]

Had Washington stuck to the idea that South Korea was not worth defending, the matter would have ended there. But with the attack underway, the United States all of a sudden found that South Korea was a vital interest. Partly, it was the memory of Munich that haunted the Truman administration; they had all lived through the Second World War and had imbibed thoroughly the lesson that appeasement ended badly. Partly, it was the much ballyhooed "loss of China." It had been a travesty, the United States felt, for China to fall to Communism; to lose South Korea to the Communist movement so soon after was unbearable. If South Korea fell, what was next? The psychological damage to the non-Communist world would be too hard to heal. Something had to be done.[63]

This was where the unfairly neglected second part of Acheson's speech came in. He had held up the United Nations as a not "weak reed" for a reason. America might not have a defense commitment to South Korea, but it could rally the UN to provide such defense. And the membership of the UN at the time was conducive to American action. Chiang's ROC held China's seat. With the founding of the PRC, Zhou had written to the secretary-general of the United

Nations, demanding that Beijing take over the Chinese seat, but the United States could and did block that demand. In those days, Washington was superb at getting votes in the UN General Assembly. When the Soviet Union and India set forth a resolution calling for the PRC to get its seat at the UN in September 1950, the United States rallied enough support to defeat the resolution. Mao's China could not hope to thwart UN action; it would remain, bizarrely, excluded until 1971. The Soviet Union could have countered the American call to respond to North Korean aggression, but it had decided to boycott Security Council meetings to protest the PRC's exclusion.[64] Getting a UN resolution to counter North Korean aggression was therefore straightforward.

By the beginning of July 1950, American-led UN forces were pouring in to beat back the North Korean onslaught. And Truman sent the Seventh Fleet to the Taiwan Strait. "The purpose of this move," he would recount, "was to prevent attacks by Communists on Formosa as well as forays by Chiang Kai-shek against the mainland, this last to avoid reprisal actions by the Reds that might enlarge the area of conflict." The official line from Washington was that this was "without prejudice to poll questions affecting Chi Govt."[65] With a war in Korea underway, adding a cross-strait war to the mix was not something the US government felt ready for.

It was one thing for Truman to decide that the question of Taiwan had been left unsettled; it was another to actually make sure it remained so. A delighted Chiang Kai-shek felt the North Korean attack was a "second Pearl Harbor": an act of war that would bring the United States to the defense of his regime once more.[66] He was not wrong. The Korean War had set a panic off within Washington. Having got involved in the conflict, the United States had to show success. That same calculus would hold true for its presence in the strait. To lose Formosa now would constitute a tremendous loss of prestige.

There were still those who thought that backing Chiang was not the worst idea in the world. General Douglas MacArthur, who would be appointed to command the UN troops in Korea, would air his very different views on what the maelstrom meant for Taiwan. Even before the war, MacArthur had been arguing that the geostrategic significance of the island was too great to permit it to fall to the Communists. It had ample bases; it had been used by the Japanese as a springboard for their invasion of Southeast Asia. Although he was unable to recommend specific measures for Taiwan's political future, MacArthur noted that the promise to return Taiwan to China "was given in consonance with a political situation entirely different than that which now exists. There is every basis from a moral standpoint to offer to the Taiwanese an opportunity to develop their own political future in an atmosphere unfettered by the dictates of a Communist police state."[67] There it was again; the idea that Taiwan and China might have to go their separate ways. The Cairo commitment could, so MacArthur was arguing, be undone.

MacArthur was perfectly willing to share his views beyond the White House. That they were loose on specifics did not bother him in the least. The general's insubordination on how to fight the war in Korea is well-known. Where Truman simply wanted to beat the North Korean forces back across the thirty-eighth parallel, MacArthur wanted to follow and annihilate them, a miscalculation that would lead to Chinese entry into the war and an eventual stalemate. But on Taiwan, too, the general and his president were at odds. Averell Harriman, special assistant to the president, was sent to talk to the general and came away with a dispiriting analysis of MacArthur's state of mind. He had, Harriman reported,

> accepted the President's position and will act accordingly, but without full conviction. He has a strange idea that we should back anybody who will fight Communism, even though he could not give an argument why the Generalissimo's fighting Communists would be a contribution towards the effective dealing with the Communists in China. I pointed out to him the basic conflict of interest between the U.S. and the Generalissimo's position as to the future of Formosa; namely, the preventing of Formosa's falling into hostile hands. Perhaps the best way would be through the medium of the UN to establish an independent government. Chiang, on the other hand, had only the burning ambition to use Formosa as a stepping stone for his re-entry to the mainland. MacArthur recognized that this ambition could not be fulfilled, and yet thought it might be a good idea to let him land and get rid of him that way. He did not seem to consider the liability that our support of Chiang on such a move would be to us in the East.[68]

MacArthur simply did not understand the morass of Chinese politics his anti-Communist fervor was plunging him into. Being an extremely self-confident man, he had no doubt that he knew what he was doing. In talks with Chiang on Taiwan, he created the impression that US cooperation with the KMT had been renewed. In a statement to the Veterans of Foreign Wars, MacArthur himself would say that Taiwan was an unsinkable aircraft carrier in the war against the Communists; there could be no compromising with the enemy, and Taiwan had to remain in friendly hands. The American government was not speaking as one. A furious Truman ordered the general to withdraw the statement, but the damage had been done.[69]

Given how the relationship between them would unravel, it is perhaps somewhat bemusing to recall that Truman and MacArthur at the beginning of the Korean War were not that far apart on the question of Taiwan. Mulling MacArthur's memo on the island's importance, both Acheson and Truman felt that it might be worth revisiting the question of Taiwan's status. Acheson inclined toward the possibility of referring it to the United Nations. The president thought it could be settled as part of a peace treaty with Japan, which had yet to be concluded.[70] In his instinct that discussions of such a treaty would be a sound venue for settling the disposition of former imperial Japanese territories such as Taiwan, Truman was correct. But if those discussions were to work, China—as the country that, barring Korea, was probably most affected by Japanese aggression—would have to be part of the conference.

This would not happen because China would enter the Korean War. Part of the issue was that, whether Truman thought so or not, his decision to send the Seventh Fleet to the Taiwan Strait *was* participation in the Chinese Civil War. The PRC certainly saw it that way. Mao recalled that Truman had said he would not interfere with Taiwan. The neutralization of the strait showed how foolish it was to place any trust in what the Americans said. So China proceeded to make it clear—the Indians were a key negotiation channel here—that the US actions constituted interference in the Chinese Civil War.[71]

The PRC had sent ethnic Koreans serving in China's People's Liberation Army to North Korea even before the war began, and they started mobilizing more troops for possible action in Korea as early as July 1950. But even then, Chinese participation in the Korean War was not a given. If there was confusion and difference on the American side, there was confusion and difference on the Chinese side as well. Mao himself wanted to join the war. There was a debt to be paid to the North Koreans who had sheltered their fellow Communists from Chiang in the civil war. Besides, Mao wanted to show strength, not cower in fear of the Americans. But his comrades felt differently. They were tired of endless war; there was a country to reconstruct and run. Gallivanting off to some adventure in Korea was just too much at the present time. The official mind of the PRC would accept the need for intervention only on October 5, 1950, when Mao summoned Marshal Peng Dehuai to address an enlarged meeting of the politburo. Peng, like MacArthur, made his case in geopolitical terms. It was not possible, he explained, to leave a hostile power in charge of both the Korean Peninsula and the Taiwan Strait and expect the country to survive. Entering the war was necessary for national security. Even then, there was some delay; it was unclear what kind of support Stalin was willing to provide. It was October 8 before Mao officially ordered Chinese troops to Korea.[72]

China's entry into the Korean War took MacArthur by surprise. So, too, did the stunning successes the Chinese troops enjoyed against his forces at the outset of what was now a Sino-American war. One of the war's casualties was MacArthur's career. The irate general wanted to broaden the attack to China, dropping bombs, even nuclear ones, on it; his public denunciations of Truman when the president refused to support this rankled. On April 11, 1951, Truman fired MacArthur. In essence, the disagreement between them was simple. Truman was fighting a war to defend South Korea; MacArthur was fighting to conquer Communism once and for all.

And if MacArthur, in his famous phrase, would "just fade away," his ideas about how to fight China were more pernicious.[73] They might disappear temporarily, but over the succeeding decades they would reassert themselves time and time again.

One of the PRC's starting points for negotiating a peace in Korea, especially after its initial victories in battle, was the evacuation of all American forces from Taiwan (the withdrawal of foreign troops from Korea and the PRC's ascension to China's seat in the UN, which was still being held by the ROC, were the others). This the Americans would not accept. So the war dragged on. After enormous loss of life, Chinese and American forces fought one another to a stalemate, winding up right back where they had started at the thirty-eighth parallel.[74]

The war also killed Truman's hope that a peace conference with Japan would settle Taiwan's status. There would indeed be a peace conference to conclude World War II. The conference took place in San Francisco in 1951. In the resulting Treaty of San Francisco, Japan renounced all claims to Taiwan and the Pescadores. But since no one could agree on whether the PRC or the ROC constituted the rightful Chinese government (the United States held it was the ROC; the United Kingdom, breaking with its American ally, maintained that it was the PRC), neither China was invited to the conference and neither China could officially accept Taiwan back into the fold. Japan came to peace with all the countries it had fought, except for the two that had suffered the most at its hands: China and Korea. The ROC would conclude a treaty with Japan in 1952, with the PRC following suit in 1978. (One problem the Treaty of San Francisco left unaddressed was that of the Senkaku Islands, which lie between the Ryukyus and Taiwan. The Japanese held and claimed these. Later, both the PRC and ROC would claim that they were the Diaoyu Islands and belonged to China. The question of which of them was China, of course, remained disputed too.)[75] The Chinese Civil War, the Sino-American war in Korea, and the American refusal to recognize the PRC meant that Taiwan's status would be left unresolved. Taiwan and China would remain divided. That division would outlast the Cold War. It is the division we live with today.

It is tempting, perhaps, to see the Taiwan problem as essentially one of decolonization mismanaged. At one level, this is correct. Taiwan had been part of an empire before another empire tore it away. It was then promised to a state that was claiming territories that belonged to an empire long gone. Chiang's China, like Mao's, sought to take advantage of decolonization to form a new empire. To FDR, these nuances did not matter. He promised and disposed of territories with all the gusto of the European imperialists he had condemned. He blithely ignored the faults of Chiang's China with a view to constructing what he thought was a better world. In this ignorance lay the seeds of the Taiwan problem.

And yet, this was only part of the problem. Even after World War II, those seeds had yet to sprout. There were paths to self-determination for Taiwan, paths that responsible American officials advocated. These paths became more difficult as time went by, but they remained within the compass of American abilities. Kennan's suggestion of using force to evict KMT troops on Taiwan in 1949 seemed extreme at the time, but it was, militarily, feasible. It would certainly have been easier than dealing with what followed.

And it would have prevented the suffering far too many Taiwanese experienced under Chiang's brutal rule.

There remained, too, the possibility of the PRC taking over China. The United States could have reached a modus vivendi with the PRC had it decided to terminate relations with Chiang Kai-shek. The path to rapprochement lay open all the way until the outbreak of the Korean War and the Truman administration's decision to intervene not just on the Korean Peninsula but in the Taiwan Strait. It was a path untaken because of domestic politics, but, especially in the era before McCarthy, it was an open, if challenging, one.

If FDR had misunderstood China during World War II, Truman misunderstood the nature of the choices available to him in the postwar world. There were options, but they were not infinite. He could choose to be neutral in the Chinese Civil War, but that would mean cutting off aid to Chiang completely. He could opt to refrain from taking a position on Taiwan, but putting the American ships in the Taiwan Strait while refusing to recognize the PRC looked suspiciously like taking a position. He could, at least in theory, revisit the question of Taiwan at a peace conference with Japan, but not without having the government in charge of China proper present. Choices come with costs and limitations. The failure to realize that would mar not just Truman's policy but that of his successor, Dwight Eisenhower.

2

Choosing Between Two Tyrannies

1953 to 1971

For someone whose reputation as a cool, competent strategist has soared of late, Dwight Eisenhower had a singularly confused China policy. He was determined to fight the world Communist movement, but that determination cost him something else he wanted: a modus vivendi with the PRC. He had hoped to persuade Chiang Kai-shek to give up the offshore islands of Kinmen and Matsu that the ROC still held. Instead, Chiang dragged him inch by relentless inch to a point where the United States was contemplating the use of nuclear weapons to defend those islands. The very organizational processes that Eisenhower is now lauded for—those weekly National Security Council meetings that imposed order and regularity on policy—would throttle strategic planning. Rarely has the gap between goals and achievements yawned quite as wide. Eisenhower would remark, somewhat ruefully, on the "the difficulty of trying to carry out U.S. policy when we were in the hands of 'a fellow who hasn't anything to lose.'"[1] It was a superb diagnosis of the problem, but it omitted the fact that it was American decision-making that had brought the Eisenhower administration into the fellow's hands in the first place.

From 1953 to 1971, this policy would leave America in an odd bind. It was committed to a China it had no desire to be bound to—and the commitment did not deepen fondness. It wanted a modus vivendi with the other China, the China it had fought, but its obligation to the ROC and its own domestic politics made this virtually impossible. The PRC's response was ineffectual, though there was a certain coherence to it. Mao was intent on getting Taiwan back and seeing Chiang defeated. To this end, he would employ a mix of force and blandishment. The shelling of the offshore islands and the fierce naval battles in the strait were an important part of his policy, but so, too, were the clandestine negotiations with ROC representatives and the propaganda targeted at ROC residents. These were the years when Mao transformed Taiwan into a cause, a means of galvanizing the people he governed. That transition would outlast the Sino-American estrangement.

For Mao wanted a rapprochement with the United States. He would use the same blend of force and diplomacy in pursuit of that objective. The PRC was not shy about using force against the United States: American planes could be shot at in PRC airspace and Beijing would provide significant assistance to the North Vietnamese war effort. But Mao kept reaching out to the Americans too. Surely a better relationship between the two countries was possible. It was a long wait. Only with Richard Nixon's ascension to the presidency was the US-China rapprochement achieved. But that was made possible by leaving the Taiwan question unresolved, its fate to be decided by what Nixon's national security advisor, Henry Kissinger, called "basic evolution"—allowing the outcome to be determined by the balance of power.[2] The problem was that basic evolution would go in very different directions from what either China or the United States had expected.

Harry Truman left office in 1953 with the Taiwan Strait officially neutralized. With the outbreak of the Korean War, he had sent the Seventh Fleet to the strait, with the mission both to deter and to protect the Communist forces in China. It was meant to prevent an attack by the Communists on the KMT; it was also meant to stop Chiang Kai-shek from trying to launch an assault on the mainland. Eisenhower came to office determined to change this. The worldwide Communist conspiracy was not meant to be coddled. It was absurd for the United States to be protecting Chinese Communists in the Taiwan Strait while fighting them on the Korean Peninsula. Part of this toughness stemmed from the president's own conviction that one did not deal with enemies lightly. Part of it came from the shrewd recognition that anti-Communism was now the predominant force in American politics. Joseph McCarthy had ensured that, for the foreseeable future, no president would wish to be seen as soft on Communism or soft on China. It is difficult, even now, to understand the sheer terror McCarthy inspired in American politicians. He had been willing to accuse that towering figure, George

Marshall, of sympathizing with Communism. How else, McCarthy asked, could one explain the general's failures in the China mission? One would have expected Eisenhower to defend Marshall, but even the American president, genuine war hero though he was, shied away from confronting McCarthy. The strength of the country's anti-Communist fervor was too great. China policy would have to reflect that anti-Communism. In his first address to Congress, therefore, Eisenhower announced that the Seventh Fleet "would no longer be employed to shield Communist China." Not, he hastened to reassure his audience, that this implied any "aggressive intent on our part."[3] But Truman's policy of neutralization—defending the Chinese Communists as much as deterring them—had come to an end.

This was a significant change, and other countries were swift to point it out. Indian prime minister Jawaharlal Nehru would hearken back to the Second World War and demand a full discussion at the UN. The British, who had been warned in advance and who had diplomatic relations with the PRC, grumbled about "unfortunate political repercussions." But they were being told, not asked. The policy had officially changed. The best Anthony Eden, the British prime minister, could do was remind his fellow parliamentarians that Eisenhower had promised no "aggressive intent."[4]

It was one thing, however, for Eisenhower to abjure "aggressive intent"; it was another to make sure that other members of his government, to say nothing of Chiang Kai-shek, did the same. Even before Eisenhower's change of policy, the KMT had launched "raids" against CCP forces. This had troubled the British, with their firm conviction that neutrality was the best course in dealing with China. With the United States no longer shielding the CCP, the Nationalists had even freer rein—and so did those within the American establishment who wanted a tougher line on China. On February 5, 1953, William Chase, head of the Military Assistance Advisory Group (MAAG) in Taiwan, wrote to General Chow Chih-jou, the chief of the general staff of the ROC military. Chase began by reminding Chow not to undertake any "significant attacks on Communist-held territory without first consulting me." But Chase then proceeded to outline a scheme that could hardly be described as nonaggressive in intent:

> I suggest that immediate thought be given and plans be made to blockade the China mainland, with respect to Chinese Communists shipping only, from Swatow to Da-chen, both inclusive, and that I be informed of these plans in order that Navy Section, MAAG, and Air Section, MAAG, be enabled to assist in every possible way. Before any blockade is put in operation, however, I desire to be informed. . . .
>
> I recommend that plans be made at once to increase the frequency of raids, not only from the "off-shore" islands, but also from Formosa and the Pescadores, and that both little raids and big ones be planned and executed on a wide front in order to obtain prisoners and worry and confuse the Communist coastal defenses. Again I suggest that I be informed of these plans so that my General Staff and MAAG sections may assist to the maximum degree.

Virtually overnight, the US stance in the strait had shifted from neutrality to belligerence. A blockade, support for raids—these were acts of war. The needle had veered from "no aggressive intent" to plotting military action against the PRC with barely a pause to take stock of the change. Chase closed his letter by expressing his "complete satisfaction and pleasure that Formosa and the Pescadores have been deneutralized."[5] One could now get down to actually fighting the enemy, though the ultimate objective of that fighting was left unresolved.

This, of course, was exactly what the Nationalists wanted to hear. The ROC was swift to follow up on news of the change in American policy with a request for further assistance in improving its air force and navy. It also called for deeper coordination in military planning between the ROC and the United States. Such coordination posed problems. It was all very well to defend Chiang Kai-shek, but the possibility of getting embroiled in a larger, nuclear war was a very real one. The CCP enjoyed an alliance with the Soviet Union, and Moscow had successfully tested a nuclear weapon in 1949. If Chiang were to drag the United States into a conflict with China, therefore, that war that could easily widen to encompass the Soviet Union. At that point, a nuclear holocaust was a distinct possibility. Getting tough on Communism came with significant risks. At a meeting discussing what kind of support could be extended to the KMT, General Hoyt Vandenberg warned that the decision to assist Chiang could mean a war with the Chinese and the Soviets. As Vandenberg saw it, "Chiang Kai-shek is a strong-headed sort of person. He is going to have planes with which he can, if he wants to, attack the Communist mainland. If he does, and if there are Communist attacks in retaliation, I think we should fully understand the kind of flypaper that we are stuck on."[6]

The first hint of how sticky that flypaper could get came with the delivery of the planes. The United States had been supplying the ROC with jet bombers. With the Communists no longer protected, there was nothing to stop Chiang from using them. Both the State Department and the Joint Chiefs were worried about what this might portend. When the problem was brought up at the National Security Council, Eisenhower was wry. The problem had come up, he observed, "when the present Administration had taken the wraps off the Seventh Fleet." It was news to him, the president continued, that Chiang was "not already under a commitment to play ball with the United States."[7] It was a moment of astonishing naivete. He had not put in place any measures to ensure that Chiang would "play ball." His own administration had been the one to undo neutrality; it should have been obvious—had been obvious to Vandenberg—that Chiang might well take advantage of that. But here was the president, bemused at where his policies had led.

The NSC decided, therefore, to seek Chiang's commitment to refrain from offensive operations against the Chinese Communists that Washington considered "inimical to the best interests of the United States." More aircraft would not be delivered until such a commitment had been made. Chiang was not above procrastinating on this issue. He was happy to agree in principle, but he wished for clarity on what would be inimical to American interests. The guerilla raids, for example, might not allow time for consultation. Besides, Washington and Taipei might differ in their assessment of the situation. Even here, the divisions within the American government were evident. The US ambassador to China, Karl Rankin, sympathized with Chiang's line of questioning and asked Washington that the planes not be held up while waiting for a formal commitment. Admiral Radford, who had become friendly with Chiang, emphasized that in view of the informal understanding he already had with ROC forces on the subject, there was no need to delay aircraft delivery. Chiang eventually did make the required commitment, and the planes came pouring into the ROC. But even before then, the back-and-forth concerning the planes had made certain points clear. First, that the Eisenhower administration could and would pull in different directions on China policy. General James Collins, then chief of staff of the US Army, would remark that if the armistice negotiations in Korea dragged on, the United States might find itself glad that the ROC could launch aerial offensives. Ambassador Rankin would beg for improved US conduct toward Free China, returning "friendship for evidences of friendship." It was a very different concept of how to deal with the ROC than the one the president had endorsed.[8] Second, Chiang could, if he wished, run ahead of where the Americans wished him to go. He could be asked not to—he was, as Radford said, a "smart fellow"—and in this case, he had, for the time being, desisted. But there was no telling how far his restraint would extend.

Sharing reconnaissance intelligence with Chiang, therefore, was courting trouble. But this is precisely what Secretary of State John Foster Dulles urged Eisenhower to do on June 16, 1954. American reconnaissance flights would often spot Soviet ships heading toward Communist China. Dulles wanted to turn the information over to the ROC, which could then stop the ships. Had the Americans stopped the ships themselves, it would have been an act of war. But for the Chinese Nationalists to stop ships supporting an enemy in their civil war would, Dulles felt, be different:

As to our moral position, & whether we're acting in good faith . . . it isn't the kind of thing we would do openly. We're not sending American boat or plane to round up & stop this traffic. We do encourage the Chinese Nationalists who are theoretically in state of civil war. They do it in exercise of their own belligerent rights, & prevent their enemy from getting necessary materials. They take off cargo & let ships go. . . .

We make the decision to extent of reconnaissance to enable them to pick these boats up. Our plane flies high, spots these boats, tells Chiang where they are, & he picks them up. He himself has insufficient reconnaissance, & can't have effective blockade. Boats are picked up on the high seas. No different from international law. Mentioned that British exercised control of picking up ships on high seas. Of course, we are doing same thing today in relation to Guatemala; it's a little illegal, but no one so far has picked it up. . . .

This is just a case of our giving them private help, & tipping off [Nationalist] Chinese. We don't automatically tell them. They treat our notification to them as being acquiescence, or invitation to action.

Quite aside from it being "a little illegal" (how Dulles squared this with being "no different from international law" is a bit of a mystery), this was a significant risk to take. America was enabling a violation of freedom of navigation, a principle it had enshrined in the Atlantic Charter. Perhaps having engaged in similar operations off Guatemala had rendered Dulles more cavalier; it normalized a practice that was both illegal and dangerous. There was no guarantee that Chiang would just let the ships go. But neither Dulles nor Eisenhower paused to consider that possibility. The Chinese Nationalists, thought Eisenhower, "might get themselves in a fix," but he did not see the Soviets going to war over the matter. So the president authorized sharing the intelligence.[9]

Chiang's response was decisive. On June 23, 1954, his forces seized a Soviet tanker, the *Tuapse*, somewhere between the Philippines and Taiwan. He then proceeded to detain the *Tuapse* in the southern Taiwanese port of Kaohsiung. By July 9, Dulles's department was getting concerned. It knew of no legal grounds for keeping the tanker and advised that Chiang be asked to release it immediately. Chiang's response was a lofty silence. The Americans were eventually informed that the *Tuapse* was being held "pending further investigation." The lesson was obvious.[10] Chiang was flouting the American directive and would do as he saw fit.

Chiang had become confident in his capacity to handle the Americans. He was a sensitive man, and his sensitivity would not allow him to brook the condescension that his patrons sometimes treated him with. Because he was also deeply manipulative, he knew how to get them to back off from the demands he considered most outrageous. In a heated exchange in 1953, he ticked off a visiting senator on the Senate Foreign Relations Committee and the commander of the First Fleet. The United States had no Far Eastern policy, Chiang declared. The Americans' fruitless expenditure of resources on Korea and Indochina (as opposed to investing more in his own struggle against the CCP) had given the Soviets exactly what they wanted. What the United States needed to do was to focus on driving the Communists out of China. Admiral William K. Phillips, who was not used to being castigated in this manner, flung out the possibility of America going home. Chiang backed down, but the exchange showed how comfortable he felt in his relationship with the United States. He was not wrong. Rankin, who had arranged the meeting, would soothe the ruffled feathers of Senator H. Alexander Smith. There was no point, said Rankin, in taking the generalissimo literally. His outburst showed how disappointed he was in the policy of an administration that had offered so much hope with its tough stance against the Communists.[11] Chiang was calculating that the Americans dared not cut him loose, for that would make them look soft on Communism. The Eisenhower administration needed him as much as he needed them.

This calculation was correct. Eisenhower would soon preside over a treaty that would bind the ROC and the United States even closer. Chiang had been deeply unhappy about the ending of the Korean War; with the possible exceptions of Syngman Rhee and Kim Il-sung, no one was more so. Mao himself was not fully satisfied, but he learned to make his peace with it. The Americans had held firm that Chinese prisoners of war would have a choice about which China they wished to be repatriated to. More than fourteen thousand of them chose Taiwan. This was outrageous to the PRC; it alone represented the true China, and the undermining of its legitimacy in this fashion caused the negotiations to drag on far longer than they otherwise would have. It was something that would have to be lived with, however, and after three years of fighting, Beijing was willing to come to terms. To Chiang, the Korean War had not been meant to end in an armistice. It was supposed to have expanded to other fronts, so that he could come roaring back in triumph to conquer China. Instead, Eisenhower was busily seeking a truce. Chiang would warn darkly of the Soviet "peace offensive," but, absent the security of absolute war against the Communists, he needed assurances that the United States would defend his little regime. Accordingly, Chiang wrote to Eisenhower informing him that the United

States would need to sign defense pacts with Asian countries menaced by Communism, including the Republic of China.[12]

The United States was somewhat hesitant about this. It would, after all, be wading into a civil war. The KMT and CCP were still engaged in hostilities, and the pact could render America a party to them. Therein lay danger. China, as Dulles reminded the ROC ambassador Wellington Koo, was a vast country where even the Japanese had got "bogged down." The United States had no appetite for a war there. Dulles suggested that there might be an advantage to the ROC in not having a defense pact with the United States; it would allow the ROC to launch offensive action against the Communists without the restrictions of a formal pact. In Korea, the US security pact with South Korea had followed the armistice, and now the conflict was frozen, with South Korea unable to attack the North. This was not a situation Dulles was particularly keen on seeing in the China theater. As he reminded Koo, the United States wanted KMT operations against the Communists in China to continue without joining those operations itself. A treaty would complicate matters: the United States might find itself compelled either to join the operations or to limit them. Nevertheless, he agreed to keep the matter under consideration.[13]

Eventually, the idea began to find favor. Chiang Kai-shek floated the idea that he would refrain from major military actions without US approval if granted a treaty. After the saga of the *Tuapse*, one can see why the assistant secretary for Far Eastern affairs found this prospect tempting, though it took a certain gullibility to believe that the generalissimo would abide by that commitment. Thus far, Chiang did not have a general US commitment to defend him. Following the Geneva agreements that partitioned Vietnam, the United States, along with Australia, Britain, New Zealand, Pakistan, the Philippines, and Thailand, would form the Southeast Asia Treaty Organization (SEATO) in September 1954. It was a mutual defense pact, aimed at combatting Communist aggression. As a demonstration of the American resolve to keep the rest of the region free of Communism, this was an important step. But SEATO pointedly left the ROC out. It would have been impossible to include it; there was no way the other members of the pact would have signed on to protecting Chiang. But Washington needed to be careful of implying that it cared less about Taiwan than about other places in Asia.[14] Such careless exclusion, after all, had been what led to the Korean War and the Taiwan tangle in the first place. One wanted to be sure that the Communists understood that Taiwan was off-limits. A defense pact would send that message unmistakably.

But if the benefits of a separate defense pact with the ROC were obvious, so, too, were the difficulties. The ROC was a belligerent in a civil war. And it was unclear what territory the pact was to include. That the United States wanted to defend Taiwan and the Pescadores was a given. But what of the offshore islands—Kinmen and Matsu, Dachen and Nanri—that lay so close to mainland China but remained, for the time being, under KMT control? On this the United States was undecided. Clarity on what the Americans were willing to defend would be necessary before committing to defense. As late as September 1, 1954, Dulles was inclined to delay a decision on a US-ROC defense pact because of the questions raised by the offshore islands.[15]

It was Mao Zedong who forced the decision. Word of the possible pact between Chiang and the Americans had reached Mao and he wanted to kill it immediately, not least because such a pact would damage the prospects for improved relations between the United States and the PRC. The Americans had malevolent intentions of course: SEATO was their attempt to wreck the peace that the Geneva conference had brought to Indochina and the surrounding region. But while China could live with America making trouble in Southeast Asia, signing a pact with Taiwan would be taking things too far; it was the difference between interfering in China's near abroad and interfering in China's civil war. China had to liberate Taiwan, and the Americans would have to understand that. It was a twisted way of thinking, but it made a certain sense. China wanted better relations with America. America was contemplating a step that would jeopardize the prospect of improved relations. America therefore had to be deterred from that step. A show of force would discourage the Americans from buttressing Chiang's regime, and would thereby prevent further deterioration to US-China relations. Mao Zedong launched shells at Kinmen in September 1954.[16] Thus began the first Taiwan Strait crisis.

Mao's military activities during the crisis were straightforward. In addition to Kinmen, he shelled Matsu. The PRC navy would attack and eventually take the Dachen island group.[17] But Mao had miscalculated the American reaction. Rather than deterring America, China's conduct caused a slow but steady hardening of Eisenhower's thinking on Taiwan. Mao wound up doing precisely the harm to US-China relations he had wished to avoid.

This did not happen overnight. The crisis found the Eisenhower administration deeply uncertain about just how important the offshore islands really were. Most of the Joint Chiefs felt the islands needed to be held. The psychological blow of losing them, they argued, would be too great. The exception was Matthew Ridgway, who had succeeded General Collins as chief of staff of the army. The defense of Taiwan and the Pescadores, Ridgway held, was unaffected by Kinmen. It was not that he was dismissing the "political and psychological importance" of the islands; it was just that he believed the Joint Chiefs were not competent to evaluate that importance. (In a world where generals opined freely on international politics, Ridgway was an exception. There were realms where he was an expert and realms where he was not—and he was secure enough to differentiate between them openly.) Dulles believed that if they could be held, the offshore islands should be defended. The "if" was crucial; there was no point putting prestige on the line for a goal that could not be achieved. All the while, Chiang was pushing for the mutual defense treaty. The ROC was the only "free" country in the region, he hectored Dulles in five hours of talks, that did not enjoy such a treaty.[18] It had been left isolated, and it was time its contributions to the anti-Communist struggle were properly rewarded.

Dulles was deeply conflicted. He had tried, even after the shelling had begun, to persuade Chiang that the ROC was better off without a treaty. He also wanted to take the matter up at the United Nations. This, he argued, would help with getting congressional support for American action as well. But there were problems here too. Taking it up with the UN would limit American room for maneuver; other countries would have a say, and even if the Soviets decided to let the matter proceed, the United Kingdom and other US allies might not side with Washington. Eisenhower was also torn. The United States needed to defend the Pacific, but he was beginning to wonder just how important the islands Chiang controlled really were. Kinmen was only of psychological importance, he pointed out. Did the Americans even really need to defend Taiwan? Even if they abandoned it, they would by no means abandon the entire Pacific. It was a fascinating outburst. The president—with all his genuine expertise in geopolitics—was rejecting the idea that giving up Taiwan would cause irreparable damage to the American posture in the Pacific. Besides, Eisenhower said, he was always getting letters from Americans who asked, "What do we care what happens to those yellow people out there?" There were also, of course, as Secretary of Defense Charlie Wilson would point out, plenty of Americans who felt the United States should have backed Chiang Kai-shek all the way in his war with the Communists in the first place.[19] Nothing was resolved. It was a divided, confused administration, which reflected a divided, confused country.

Even with the first Taiwan Strait crisis underway, then, the United States was willing to contemplate abandoning the ROC. But the idea that Taiwan was vital to US national security, which Admiral Radford and others had argued so forcefully for, was difficult to dislodge. Meeting by meeting, the National Security Council kept reemphasizing how important the ROC was. General James Van Fleet, who had been asked to evaluate American military assistance programs in the region, penned a paper calling for a mutual defense treaty with the ROC. And the constitutional implications of his administration's current military posture were beginning to dawn on Eisenhower. If Taiwan was vital to American interests, it had to be defended. If it had to be defended, that had to be done by constitutional means. He was suddenly, painfully aware that he lacked the authority to use the Seventh Fleet to defend Taiwan. Doing so without proper congressional authorization could lead to impeachment. The path to that authorization was to sign a treaty and then get it ratified by Congress.[20]

The requirements for passing the treaty were clear enough. It would need to be specific on the territories to be defended. It could not include all of China, which Chiang did not possess; that would raise the awkward question of whether the United States was obligated to help Chiang reconquer the mainland. There had been enough debate about the offshore islands that including them was not certain. The United States would have to retain the right to build military bases on Taiwan. Then there would need to be an assiduous courting of key senators. The eventual text of the treaty limited the territories covered to Taiwan and the Pescadores. The offshore islands were left uncovered. It also provided the United States "the right to dispose such United States land, air and sea forces in and about Taiwan and the Pescadores as may be required for their defense, as determined by mutual agreement." The treaty would be formally ratified in March 1955. Despite the Democrats controlling the Senate, the resolution calling for ratification passed overwhelmingly. Eisenhower's stance on China had broad bipartisan support. But well before ratification, the PRC's military activities were testing the full scope of American obligations. The formal exclusion of the offshore islands had not led to a complete abandonment of them. Dulles had wanted to "fuzz up" the language; fuzziness, he argued, would leave doubts in the minds of the Communists about just what the United States would do, and creating doubt in the mind of the enemy was all to the good.[21]

The problem with the fuzziness was that it created doubt within the US government too. Having formally excluded the defense of the offshore islands from its treaty responsibilities, it still found itself wondering about them. Chiang was quick to exploit that confusion. He had no desire to give up any inch of his territory, and the ROC asked for help in defending the Dachen Islands. The Dachens were a problem: they could not be defended, and yet their loss would harm morale and prestige. So Dulles, at the National Security Council meeting on January 20, 1955, would come up with a formula. The Dachens had to be abandoned, and the United States would have to help Chiang evacuate his forces there. But to offset the loss of prestige and to make American resolve clear to the CCP, the United States should commit itself to the defense of Kinmen and Matsu. Dulles had already sounded out congressional leaders on the possibility. Fuzziness had failed to create sufficient doubt among the Communists. It was time to get tough.[22]

This was by no means a position that everyone in the Eisenhower administration shared. Secretary of Defense Charlie Wilson thought "it was foolish to fight a terrible war with Communist China simply in order to hold all these little islands. . . . We should defend only Formosa and the Pescadores and let the others go." National Security Advisor Robert Cutler was alert to the danger that the defense of islands so close to the mainland would increase the risk of general war with China. (On this, Cutler was right. There was a risk. Mao, however, gave orders that the PLA was not to attack foreign forces needlessly. The goal in using force, after all, had been not a war with the Americans but, ideally, a peace with them. Mao's restraint, belated as it was, was a key factor in the peaceful resolution of the crisis. He could have chosen to escalate. Eisenhower got lucky.) But Eisenhower, by this point, had had it. Further delay was risky and he needed a congressional resolution. "If the Chinese Communists wanted to make general war out of anything the United States did," he snapped in response to Cutler's concern, "there was nothing we could do to prevent it."[23]

The resolution Eisenhower got from Congress authorized him to "employ the Armed Forces of the United States as he deems necessary for the specific purpose of securing and protecting Formosa and the Pescadores against armed attack, this authority to include the securing and protection of such related positions and territories of that area now in friendly hands and the taking of such other measures as he judges to be required or appropriate in assuring the Defense of Formosa and the Pescadores." This authority was given because American national security was seen as dependent on the possession of the West Pacific island chain—stretching from the Kurils through the Japanese archipelago, onward to Taiwan, and then to Southeast Asia—by friendly governments. The resolution would last as long as Eisenhower saw fit. (It was, in some ways, a harbinger of the Gulf of Tonkin Resolution that would later allow Lyndon Johnson to wage war in Indochina: it abdicated congressional responsibility to decide on war and peace, ceding extra power to the president in the name of security.) But even this was not enough for Chiang Kai-shek. He would, he threatened Ambassador Rankin, refuse to ask for help evacuating from the Dachens until the United States clarified its position on Kinmen and Matsu. To do otherwise, the generalissimo insisted, would be to betray Free China. It was time the Americans realized they were not "dealing with children."[24]

This was a remarkable tone for a man whose defenses relied so heavily on the United States. And though Chiang failed in his attempt to get the United States to make a public statement affirming its commitment to Kinmen and Matsu, he was capable of issuing a statement of his own. He would, he declared in a press release on February 7, 1955, be redeploying the forces evacuated from the Dachen Islands (he had eventually resigned himself to their loss) to

Kinmen and Matsu after consultation with the United States. The United States had assured him of its commitment to defend Taiwan and the Pescadores, as well as any territories deemed crucial to that goal. The statement was issued without waiting for US approval. The treaty might have made no explicit mention of Kinmen and Matsu, but they were there, weighing heavy upon the official mind. The Eisenhower administration's haplessness was crystallized in Dulles's wistful phrase: "How fortunate it would be if these islands sank to the bottom of the sea."[25]

It was at this juncture that the specter of nuclear war was raised. The PRC had succeeded in taking Nanri Island, which lay close to China's shore between Kinmen and Matsu. The two ROC-held islands were looking vulnerable. On March 6, 1955, Eisenhower told Dulles that he was willing to use "atomic weapons as interchangeable with conventional weapons" to defend Kinmen and Matsu. Dulles began to work on creating "a better public climate for the use of atomic weapons." This was reckless beyond belief. Had Eisenhower taken this step, he might well have initiated a nuclear holocaust. As it was, he backed off the idea. By April 1, he was hoping that it would somehow be possible to get the generalissimo to abandon the islands voluntarily.[26]

This did not happen. What did happen was that Zhou Enlai declared at the Bandung Conference in April 1955 that China was willing to negotiate with the United States to dial the tension down. China never had given up on the idea that "peaceful coexistence" with the United States was a possibility.[27] Deterrence had clearly failed in achieving that goal—the Americans now had a treaty with the ROC—so it was time to see if negotiation might be more fruitful. Having triggered the crisis, the PRC now saw fit to end it. America did not have a monopoly on confusion after all. The change of tack from the PRC staved off further reconsiderations on Eisenhower's part. The question of whether to defend the islands could be shelved for the time being. The first Taiwan Strait crisis was over.

The United States had, with a somewhat unwarranted optimism, assumed that Chiang would give up Kinmen and Matsu in due course. But Chiang, who was incensed when told that Eisenhower had changed his mind on defending the islands, had no intention of doing so.[28] The generalissimo would instead move to strengthen his position there (American aid, of course, made such strengthening possible). And that meant that, when the second Taiwan Strait crisis came in 1958, it would be that much harder for the Americans to compel an ROC evacuation from Kinmen and Matsu.

There were several motives underpinning Mao's decision to shell the offshore islands again in 1958. The most important, perhaps, was Mao's idea that conflict could galvanize the population behind a common goal. He was obsessed with the Great Leap Forward: an ambitious, tragic plan that sought to surpass the Western powers' industrial strength by bringing massive communes to China and boosting industrial production. The transformation would be wrenching, but if the Chinese were given an enemy at the same time, they might unite behind the chairman's plan. "To have an enemy in front of us, to have tension, is to our advantage," said Mao on August 17, 1958, as the assembled CCP members contemplated both the Great Leap Forward and shelling Kinmen.[29]

There were foreign policy considerations too. The relationship with the Soviets had never been entirely free of friction, and Mao had suspected that they were treating China as a subordinate. The Soviet suggestion of a joint submarine fleet struck the chairman as an attempt to control China's coast. He raged heatedly at both the Soviet ambassador and Soviet leader Nikita Khrushchev about the matter, to make sure they understood that China could not be bullied. Taking the initiative to shell ROC territory would show the Soviets that China was a power to be reckoned with and was not answerable to Moscow. The Soviets, who had been rather discouraging of China's ventures in the strait, had to be taught that the PRC could act independently.

At the same time, American troops were being criticized for their activities in Lebanon—they would pull out as the crisis started—making this an opportune moment for an attack. The final motivation was that Chiang had been fortifying Kinmen and Matsu, and his forces continued to bombard China with propaganda aimed at fomenting an uprising. ROC and US forces had choked the life out of the Chinese city of Xiamen, which had once been a bustling, thriving port. It would, in days to come, become crucial to the PRC's economic opening and reform. But in 1958, it was a place shuttered, its potential a casualty of cross-strait tension.[30] So in August 1958, Mao kicked off the second Taiwan Strait crisis.

For an adventure that could have triggered the United States into using nuclear weapons, it is surprising just how carefully calibrated Mao's use of force was. The shells flew on August 23, 1958, but there were no attempts to seize the islands. Mao wished to avoid initiating an attack on the Americans. The idea was to make a show of force, not to conquer Taiwan.[31] That careful calibration was lost on Washington.

Dulles, by this point, had teetered back to the position that the defense of Kinmen and Matsu was essential. As the secretary saw it, Chiang's efforts at fortifying those outposts had rendered them more

integral to the Republic of China and therefore more worth defending. Eisenhower was still ambivalent but remarked that American
involvement with the islands would be solely "to sustain the morale
of the GRC [Government of the Republic of China] which had deliberately committed major forces to their defense contrary to our 1954
military advice." US involvement in defending the islands was in
essence a reward to Chiang for crises he had had no small role in creating. There was good reason to put an end to such rewards. But the
problem with having considered the use of nuclear weapons once,
as the Eisenhower administration had in 1955, was that it had normalized the idea; it would now always be there, within the realm of
acceptable statecraft. Dulles would once again invoke the possibility.
He admitted it might cause "revulsion," but perhaps a small-scale set
of detonations would meet with limited public outcry.[32] The sheer
confusion the Eisenhower administration had allowed to fester had
left it in a place where the use of nuclear weapons was considered
practical policy.

Dulles would eventually go back to Taiwan to try to talk Chiang
into reducing his forces on the islands and thereby pave the way to
an informal armistice. He failed. Chiang, as ambassador to the ROC
Everett F. Drumright noted, was sensitive to the charge of being a
US "puppet." Dulles's proposal, the ROC declared, was tantamount
to terminating its government and consenting to the dreaded "two
China" policy. When Dulles pointed out that the defense of Kinmen
and Matsu might involve the use of nuclear weapons comparable in
effect to those used against Hiroshima and Nagasaki, Chiang dismissed the idea loftily. He was no weapons expert, but some means
would be found. Dulles came away with one small consolation. Chiang had promised not to liberate the mainland by force. Given that

KMT forces landing on China would almost certainly be annihi-
lated, this might not have been quite as important an achievement as
Dulles made it out to be.[33]

Once again, it was China that brought the crisis to an amicable end.
Mao decided that it was all right to leave Kinmen and Matsu in Chiang's possession; it would provide a station from which to communicate
with the KMT close at hand. This would thwart any American attempt
to normalize a situation in which the offshore islands were handed to
China but Taiwan was not. If the PRC wanted to up the pressure on the
KMT or the Americans at some point in the future, it could always show
more force. Those were the reasons Mao gave to his fellow party members, but perhaps it was simply a way of saving face. Whatever the reason, the shelling stuttered to a close. On October 25, the PRC declared
it would shell only every other day; the ROC would do the same. The
shelling would continue in this desultory fashion for two decades until
US-China relations were normalized on January 1, 1979.[34]

It is easy to look back at the 1958 Taiwan Strait crisis with a sense
of complacency. It all worked out, after all. China did not push the
attack, and Taiwan stayed out of Communist hands. Such a reading
misses the very real danger of the situation. Just as it had been in the
1954–1955 Taiwan Strait crisis, the United States was being dragged
to a position where it was considering using nuclear weapons to
defend islands it knew it had no interest in defending. Once again, a
single miscalculation was all that lay between a crisis and a general
Sino-American war. Even if the worsening Sino-Soviet relationship
reduced the risk of Moscow getting involved automatically, the carnage of such a war would have been horrific and it might well have
ended in the use of nuclear weapons. That did not happen because
Mao chose to back down at the last moment. If he had not done

so, there is no telling how much damage the confusion inherent in Eisenhower's policy might have wrought.

American policy toward China and Taiwan during these years, then, was a mess of indecision and militarism. Starting with that seemingly simple step of declaring an end to neutrality in the Taiwan Strait, Eisenhower had slipped into committing the United States to defending islands of dubious strategic value. One cannot keep declaring that one must prevail in mortal combat with a Communist monolith without coming, at some level, to believe it. That belief, counterproductive and unrealistic as it was, infected the minds in Washington and brought the United States to the brink of nuclear war. Eisenhower was adamant that the destruction of the Chinese Communists' military power was in America's long-term interests; he was appalled when General Ridgway would question that belief. The Joint Chiefs would insist on enshrining the ultimate removal of the CCP into NSC directives. When it was pointed out that this was not a practical objective, they would counter that there was no harm in having it as a long-term aspiration, even if it was unachievable now.[35] This was, at a certain level, understandable. McCarthyism aside, America had just fought a war with China in Korea, and there was anger and trauma to process. But having the destruction of Chinese Communist power as a long-term aspiration meant that the loss of Taiwan was unthinkable. By 1958, the loss of Kinmen and Matsu—once considered worthless outposts that Chiang had to somehow be persuaded to abandon—became impossible to countenance. So even as Chiang proved a feckless ally, the United States was threatening nuclear war on his behalf. Each time a meeting invoked the need to counter Communism, the pressure to do so felt more intense. Each time the commitment to Taiwan was mentioned, the harder it became to question. The sheer bureaucratic weight of the meetings devoted to keeping Chiang going and forcing Mao out overpowered more practical considerations.

For there were more practical considerations. Charlton Ogburn, the regional planning advisor for Far Eastern affairs at the State Department, would state bluntly that "to suppose that the future of China lies in any sense with the National Government seems to me to ignore all the evidences of reality we have. . . . It seems to me that our present policy toward the Chinese Nationalists . . . is based not upon a reasoned estimate of the situation and of our national interests, but upon a desire (by no means discreditable) to make amends for what we consider our shortcomings in the past." It was completely unrealistic to hope that the CCP was going to disappear and that the KMT could represent China. It was completely unrealistic to hope that defending Taiwan more staunchly would cause the PRC to split from the Soviet Union—something Dulles and Eisenhower desperately wanted to achieve. The president himself would occasionally have a glimmer of realization that the United States could not sustain its present China policy. On April 13, 1954, for example, he would ask if there was some way of trading with the PRC. When Secretary of Defense Wilson said this was incompatible with refusing to recognize China, the president snarled that he was talking "of peoples, not governments. He was insisting upon some way of reaching the mass of the Chinese people." (It was the same instinct that would later cause Nixon to seek rapprochement with China: one could not leave that many people outside the international system.) Had there been a study, Eisenhower would ask, even as he prepared to sign the defense treaty with the ROC, of what circumstances it would take for the United States to recognize the PRC? After all, as he would acknowledge in a moment of crisis, the defense of Formosa itself was not as important as that of Japan or the Philippines.[36]

Pursued to their logical conclusion, such thoughts charted an alternative course for American policy. Once one resigned oneself to the notion that the CCP was not going to vanish, the question became how best to live with it—at which point, one was essentially contemplating the kind of rapprochement that Nixon and Kissinger would later achieve. Had Eisenhower commissioned a study on the conditions it would take to recognize the PRC, he might well have found it achievable. A compromise on Taiwan—and for all the support extended to Chiang, the Eisenhower administration was thoroughly sick of the generalissimo—would have been difficult, especially after the defense treaty with the ROC was ratified, but it was by no means impossible.

But these thoughts never shaped broader policy; they died in the moment, and the question of how to defend Taiwan took their place. The president's own anti-Communism made it impossible to follow up on the alternative ideas he raised. When it came to the China and Taiwan conundrums, Eisenhower was his own worst enemy. He never managed to make up his mind on what was vital and what was not. The pressures of McCarthyism and the convictions of his bureaucrats made the careful parsing of possibilities even harder. The result was strategic drift: a thicker entanglement with the ROC and continuing estrangement from the PRC, achieved in a fit of irresolution.

The basic contours of Eisenhower's China policy outlasted his administration. This persistence was all the more remarkable because, even in the later Eisenhower years, it was becoming clear the PRC and the Soviet Union were falling out. The 1958 Taiwan Strait crisis had exposed major differences between Moscow and Beijing. By 1960, the Soviets were recalling their advisors from China, and tensions were high along the China-USSR border in Xinjiang. By 1964, Washington was able to reach out to the Soviets to ask if Moscow might be interested in pursuing a joint strike on China's nascent nuclear program. Moscow turned the offer down, but the very request showed Washington's awareness of the fact that there was a schism between the two Communist giants. Under these conditions, surely it was conceivable that America and China might achieve some sort of rapprochement. The possibility was occasionally raised in the Kennedy-Johnson years. John F. Kennedy does appear to have thought about some sort of rapprochement with the PRC—it might have happened in the second term he did not live to serve—but he died without having altered the China policy he inherited. JFK's successor, Lyndon Johnson, was mired so deep in Vietnam that reaching a modus vivendi with the PRC—which was supporting the North Vietnamese war effort—would have been well-nigh impossible for him. LBJ was not going to let it be said that JFK had been tougher with the enemy than he was. The fear of appearing weak on Communism paralyzed American policy.[37]

This paralysis rendered Mao's policies ineffectual. Mao's strategic outlook was defined by a peculiar mix of risk-taking and prudence.[38] His conduct during the Taiwan Strait crises saw his country edging right to the brink of general war, even as it sought improved relations with Taiwan and the United States. Where Eisenhower's administration was confused about its goals, Mao knew what he wanted—and he would blend military threats with diplomatic outreach to get it.

There would be missiles lobbed at Kinmen and Matsu, not to mention heavy investment in the air force and navy; one would need air and sea power to take Taiwan. China's quest for a nuclear bomb would be fulfilled in 1964. But there would also be a steady stream of communication indicating that Beijing was open to a rapprochement with both the KMT and Washington.

Just what form such a rapprochement with the ROC would have taken is unclear. One model was proffered in 1957, when Chiang sent an envoy, Song Yishan, on a secret mission to Beijing. There, Song met with Li Weihan, who headed Beijing's United Front Work Department. Li's offer to Chiang was deceptively straightforward. Both the CCP and KMT could work toward peaceful unification. Taiwan could be designated a special autonomous region. This was a designation Xinjiang already had and that Tibet would get in 1965. The designation itself had little to do with the day-to-day realities of governance; the heyday of Tibetan autonomy had been between 1951 and 1959. By 1965, the designation was just the PRC's way of saying it was in complete control of Tibet. In Li's proposal, Taiwan would be left under Chiang's administration; the CCP would refrain from sending officials to interfere. Chiang was welcome to send KMT officials to China to participate in the central administration. The condition was that American forces would have to leave the Taiwan Strait.[39]

Chiang, of course, rejected the offer. Part of the problem, one suspects, was his innate unwillingness to share power—there was no way these Communist bandits could be allowed to assume parity with him in governing China. But there was a sensible reason for rejecting the offer too. There were no guarantees that the CCP would keep the peace. Once American forces had left the strait, there was nothing binding Mao to his word. The offer was a harbinger of what would later be designated "one country, two systems," and it suffered from the same problem that model did: the autonomy of the second system could be changed on a whim, as Tibet would find in 1959. To accept the CCP's offer was to surrender, and much as the United States worried about the possibility, that was something Chiang would never do.

Chiang's refusal to come to terms did not mean that Mao would give up on outreach. During the civil war, the CCP had won significant territories by convincing the warlords working for Chiang to switch sides. Persuasion was so much easier than warfare; it could certainly be tried with Taiwan. This never quite brought about the complete handover of Taiwan that the PRC would have hoped for (though, with the Americans prowling the strait, it was a far likelier path to victory than a naval conquest), but it did lead to some of Chiang's erstwhile cronies defecting to the PRC. Wei Li-Huang, one of Chiang's generals who had fallen out of favor, had fled to Hong Kong. In 1955, he made his way to China, where he was soon clinking glasses with Mao Zedong. Wei would write a note to his Taiwanese compatriots, celebrating the economic strides Mao's China had made, denouncing Chiang and the defense pact he had signed with America, and declaring that Taiwan was a part of China that would have to be liberated. It was exactly what Mao wanted Taiwan's residents to hear. Mao himself was careful to remind people that the KMT and CCP had cooperated twice before. There was no reason they could not do so again—and Wei's arrival in China was proof.[40]

But by far the biggest fish to return to the mother country was Li Zongren, the ROC's former president and Chiang's bitter rival. Li had been in the United States ever since his medical leave back in 1949. He had spent most of his time grumbling to the Americans about their support for Chiang, whose temporary cession of power, he maintained, was just a charade. Li had been a warlord, and switches of allegiance came easily to him. Like Zhou Enlai, he had been calling for internal Chinese cooperation to solve the Formosan problem. Both the CCP and the KMT were bitterly opposed to the idea that the UN might take up the Taiwan issue. The UN, after all, might well decide on a plebiscite of some sort, which could lead to Taiwanese independence. And Taiwan, both parties agreed, was a part of China. The question was always which party would be in power over China as a whole, not whether Taiwan could go its own way. That made Taiwan an internal matter, best settled by the Chinese themselves.

In 1965, Li decided it was time to return home. Home was China. When asked what had changed his thinking, Li cited the atomic bomb. Nuclear power had been the province of the great powers: the United States and the USSR. Now, China had a bomb, had shown it could stand up as a great power in its own right. On top of that, it had gone to war with and defeated India in 1962, evidence that the CCP could and would protect the motherland. In Li's philosophy of life, power made for legitimacy. The military prowess the PRC authorities had shown made them the rightful masters of China. (It was a nice way of underscoring Chiang's incompetence too.) Li made his way to Europe and then to Pakistan, from where he flew onward to China. There he was met by Zhou Enlai. His reception was cordial. A fallen leaf had returned to the roots.[41]

The PRC did not confine itself to keystones in Chiang's power structure. Its own origins had been as mass revolutionary movement, and it sought to inspire something similar on Taiwan. Over a million propaganda leaflets made their way to the offshore islands.

Radio broadcasts boomed out in Taiwan for twelve hours at a stretch. Newspapers and magazines across the Chinese-speaking world—Japan, Hong Kong, Southeast Asia—carried pieces encouraging the liberation of Taiwan. Those in China who had relatives serving in the KMT were encouraged to send letters stressing the need for liberation.[42] If sufficient numbers were convinced, Taiwan might throw off the KMT yoke on its own.

The propaganda had many points to make—the duties of a true patriot, the glories of life under the PRC, the evil of Chiang Kai-shek—but one point was particularly potent: American imperialism. There was a foreign power running Taiwan; it was foreign money and weapons that made Chiang's regime possible. Propaganda has its greatest chance of success when there are genuine grievances to exploit. The American presence in Taiwan was a genuine grievance. Here they were, these benevolent overlords, propping up a police state and swaggering around as though the laws did not apply to them. It was not surprising that, even without CCP influence, a group of angry Taiwanese stormed the US embassy in Taipei in 1957.

The anger came from a simple spark. An American soldier, Robert Reynolds, shot and killed a Taiwanese man, Liu Ziran, on March 20, 1957. Reynolds claimed self-defense, and he was acquitted in the court-martial that followed. Liu's widow stood outside the embassy with a banner of protest. Was the killer Reynolds innocent? She would object; she would resist. A crowd gathered in solidarity. Then, it stormed the embassy, destroying everything it could find. No major injuries were suffered by the Americans, but the building was a wreck. The indifference of the police—the protesters were left in the embassy for hours and the police did not open fire—led the Americans to suspect that ROC officials might have helped organize the riot (Chiang Ching-kuo, the generalissimo's son and spy chief, was rumored to have had a hand in the matter). This was something the generalissimo vehemently denied. But he grumbled about the court-martial; it reminded everyone that Americans answered to a different law. He asked that Ambassador Rankin convey "his profound regret and his assurance that the events of May 24 do not reflect anti-Americanism in Free China, but simply resentment at the verdict of a court martial." This, Rankin did. He, too, believed that anti-Americanism in the ROC was not terribly strong; it was part of anti-Westernism, rooted in the colonial era. It was possible, Rankin and Dulles believed, that the authorities had allowed the riot to go as far as it did in an attempt to apply some pressure to the United States. There was a status of forces agreement to conclude, and the United States had been slow in sealing it.[43] What was remarkable was the refusal to gauge the full depth of the anti-Americanism. For it was there—powerful, hidden from men like Rankin who got their information solely from Chiang and lacked the curiosity to dig further, but waiting to burst out. The ROC was on the American side. Why, then, would it be subject to anti-Americanism? It was a blindness that would persist into the present day.

There was no evidence that the CCP's propaganda efforts had had anything to do with the riot. But one could see why the CCP had hopes that the propaganda might work. There was fertile ground for it to take hold. With a corrupt, despised regime, significant anti-American sentiment, and general discontent, the ROC would have seemed an excellent candidate for a revolution. The general uprising never happened, but the possibility was always there.

Meanwhile, Mao reached out to the Americans too. Dulles had famously refused to shake Zhou Enlai's hand when they met at

Geneva in 1954 to bring a peace settlement to Indochina, but this had not stopped the premier from signaling his country's willingness to talk to the United States at Bandung the next year. Talks began to discuss swapping prisoners. These grew into the Warsaw channel, where ambassadors from the PRC and the United States would meet and talk. At first glance, the talks would seem a complete and utter failure. The PRC wanted recognition. The United States wanted to reach a modus vivendi but refused to renounce its defense pact with the ROC and would insist that the CCP vow not to use force for reunification. To the PRC, the ROC was not a state but a rogue part of China; it had no right to conclude a defense pact, and America had no right to make one with it. Wang Bingnan, the Chinese ambassador, would go so far as to suggest that if America would only abide by Truman's statement—the president had vowed that America was neutral when it came to the Chinese Civil War—the problem would be half solved.[44] Thus the Warsaw talks would wind on, from promise to recrimination and back again. But there was one thing they did achieve. They brought the two sides face-to-face. They were shouting at one another, but there was a channel of communication, one that allowed them, if only subconsciously, to register each other's basic humanity.

The value of this banal recognition made itself felt in the summer of 1962, when Chinese troops started massing along the coastline opposite Kinmen and Matsu again. Official Washington was not sure what this meant. It could be preparation for another assault on the offshore islands. But it could also be a response to Chiang's own plans for an assault on the mainland. Chiang had taken heart from the Tibetan uprising of 1959. As he saw it, his time had come: now was the moment to launch a three-pronged assault on the despised

Communists, attacking from Tibet, the southern provinces, and the coastline. Observing Chiang's preparations, the PRC would have been irresponsible to leave itself unprepared for a coastal assault. US ambassador to Poland John Cabot met with Ambassador Wang in Warsaw to discuss the matter. Cabot's summary of the conversation is telling:

> Reverting to an earlier remark by Wang that our talks could not continue if an attack were made, I said that such attack if made by GRC would be without support of US. It would seem to me most important under those circumstances for our talks to continue in order to restore peace. We would clearly disassociate ourselves from any such attack. . . .
>
> I then asked for assurances from him that ChiComs [Chinese Communists] would not attack Taiwan. There was a long pause and Wang then replied question of ChiCom attack does not arise. The question is of Taiwan organizing an attack on Mainland. . . .
>
> *Comment*: Although discussion throughout was serious, atmosphere not particularly tense. I think this summary of conversation, which comes from almost word for word transcript made by Embassy officer, gives flavor better than anything I can add. Wang was relaxed and friendly when offering us tea after formal exchange.[45]

There was a direct way, this time, for the PRC to communicate its intentions—and, perhaps even more important, its emotion. Cabot could look his counterpart in the eye, register the friendliness behind the offer of tea. Wang could realize that the man negotiating with him would respond to that offer in a friendly fashion and had his own concerns that he would attempt to convey in all honesty. They had moved from an abstract Communist and imperialist to slightly more complicated human beings. They would continue to accuse one another of sabotaging peace, but there was now a capacity for something approaching understanding. China would not renounce the right to use force if it had to; that would be caving on the principle that what happened on Taiwan was an internal affair. But Chinese diplomats would signal through the British that they were in no hurry to launch an invasion of Taiwan.[46] The mere opening of communication helped avert a third Taiwan Strait crisis for the time being.

This was a massive improvement on the Eisenhower years. But the basic contours of America's China conundrum had remained the same. The United States was still refusing to deal with the PRC as the government of China; it was still tied, however resentfully, to a rump regime on Taiwan whose delusional intentions of taking back the mainland remained as powerful as ever. It would take Richard Nixon's arrival in the White House to change that. Much of the credit for the famous opening to China has gone to Henry Kissinger, who made the dramatic secret trip in 1971 that led to the breakthrough. Kissinger's immersion in European history had left him with certain ideas about how diplomacy should work. He believed, like Prussian statesman Otto von Bismarck, that facts could not be changed, only used; he believed, too, in being closer to other great powers than they were to one another. He would bring these ideas with him to his role as Nixon's national security advisor.[47]

Putting those ideas into practice naturally meant seeking a rapprochement with China. But absent Richard Nixon, they might well have just remained academic fantasies, not practical policy. "There's an old Vulcan proverb. Only Nixon could go to China," said Spock on *Star Trek*. Spock was highlighting how Nixon's reputation as a ferocious anti-Communist made the visit possible; no one could convict him of being soft on Communism. But there was more to Nixon than political armor. His grasp of the balance of power was perhaps even deeper and farther reaching than Kissinger's, and he had learned much from his experiences as Eisenhower's vice president. He had traveled to Asia in 1953 and been impressed by Hong Kong governor Alexander Grantham's argument that Communist China sooner or later had to be admitted to the "family of nations." As president, Nixon had the capacity to act on that belief. Eisenhower had been imprisoned by his national security bureaucracy; his decisions emerged carefully threshed through the NSC. Nixon decided to cut right through. He had no desire to have his instincts quashed by a relentless set of meetings, and his decisions were made in secrecy. The secretaries of state and defense would be unaware of the president's maneuverings toward a Sino-American rapprochement. Nixon also gloried in duplicity. There was no reason to stay tied to the ROC—and there was no reason to tell the ROC the truth until he was ready. Having assured Taipei that there would be no change in policy, Nixon dispatched Kissinger to Beijing in 1971.[48] The national security advisor's mere appearance confirmed that the rapprochement was underway.

Beijing was in a receptive mood. A falling out with the Soviet Union—caused, in part, by Nikita Khrushchev's refusal to back the PRC in its bombing of Kinmen and Matsu—had yielded violent clashes on the China-USSR border in 1968–1969, making Beijing all the more eager for friends. The PRC would never close off the possibility of improved relations with the Soviet Union, but it would not hurt to befriend the United States while waiting. This would involve some compromise on Taiwan, and that compromise was struck almost immediately. Kissinger admitted that had the Korean War not happened, Taiwan would have been part of China. The United States could not offer a switch of recognition soon, though Kissinger hoped to see progress on that front early in the president's second term. But it could dial down its forces on the island. With Nixon and Kissinger eager to wind down the Vietnam War, the United States could commit to a complete evacuation of its forces from Taiwan in due course.[49] What counted was not the legal status of Taiwan or the formality of recognition but the cordiality and goodwill being offered. This was something more delicate, but potentially more lasting, than an agreement. It was a relationship.

This was an approach that suited Beijing. The PRC would have liked even greater concessions on Taiwan—in an ideal world, the Americans would simply have handed it over—but the overall relationship mattered more than the island. "I say that we can do without Taiwan for the time being," Mao would later announce grandly, "and let it come after one hundred years. Do not take matters on this world so rapidly." It was just what Kissinger, who was busily explaining how he could not sever relations with Taiwan immediately, wanted to hear. The Shanghai Communiqué of 1972, which set out the new understanding between China and the United States, therefore left the question of Taiwan unresolved:

The Chinese side reaffirmed its position: The Taiwan question is the crucial question obstructing the normalization of relations between China and the United States; the Government of the People's Republic of China is the sole legal government of China; Taiwan is a province of China which has long been returned to the motherland; the liberation of Taiwan is China's internal affair in which no other country has the right to interfere; and all U.S. forces and military installations must be withdrawn from Taiwan. The Chinese Government firmly opposes any activities which aim at the creation of "one China, one Taiwan," "one China, two governments," "two Chinas," and "independent Taiwan" or advocate that "the status of Taiwan remains to be determined."

The U.S. side declared: The United States acknowledges that all Chinese on either side of the Taiwan Strait maintain there is but one China and that Taiwan is a part of China. The United States Government does not challenge that position. It reaffirms its interest in a peaceful settlement of the Taiwan question by the Chinese themselves. With this prospect in mind, it affirms the ultimate objective of the withdrawal of all U.S. forces and military installations from Taiwan. In the meantime, it will progressively reduce its forces and military installations on Taiwan as the tension in the area diminishes.[50]

In essence, this was a decision to leave the Taiwan question unresolved for the time being. Both sides had stated their positions. Those positions were not, strictly speaking, in conflict. The Americans had made a major concession by agreeing to withdraw their forces. Had Beijing wanted to be persnickety, it could have pointed out (as it had at Warsaw) that Washington's avowed interest in a "peaceful settlement of the Taiwan question" smacked of interference in China's internal affairs; it came perilously close to telling China how to manage the relationship. But Beijing was not in a mood to carp. The Americans were withdrawing their forces, and the important thing was the overall Sino-American relationship.

The Shanghai Communiqué ushered in a new era of Sino-American bonhomie, but it did so at the expense of clarity on the subject of Taiwan. And if the sacrifice seemed necessary, it was also one that could, in due course, become dangerous. Kissinger and Zhou evinced an understanding that Taiwan would, after a face-saving pause for the United States, return to China. (There is no reason to doubt Kissinger's sincerity in his assurances to Zhou on this particular point. His philosophy of great power politics was such that it would have made eminent sense to him and even seemed well-nigh inevitable.) But the understanding could, as the PRC would find, change with the next American administration. It was all very well for Kissinger to confess to Zhou that in the absence of the Korean War, Taiwan would long since have been part of the PRC, but Kissinger had not convinced his own country of that view.[51] Nor could the CCP return to the 1930s and 1940s, when the concept of what China would encompass was something that could be played with, reshaped to suit reality. If Kissinger could not overcome the anti-red nationalism in the United States, Zhou could no more overcome the nationalistic fervor that China had whipped itself into over the Taiwan question. There were forces larger than the diplomats that had been let loose in the countries they governed, forces that would outlast any understanding they thought they had reached. That made fudging the Taiwan question yet again a very risky move indeed.

There was a reason the Chinese listed their objections to "one China, one Taiwan," "independent Taiwan," and "the status of Taiwan remains to be determined": the Taiwan independence movement. This was not (as it is often misunderstood to be) a move to create a separate Taiwan under Chiang Kai-shek; it was, instead, a move to overthrow him and establish an independent Taiwanese state. Chiang's relocation to the ROC had allowed him to oversee significant economic reform. Land reform was a massive accomplishment. The foundations were laid for Taiwan's emergence as a key player in global fisheries. But politically, the ROC remained what it always had been: a police state. Chiang and American officials (Rankin was especially fond of doing this) called the Republic of China "Free China." (Embarrassingly, there are Americans who insist Taiwan should embrace that name to this day.) It was nothing of the sort. Chiang had the governing instincts of an authoritarian ever fearful of falling from power. In Taiwan, those instincts were given free rein. Opponents were subject to torture, imprisonment, and execution. Anyone who objected to Chiang's government was by definition colluding with the Communists and therefore out to overthrow the state. The reason for violating due process was the reason American-supported authoritarians everywhere gave: there were Communists around and one needed to be tough to keep them from overthrowing the state. This was as self-serving as it was untrue. The best way of undermining the lure of Communism at home would have been to simply and immediately declare that the 228 incident had been a crime, that there would be justice for that crime, and the government was committed to free and fair elections. But this was not the Chiang Kai-shek or Free China way. Chiang's son, Chiang Ching-kuo, was the fierce, cruel spy chief. Even Dulles, at one point, would suggest that he might want to be less rough in his methods.[52]

Dulles's request did not stop the arrests, torture, and executions. And the tyranny accomplished what tyranny often does: it intensified the rebellion. For all its ferocious policing, the KMT never quite snuffed the flame of Taiwanese independence out. There were fishermen weaving along the coast, trafficking messages of independence and lethal weapons. In hideaways ranging from Japan to the United States, Southeast Asia to Taiwan itself, angry Taiwanese plotted how best to overthrow the government, and there were foreigners who were willing to support them. Literature calling for Taiwanese independence was smuggled onto buses and public transport across the island. Su Beng had just published a work on four hundred years of Taiwan's history, a book that staked out a past for Taiwan distinct from that of China. Word that Taiwan was and always had been something different, apart from China, spread. The activists even claimed there was a provisional government of the Republic of Taiwan (though, being an underground movement, it was hard to test its legitimacy). In and of itself, the talk was bad enough. It kept an idea alive, and if one believed, as Chiang did, that propaganda and words could create a movement and give it strength, the talk was dangerous. (The belief was not unfounded. Chiang had witnessed firsthand how propaganda had helped the CCP gain recruits, even when he had almost exterminated it; he had seen, too, how that propaganda allowed the CCP to grow until it came back and drove him out of China.) And the agitation did not stop at words. In 1964, Taiwanese independence activists managed to blow up railway tracks and then later bomb a military train near Wangtian station in Taichung.[53] The harder the government cracked down, the deeper the resistance ran.

This being the case, it was perfectly possible that an end to American support for Chiang might mean a revival of the idea of Taiwanese independence and the formation of a Taiwanese republic. By 1971, this was a possibility the PRC was no longer prepared to brook. Mao's authoritarianism had always drawn on populism; he won support for his goals by galvanizing his people into supporting them. Mao had sought to infuse the quest to liberate Taiwan into the very souls of those he governed. It was a solemn responsibility to be put to them, something to rouse their deepest passions. It had become a means of uniting the populace behind collectivization and the Great Leap Forward.[54] There was, by now, an almost religious fervor about the island in China. To abandon the eventual liberation of Taiwan would have been playing with fire. Somewhere along the way, the object had shifted from defeating Chiang to seizing the island. Taiwan had become a cause.

Zhou, therefore, was emphatic that there was to be no American support for Taiwanese independence activities. He was particularly concerned because Peng Ming-min had just arrived in the United States.

Even among the panoply of Taiwan independence activists, Peng stood out. He had had a distinguished academic career; he had even been enrolled in one of Kissinger's seminars at Harvard, back when the national security advisor had been an academic. Incensed by the Chiang regime, he and two friends in Taiwan had written a manifesto, which called for ousting Chiang and founding a new country. That new country was to have meaningful democracy and due respect for human rights. It was to be a real country, a participant in the international system, with proper diplomatic relations and membership in the UN. They had managed to find a printer to run copies of the pamphlet, but before it could be mailed across the island, Chiang's agents had shown up to arrest them. Peng was subjected to endless interrogation; he would recall, later, that the sheer exhaustion caused by the process rendered torture superfluous. (His interrogators were especially insistent that the Americans had been behind the pamphlet; the suspicion seems to have been that Washington was seeking to rid itself of bad assets.) Peng was sentenced to eight years in jail. The sentence was commuted, but he soon found that he and his family were under constant surveillance. The surveillance jeopardized both Peng and anyone he met with, so—at considerable personal risk—he slipped out of Taiwan and made his way to Sweden. From there, he eventually went to the United States. Given Peng's connections, the attention the case had got, and the media portraying the pamphlet as a call for "Taiwanese independence," Zhou's concerns were understandable. It did not help that Chiang had declared that it was the Americans who had helped Peng escape. As Nixon wryly pointed out, the generalissimo had not been pleased either.[55]

Kissinger's response made clear that the United States was not interested in a free Taiwan. "I told the Prime Minister," he noted, "that no American personnel . . . will give any encouragement or support in any way to the Taiwan Independence Movement. . . . What we cannot do is to use our forces to suppress the movement on Taiwan if it develops without our support." Taiwan's fate was irrelevant to Kissinger. This was about a rapprochement with China. The suppression of the Taiwan independence movement, Zhou agreed, could be left to Chiang Kai-shek. The much maligned generalissimo would be helping the PRC by making sure that Taiwanese independence did not make headway.[56] Zhou knew, as did Nixon and Kissinger, that, on the question of Taiwan being part of China, the PRC and ROC were in complete agreement. They were agreed that China was sovereign over Taiwan, agreed that it was sovereign over Tibet, agreed that it was sovereign over the disputed territories with India, agreed that it was sovereign over offshore islands whose names they did not know. The only thing they did not agree on, really, was who was in charge of that sovereign China.

But all that would soon be in the past. The Americans had abandoned their entrenched hostility against China. In October 1971, the UN General Assembly finally passed a resolution that awarded China's seat in that organization to the PRC. The fiction that the ROC represented China was at an end. Sooner or later, unification would be achieved. "Basic evolution," to use Kissinger's phrase, was bound to lead in that direction.

With the benefit of hindsight—and perhaps even without—Nixon's visit to China was Washington's best chance to return the island to PRC control. In fairness, it was not a great chance, but it was as good as it was going to get. The logical conclusion to Nixon's policy on China would have been to terminate the defense agreement with the ROC and switch recognition. Chiang and those he governed would be left to deal with the consequences of reunification.

What kept Nixon from doing this, of course, was fear of political backlash. Anti-Communism remained a powerful force, if by no means an unchallenged one, in the United States. Nixon's own election to the presidency had been underpinned by his credentials as an implacable anti-Communist. The opening to China was broadly popular, perhaps because the Vietnam War had wearied the country of crusades against Communism, perhaps because the damage McCarthy had inflicted was plain to see, or perhaps because Americans were just a little more reasonable than their leaders trusted them to be. But there were Republicans and Democrats alike who thought that the president had made far too many concessions on Taiwan. Nixon was running for reelection; he needed the support of the fierce cold warriors who were determined to stand tough against Communists.

There was only so far Nixon could go on the China question. The pro-Chiang lobby was still strong. California governor Ronald Reagan had been irate when the PRC was awarded China's seat at the UN in 1971. He had just come back from meeting Chiang in Taiwan. "The old boy" had impressed him as being "sharp as a tack." On a telephone call with Nixon, Reagan would venture the suggestion that the proper response to the UN's action was for the United States "to get the hell out of that kangaroo court. . . . That the United States would not vote, and would not be bound by the votes of the UN, because it is a debating society. . . . We'd be there, our presence would be there, but we would just not participate in their votes. I think it would put those bums in the perspective they belong." Nixon was soothing, conciliatory—nothing in his response would ever have led Reagan to suspect that the president was not altogether averse to the vote in the UN going Beijing's way.[57] There was no reason for Nixon to care about the UN awarding China's seat to Beijing; it was bound to happen sooner or later and, given his own policy of rapprochement, the inevitable transition could only help. But with Nixon's own party reacting to the PRC so vitriolically, terminating the ROC defense treaty and switching recognition might have been a step too far.

And yet, it might just have been feasible, albeit at significant cost. The American public was weary of the war in Vietnam and might well have understood that this was part of retrenchment—Reagan's grumbles notwithstanding. The abandonment of South Vietnam was shocking, but it was something the country learned to live with, despite the money and lives America had sunk into that lost cause. Cutting Taiwan loose would have been easier. And Chiang was not an ally to be proud of. He had his supporters, but there was little about his cruel, authoritarian state to excite widespread sympathy. A shrewd campaign against him, a touting of the benefits of the rapprochement in the overall Cold War, a promise that it was part and parcel of winding down the hated war in Vietnam—all this might have made the change a little easier for the American public to swallow. Swallowing it would not get easier with time. The longer the Taiwan question was left unresolved, the more entrenched the voices arguing against Nixon's policies would become. If the ROC was to be abandoned, this was the moment to do it. But the selling of foreign policy accomplishments to a domestic audience never had been a Nixon and Kissinger specialty. If they had pushed ahead to switching recognition instead of sitting back and letting events take their course, the Sino-American rapprochement might well have been complete. The PRC would have been in full possession of Taiwan. The story would have ended there. But then, how could they or their counterparts have known how different a track basic evolution was going to take? No one in Washington, Beijing, or Taipei was prepared for the remarkable developments that the succeeding decades would bring.

3

Toward Another Crisis

1971 to 1996

"They think it's great we've gone to China, we've shaken hands and everything is going to be hunky-dory. It's not going to be hunky-dory; it's going to be tough titties." Thus in March 1973 did Richard Nixon muse to Henry Kissinger about what the future of US-China relations might hold. "So now, now that we have come this far, the real game is how do you build on these great initiatives."[1] Juvenile crassness aside, Nixon's apprehensions were well-founded. Despite the Sino-American rapprochement, the difficulties of the triangular relationship between Washington, Beijing, and Taipei would prove intractable.

Part of the difficulty came from the United States itself. Washington might have decided that it wanted a relationship with Beijing, but it found itself unable to sever connections with Taipei. Nixon and Gerald Ford would leave office with the US-ROC defense pact still standing in the way of normalized diplomatic relations between the United States and the PRC. Jimmy Carter finally managed to terminate the pact and recognize the PRC—only for Congress to pass the Taiwan Relations Act (TRA), which trumpeted America's determination to make sure that Taiwan's future would be decided peacefully. The TRA left China incensed and the United States hopelessly confused about how committed to Taiwan's defense it really was. The confusion persists to this day.

For both the PRC and ROC, the decades following the rapprochement brought massive changes. Mao Zedong died in September 1976. It was a moment of tremendous significance for modern China. The impact on the Taiwan conundrum was indirect but powerful. The PRC's determination to take Taiwan outlived the chairman. And his death cleared the way for economic reform that would turn China into a superpower and give it additional leverage in its quest for the island. Under Mao's eventual successor as paramount leader, Deng Xiaoping, China became capitalist in all but name. The extraordinary growth thus unleashed gave the PRC's economy a gravitational weight that would tug at countries around the globe.[2] Burgeoning economic ties and the glittering promise of "one country, two systems" that Deng held out meant that that tug was felt by Taiwan too. There were those on the island who thought that Taiwan's future lay with the PRC. All else being equal, Deng might well have achieved that elusive goal: peaceful unification.

China's hopes for peaceful unification were lost in the unexpected maelstrom of Taiwan's political change. There was nothing inevitable about the island's transition from police state to democracy. It was a stuttering, halting transition, which could, even in the nineties, have been left unaccomplished. In and of itself, democratization might have been compatible with the "one country, two systems" model (this was well before Xi Jinping would show that the promise of two systems was easily reneged on). But in Taiwan's case, democracy came with a fierce, unrelenting embrace of it as part of Taiwan's identity—and that made unification with the PRC virtually impossible.

Left to themselves, it is difficult to say how these contending forces would have played out. If it seems likely that the PRC's heft—economic and, if need be, military—would eventually have prevailed, it is also worth remembering that small states can be extraordinarily tenacious. Deng's PRC, after all, was unable to compel Vietnam to do its will despite a war. And Taipei was pursuing a nuclear deterrent; success would have gone a long way toward evening the balance of power across the strait. However, the American commitment—unclear though it was—to Taiwan's defense raised a far more troubling question: Could China and America avoid war over Taiwan? During the Third Taiwan Strait crisis of 1995–1996, the answer could have gone either way.

By 1972, the rapprochement had been achieved, but where was the relationship to go from there? It was all very well to have grand conversations about the global balance of power and mutual friendship, but a relationship cannot live on those alone forever. It must make progress; if it fails to do so, it withers. From the rapprochement, the benchmark for progress was obvious. There would have to be normalization: proper American recognition of the PRC, an exchange of ambassadors, a restoration of full diplomatic relations.

The problem, of course, was how to reach that benchmark while still tied to Taiwan. Even before the glow of the rapprochement had faded, Nixon and Kissinger were looking ahead. Withdrawing forces from Taiwan, as they had promised Beijing, was easy enough. The Vietnam War was being wound down; there was little reason to leave troops there. But switching recognition would mean trouble.

> **Kissinger:** For the time being, what they really want from us is protection against Russia. Taiwan is subsidiary. Eventually, we may have to come to a position similar to Japan's, which is that we maintain consular relations in Taiwan and diplomatic relations in Peking, in return for a promise by them they wouldn't use force against Taiwan, but we hope that Chiang Kai-shek will have died before then.

> **Nixon:** Japan has consular relations with Taiwan?

> **Kissinger:** Yeah.

> **Nixon:** It'd be a bitch for us.

> **Kissinger:** It'd be a bastard.

The reason it was troublesome was American political opinion. (As an aside, though Japan's offices in Taiwan did perform consular functions, they were avowedly informal, which was why they would be touted by the PRC as a model for how the United States could conduct itself.) The president's trip to China had commanded broad, though not universal, support. "Chowder-headed liberals," as Kissinger would call them, were particularly keen on the relationship. But the wholesale abandonment of a treaty ally—and the ROC was, for better and worse, a treaty ally—was something the American public might find hard to swallow. Nixon could devise no better solution than giving it time.[3] In due course, surely, the public would come around.

Kissinger, perhaps, was a little too sanguine when he visited Beijing in 1973. As he sketched the timeline out for Zhou Enlai, the United States would draw down its forces on Taiwan over the course of two years. This was not a major sacrifice. Taiwan had once been an important base for US troops on their way to Vietnam—at the height of the Vietnam War, there had been as many as thirty thousand American soldiers on Taiwan—but Nixon had already begun the process of ending the war. That move meant that troop numbers on Taiwan had been cut to around nine thousand by 1972. Moving forward with further reductions promised to be straightforward. At the end of 1974, the United States would begin working on full normalization. The goal was to establish diplomatic relations with the PRC by the summer of 1976. There would, Kissinger hoped, be some understanding that the eventual settlement of the differences between Beijing and Taipei would be peaceful. To that end, he would engage to exercise "great restraint" in arms sales to Taiwan; the sale of two F-4 squadrons had already been stopped. Meanwhile, the United States could establish a "liaison office" in China, which would do much of what a diplomatic mission would, absent formal diplomatic relations. China, naturally, was welcome to do the same. Zhou was receptive to the idea. Chairman Mao had signed off on it and it was not without precedent. Japan, to take one example, had begun with trade offices in the PRC before going on to normalize relations. Japan would become the template China would hold up for the United States to emulate. It had restored diplomatic relations with the PRC, it had affirmed its full understanding and respect for the PRC's stand that Taiwan was an "inalienable part of the territory of the People's Republic of China," and it had managed to maintain what it called an interchange association in Taiwan. The association issued visas, looked after citizens' interests, and did whatever an embassy could—but it was not called an embassy, which was why Beijing was willing to let Japan keep it. Japan had normalized relations with the PRC on the basis of the "one China" principle.[4] There was no reason the United States had to be too different. It was a nice, workable plan.

One source of trouble was Watergate. Nixon's complicity with a group of burglars who raided the Democratic National Committee headquarters would end with his resignation from the presidency. Before that, however, Watergate showed Beijing a "paralyzed President," to use Kissinger's phrase, which left the Chinese uncertain about the assurances they had received. Watergate never ceased to mystify the PRC. How was one to deal with a country where a simple burglary scandal could threaten the head of state? Meanwhile, congressional delegations to Beijing had not been shy of telling Chinese leaders that they operated independently of the president.[5] If this was where the American system of rule of law and checks and balances led, perhaps Beijing would need to be more circumspect in its approach to Washington.

But there were political problems within China too. Mao Zedong's Cultural Revolution, launched in 1966, had let powerful ideological currents loose within Chinese society. The idea of revolution had become gospel to some within the party, and it proved almost impossible to get rid of. The Gang of Four—Zhang Chunqiao, Wang Hongwen, Yao Wenyuan, and Jiang Qing (who was married to Mao)—had come to exert fearsome power within the party. They were deeply troubled by the direction they saw technocrats like Zhou Enlai and Deng Xiaoping dragging their country in, and they were not afraid to criticize them. The savagery of the CCP's political infighting fused with genuine concerns about American behavior. US outreach to the Soviet Union looked as though America might, at some point in the future, conspire with the Soviets against China; one never knew what the outside world would do. Then there was the United States' continued bombing of Cambodia and its continued entanglement with Taiwan. Zhou, it suddenly seemed, had been too soft, too yielding in his meetings with Kissinger. It was time to get tough with the United States. Thus, when Kissinger hinted that it would be nice if Zhou Enlai would visit Nixon's residence in San Clemente before the president made his next trip to China, Huang Chen, the Chinese liaison officer, was blunt. The United States still had ties with the "Chiang group." Accepting a "side . . . or . . . back door" visit to the United States under such circumstances was not compatible with the dignity of the premier's office.[6] If the United States was serious about the relationship, it would have to show it by severing its connections with Chiang. There were matters of face involved.

Kissinger's 1973 visit did little to alleviate Chinese concerns. He found himself having to explain why more ROC consulates were being opened in the United States. Worse, an American cruiser, the *Oklahoma City,* had passed through the Taiwan Strait recently. Zhou would bring this up politely, and an embarrassed Kissinger would have to explain it was "stupidity. Before coming here we had pro-hibited airplanes coming anywhere close to China, but we forgot to specify ships. So I can only apologize. It was bad taste. It was legal but stupid." The ROC had not been shy about celebrating the *Oklahoma City*'s passage, and though Zhou was gracious, the incident would not have added to China's confidence in its new diplomatic partner. Who, to borrow Kissinger's famous question about Europe, did one call when one wanted to talk to America? In searching for something positive from the visit to report to Nixon, Kissinger would alight on Zhou's proposal demanding "only that the 'principle' of one China be respected as we normalize relations."[7] The small matter of what respect looked like in practice had been left unresolved.

The negotiator whom Kissinger would deal with the following year was a very different man from Zhou Enlai. Zhou's was a charm of gen-tle courtesy. Deng Xiaoping's, by contrast, had an earthy candor to it, a bustling, impatient practicality. In dealing with Deng, there would be no subtle hints, no grandiloquent gestures with the details left unre-solved. He would hawk into his spittoon and plunge into the concrete details that his interlocutor wished to elude. He was more than happy to flesh out what respecting the "one China" principle should look like. On a visit to New York, he was dismissive of Watergate—"such an issue is really incomprehensible to us"—and had the vice foreign min-ister, Qiao Guanhua, make clear that US-China relations would have to follow the "Japanese pattern." He hoped it would happen soon, but if it did not—this was vintage Deng—there was no hurry.[8]

The full blast of his candor would be turned on Kissinger when the latter visited Beijing in 1974. Kissinger came hoping for under-standing. The United States had certain considerations that Japan did not. It had a defense treaty with the ROC that was law; it wanted certain assurances that reintegration would be peaceful. If those things could be borne in mind, perhaps China would be willing to proceed with normalization. Deng was having none of it. Normalization could proceed only under a "one China" principle—and that meant that any signs of diplomatic relations with Taiwan were unacceptable. The United States would have to shut down its diplomatic offices on Taiwan and terminate its defense treaty with the ROC. "Well, since you can formulate a law," Deng scoffed of the defense treaty, "naturally you can also do away with it." As to how Taiwan was reunified with the mainland, that was China's own business. No outside country had the right to interfere. (This was, of course, the same line China had taken in the talks with the American ambassador at Warsaw before rapprochement. It was a line that almost never changed.) If the United States still needed Taiwan, China could wait. China would issue an invitation to the American secretary of defense, and of course the new president, Gerald Ford, was welcome to visit. But it would not normalize relations at the expense of clarity on its sovereignty over Taiwan.[9]

Kissinger was in the deeply uncomfortable position of wanting progress on the relationship more than the Chinese did. He desperately needed something to show for all these visits to Beijing. The weight of expectation was heavy: Ford had told Congress that he was interested in visiting China so that normalization could proceed apace. "All the liberals," as Kissinger reminded Ford, wanted it too. But China was not prepared to move toward normalization without an acceptance of three conditions: the removal of US troops from Taiwan, the termination of American diplomatic relations with the ROC, and the abrogation of the defense treaty. Ford was welcome to visit, but issuing a communiqué that hinted at progress when there had been none was something Beijing was loath to do. An annoyed Kissinger remarked that it was "difficult to explain to the American public that we are going to China for no other purpose than a visit," but Beijing refused to budge. There had been no progress on Taiwan, and the Chinese would not issue a communiqué that suggested otherwise. The United States, Kissinger found, had little choice but to go ahead with the presidential visit. Geopolitical costs aside, if Ford called the trip off, "it would give the Chinese a chance to invite all the Democratic candidates over to say you screwed up the Chinese policy." Ford did wind up going to Beijing, with nothing to show for it but the visit itself—and a reminder from Deng on what normalization would take. Kissinger tried to put matters in a positive light to the president; they had wanted the visit, he claimed, and "our kicking them around . . . really paid off."[10] But the visit had gone exactly as Deng had indicated it must. America had thought it could pry more out of China than China was prepared to give. And it had failed.

Chiang Kai-shek died in 1975. The generalissimo had been ailing since 1972. Age, pneumonia, and perhaps the shock of the American abandonment had sapped him of his strength. In death, as in life, he did not give up on conquering China again. His last testament to his people read: "My spirit will be always with my colleagues and my countrymen to fulfill the three people's principles, to recover the mainland and to restore our national culture. . . . We have been fighting the Communist evils on the China mainland, engaging in political warfare against them." Even in death, he was capable of rallying the forces in American politics that would never abandon Taiwan. Senator Barry Goldwater, staunch conservative and avowed friend of Free China, had been quick to signal that whatever the president might think, there was no way he was going to sever connections with the ROC. When Chiang died, it was Goldwater who rallied members of Congress to scupper any changes in the relationship with Taipei.[11]

Part of what motivated these legislators was probably the money pouring in from ROC lobbyists. Part of it was the shrewd political sense that being tough on the PRC won votes. Part of it might have been genuine conviction. Whatever the reason, a set of forces in American politics was ranged against the conditions the Chinese had set for normalization. Nixon, the proud, the canny, the swaggering Nixon, might have had it in him to fight them; he was of their party and his standing when he won reelection had been high indeed. But Ford did not have that history of political triumph. He was trying to carry on with the accomplishments of another man. Goldwater and his comrades in arms were too powerful for Ford to take on. Ford and Kissinger felt that he needed this faction for reelection. The president, who had planned to send the secretary of agriculture to Chiang's funeral, found himself cornered into sending the vice president instead. Then the president found his party vowing, in the platform it put forth for the 1976 election, that "the United States government, while engaged in a normalization of relations with the People's Republic of China, will continue to support the freedom and independence of our friend and ally, the Republic of China, and its 16 million people. The United States will fulfill and keep its commitments, such as the mutual defense treaty, with the Republic of China." Kissinger could grumble about the "outrage," but he knew that if Ford tried to say he was not bound by the platform, Reagan would "assault" him. Gaffes did not help America's case with China. In a presidential debate on October 6, 1976, Ford claimed that the Shanghai Communiqué had stated that the PRC and Taiwan would resolve their differences peacefully. This was not what the communiqué had said, of course. The Chinese side had maintained that "the liberation of Taiwan is China's internal affair in which no other country has the right to interfere." The American side had simply reiterated "its interest in a peaceful settlement of the Taiwan question by the Chinese themselves." An embarrassed Kissinger would tell the Chinese foreign minister, Qiao Guanhua, that Ford had misspoken on the Shanghai Communiqué, only to be asked why former Pennsylvania governor (and serving US ambassador to the UN) William Scranton had supported Taiwan's readmission to the UN in an interview. Kissinger was shocked. "Ridiculous, outrageous!" he said. "Perhaps you can't believe me when I say I didn't know about this until you told me just now." American malevolence or American cluelessness—whichever way Beijing chose to see matters, it did not inspire confidence. The best Kissinger could do was to assure the Chinese that the Republican platform was meaningless and that, after the election, China would see "discipline and cohesion" in American policy.[12] One could forgive Beijing for placing little faith in such assurances.

The fact that it would fall to Jimmy Carter's administration to normalize relations was rich in irony. Here was a Democrat administration embracing the policy Nixon and Kissinger had launched wholeheartedly—this while Kissinger's own party seemed hell-bent on obstructing his China policy. Ford and Kissinger had been contemptuous when Deng told them that Cyrus Vance—lawyer, vice-chairman of the board of the Council on Foreign Relations, and chairman of the Rockefeller Foundation—had brought a delegation of "world affairs organization people" to Beijing earlier. (Vance had come with a delegation sponsored by the National Committee on US China Relations, an organization that aimed to promote

Sino-American cooperation. The delegation had comprised Americans working on public education pertinent to international affairs. It was one more sign of how far the Sino-American relationship had come since Kissinger's first visit that such delegations were now possible.) Kissinger compared Vance to the Dalai Lama—they both had a "government in exile"—while Ford assured Deng that Vance was unlikely to return to government. Barely a year later, on January 8, 1977, Kissinger's last act in this particular drama would be to introduce Vance to the Chinese as his successor in the role of secretary of state and assure the PRC that there would be continuity of policy. And continuity there was. Vance and Carter's new national security advisor, Zbigniew Brzezinski, had their differences, but on the need to normalize relations with China they were agreed. For Brzezinski, it would almost seem as though the idea was to outdo Nixon and Kissinger. "Compared to what was then being said," he would tell Carter after reading the Nixon-Kissinger conversations with their Chinese counterparts, "one cannot avoid the conclusion that the present state of US-Chinese relations is rather dormant."[13] A Republican administration might not have felt quite the same urgency about moving US-China relations to a normalized level.

Most surprising of all, perhaps, is Jimmy Carter's own role in normalization. Carter is remembered as a hapless president when it came to international affairs—indecisive at best, downright weak at worst. And yet when it came to China, there was surprisingly little hesitation. "My own inclination is to be bold about it. My experience in life has been that it never pays to procrastinate," he said at a meeting discussing normalization and how it might be accomplished. "If we are sure our position is correct, I am prepared to move ahead as soon as possible."[14] It was a remarkable statement, almost naive in its approach to a complex issue, and yet naivete was perhaps what the decision needed. There had been so much weighing up of pros and cons, so much thought of credibility and domestic politics. If America wanted a normalized relationship with China, it would simply have to get on with it.

Carter proceeded to get on with it. Vance was dispatched to Beijing in August 1977 with a formula that would, so the Carter administration hoped, prove acceptable to Beijing. Vance came willing to switch diplomatic recognition and promising to let the detested defense pact lapse. This was all well and good, but there were two points that Deng (who was just beginning his ascent to the role of China's paramount leader) balked at. The first, of course, was the American hope for a commitment that China would not use force. This constituted interference in internal affairs. The second was Vance's suggestion that the United States maintain a liaison office in Taipei. As far as Deng was concerned, this was just "an Embassy that does not have a sign on its door." He was all the firmer in this conviction because the United States had enjoyed a liaison office in Beijing. Deng left a silken threat hanging in the air: "We have stated on many occasions that we are patient," he reminded Vance. "But we hope you do not misunderstand this and take it as meaning that the Chinese will tolerate unlimited procrastination with regard to this issue."[15]

That same flintiness was in evidence when Brzezinski visited Beijing. Carter, Deng said, needed to make up his mind. This the president had done, Brzezinski explained. The national security advisor had come prepared to make concessions. The United States asked only for the "hope and expectation that the internal and purely domestic resolution of Chinese problems would be such that it would be peaceful and that our own hopes in this respect would not be specifically contradicted." This, he emphasized, was not a "condition." It was a plea for understanding. Deng's response was typically blunt and practical. The United States was willing to express its hopes and expectations; China would do the same. And of course, the United States was welcome to maintain nongovernmental and trade relations with Taiwan, just as Japan had.[16] Deng was willing to respect existing US interests in Taiwan. He simply wanted the Americans to respect his country's claim to the island.

The basic conditions for normalization, then, had been met. Carter had agreed to sever the defense treaty with the ROC—it would take a year from notification for the treaty to lapse—and switch recognition. The Americans could express their hopes for peaceful unification, but there was no commitment from China that it was bound by those hopes. The one concession Deng made was on the question of arms sales to Taiwan. The Joint Chiefs had been vociferous in their insistence that the "continued security of the people of Taiwan" required America to continue supplying the island with weapons. Deng was willing to tolerate the sale of defensive weapons to Taiwan (though he was careful to ask that such weapons not be sold during the year the treaty remained in effect), but he would not tolerate it with good grace. Arms sales could damage the prospects for peaceful reunification, he made clear, and he would castigate the Americans for such sales if the matter came up.[17] But Deng had won crucial ground. He had no intention of invading Taiwan in the near future; he could afford a touch of magnanimity. On January 1, 1979, the United States and the PRC finally established normal diplomatic relations.

At first glance, everything seemed to be, as Richard Nixon would have said, "hunky-dory." True, there had been a slight change of wording in the Chinese text of the normalization communiqué—the Chinese now used *chengren* instead of *renshi dao*, which a linguist could argue constituted recognition rather than acknowledgment—but the Americans felt comfortable deeming the English text, which was consistent with the Shanghai Communiqué, authoritative. (The change of words was perhaps far less important than it was considered both at the time and today. A linguistic debate about what had and had not been agreed to was irrelevant to the broader spirit of the agreement. What mattered to China was not whether the Americans had recognized or acknowledged its position on Taiwan but how much the Americans would interfere in the matter. What mattered to the United States was not whether it had recognized or acknowledged the Chinese position on Taiwan but how easily it could pursue its objectives in the region. The communiqué was just words. It was behavior that counted.) The ROC, predictably, was outraged—in Taipei, an incensed mob smashed American ambassador Leonard Unger's spectacles, with the police doing little to help—but that was to be expected. The important thing was that Deng had arrived in Washington. Defense officials were talking. There were discussions on scientific exchange. Business deals were being struck. Carter's decisiveness had paid off. Then on March 3, the Chinese ambassador to the United States noted his country's displeasure at a debate unfolding in Congress. Foreign Minister Huang Hua called in the US ambassador to China. If Congress had its way, Huang argued, it would be maintaining the soon-to-be-defunct defense treaty and in essence recognizing Taiwan as a country. This was unacceptable.[18]

Carter had anticipated trouble with Congress. Goldwater had been very far from resigning himself to events. He had sued the president for the termination of the defense treaty, arguing that it was illegal to do so without congressional consent. The case wound up in the Supreme Court, where a plurality ruled that it was a "nonjusticiable political question." In other words, the executive and legislative branches of government would have to settle this between themselves. (It is interesting to note that a district court had observed that the legislation that had originally passed the treaty had not specified the need for Congress to be involved in its termination.) Congress therefore took it upon itself to settle the matter. The Taiwan Relations Act passed both chambers of the legislature in 1979, and it laid out the ambiguous terms that would govern US relations with Taiwan. The act, as it passed:

> Declares that peace and stability in the area are in the political, security, and economic interests of the United States, and are matters of international concern. States that the United States decision to establish diplomatic relations with the People's Republic of China rests upon the expectation that the future of Taiwan will be determined by peaceful means and that any effort to determine the future of Taiwan by other than peaceful means, including by boycotts or embargoes is considered a threat to the peace and security of the Western Pacific area and of grave concern to the United States. States that the United States shall provide Taiwan with arms of a defensive character and shall maintain the capacity of the United States to resist any resort to force or other forms of coercion that would jeopardize the security, or social or economic system, of the people of Taiwan.
>
> Reaffirms as a commitment of the United States the preservation of human rights of the people of Taiwan.

Declares that in furtherance of the principle of maintaining peace and stability in the Western Pacific area, the United States shall make available to Taiwan such defense articles and defense services in such quantity as may be necessary to enable Taiwan to maintain a sufficient self-defense capacity as determined by the President and the Congress. Requires such determination of Taiwan's defense needs to be reviewed by United States military authorities in connection with recommendations to the President and the Congress.

This was, in effect, a declaration of intent: America would interfere in what it had acknowledged to be internal Chinese affairs. It was not a defense treaty, but it took responsibility for Taiwan's defense upon the United States. And it made clear that there would be consequences for China if it sought to exercise its right (as acknowledged by Nixon, Ford, and Carter) to unify Taiwan by force. It was all very well for the president to reassure China by suggesting he would see to the implementation of the act and, in doing so, would ensure it was consistent with the Sino-American understanding.[19] American presidents had come to China bearing assurances in the past, only to be undercut by the US Congress. How on earth was China to deal with a country that could not speak with a united, consistent voice?

The bizarre combination of normalized relations and the Taiwan Relations Act crystallized America's fundamental confusion about its China-Taiwan policy. The United States wanted proper relations with China (the act notably stressed the desire for close relations with China and did not repudiate normalization), but it also wanted a say in what happened on Taiwan. It was not just the legislative branch that had trouble cutting its ties to the ROC. Carter's administration had thought long and hard about the island's future and had been unable to bring itself to terminate arms sales. It never quite managed to articulate why it cared about Taiwan, but it cared enough to make complete abandonment impossible.

This basic confusion would define US-China relations from this point forth. Beijing and Washington would continue to deal with one another. The Taiwan issue would flare up from time to time, then subside for a while before popping up again. There was one period when it seemed that this dynamic would be upset, and that was when Ronald Reagan campaigned for the presidency. Reagan vowed that, as president, he would recognize Taiwan again—a move that would, Deng warned, do significant harm to US-China relations. Reagan's vice presidential running mate, George H. W. Bush, had been stationed in China as unofficial ambassador; he knew Deng and promised him that Reagan had no intention of making good on his word. It was quite a moment: a presidential candidate proclaiming a policy change to the American public, and the vice presidential candidate promising Beijing that that policy change would never happen.[20]

Bush, it turned out, was correct. Reagan found himself first unable and then unwilling to recognize Taiwan. Republicans informed him that it was a bad idea to undo an initiative that had had so much support; the threat to invite Taiwanese officials to his inauguration was walked back. He was beginning to discover, as his predecessors had, that there are limits to the powers of the presidency. Presidents proclaim their determination to chart a new course. Civil servants and politicians then weigh in on initiatives and can bog change down. As it was, Reagan found, to his delight, that the Chinese were willing to cooperate with him against the Soviets; the intelligence they shared during the Soviet invasion of Afghanistan was valuable. He would, therefore, content himself with giving Taiwan his famous six assurances. The assurances seemed banal enough on the surface, but they would, along with the Taiwan Relations Act, become almost canonical when it came to US policy toward Taiwan. America had not agreed to set a date for terminating arms sales, it had not agreed to consult China on arms sales, it had not agreed to mediate between Beijing and Taipei, it had not agreed to revise the TRA, it had not agreed to take a position on the issue of Taiwan's sovereignty, and it would not exert pressure on Taiwan to negotiate with the PRC. In essence, these assurances amounted to little more than abiding by the terms of the Shanghai Communiqué and the TRA. And yet, that line on sovereignty would be subject to deliberate misinterpretation. Ambitious members of the US Congress would, starting in 2005, cite it when introducing resolutions—and they would do so with a twist. The six assurances, it was argued, held that the United States would not recognize China's sovereignty over Taiwan. This was incorrect; they stated only that America would not take a position on the matter, and a refusal to recognize was very much taking a position.[21] For a long while, the resolutions would prove ineffectual, but they showed that the idea of undoing the "one China" policy had not altogether vanished. If the mood in the United States were to change, such resolutions might gain traction.

But all that lay in a distant future. Having delivered the six assurances, Reagan decided to stick with the China policy he had inherited from Carter. That basic policy would remain intact for a long while. Even the Tiananmen Square massacre did not alter it. Bush, now president, sought quietly to patch matters up with his "old friends." He would fight to renew the PRC's most-favored-nation trading status even as Congress asked that Beijing be called to account for its human rights record. When Taiwan sought to take China's place in the General Agreement on Trade and Tariffs, the Bush administration would work to prevent it.[22] Taiwan would become a member of the World Trade Organization (WTO) in 2002. The United States would tilt heavily toward dealing with Beijing. But every now and then, it would find itself lurching Taipei's way—with Beijing's ire aroused.

There would be anger in the ROC too. How, demanded one diplomat, could a deal between "disgraced and dead" leaders be allowed to come to fruition? The ROC had tried, since 1969, to reach out to the Soviet Union; in the wake of the Sino-Soviet split, tilting toward Moscow was always an option. The effort went nowhere—and Deng Xiaoping was perfectly confident that he could handle it if need be—but it did show that what bothered the KMT was not Communism but Chinese Communism and the challenge it posed to KMT authority.[23] What made matters worse was that the United States insisted on depriving the ROC of the one thing that might have assured it of safety: a nuclear deterrent.

Even before Nixon's rapprochement with China, Chiang had been trying to develop nuclear weapons. By the 1970s, there had been progress enough that American clandestine intelligence on the program generated serious concern in Washington. Carter, to whom nonproliferation was vital, demanded that Taipei abandon the program, and it did. It needed the United States not least because that was where the bulk of its functional weaponry came from. But the ROC had not quite resigned itself to being defenseless. The program picked up again in the 1980s. Once again, Washington noticed the activity, and once again the ROC was told to desist. American worries about the program were an odd mix. The United States feared the impact on cross-strait relations, especially at a time when Taiwan was on the verge of a murky leadership transition. It also feared the impact on Taiwan's relations with neighbors who had signed on to the Nonproliferation Treaty: Japan, South Korea, the Philippines. Deep down, the most powerful motive was probably a simple instinct against nuclear proliferation. Taiwan, once again, was stopped in its quest for the bomb.[24] Having taken on the responsibility for supplying the ROC with defensive weapons, the United States was also going to make sure that the ROC did not produce on its own weapons that blurred the line between defensive and offensive. It was yet another example of the perils of dependence, one more grievance to add to the roster.

Normalization and the Taiwan Relations Act, then, had left everyone dissatisfied but resigned. The United States had slipped out of one commitment to the ROC, only to argue itself into another. The PRC had got normalized relations with the United States, but the Americans never quite made good on their promise to sever relations with a rival regime. The ROC had lost recognition and a defense treaty, but it had won at least an ambiguous commitment to its survival. It was not ideal, but it was better than complete abandonment.

There were several reasons Deng did not react with even greater ire to American ambivalence. One was the recognition that there were larger stakes to the relationship than just Taiwan. The Taiwan Relations Act was an outrage. How would America feel, as one Chinese diplomat put it, if China passed a Hawaii or Alaska act? But against this frustration, Beijing had to set the geostrategic and economic gains its relationship with America brought. When Reagan threatened to switch recognition, Deng found it appalling, but his message to Bush was that Reagan had to be schooled in the full significance of the Sino-American relationship. He seemed to have faith—justified, in the event—that this could be done. There was too much at stake for both sides; the Americans would probably see that.[25] Finally, there was the fact that Deng had no intention of liberating Taiwan by force. Not that he was renouncing that right; it was simply that it was easier to achieve reunification peacefully. Deng was a man of eminent practicality. That practicality underpinned the policies known as "reform and opening" that would transform China's political economy. The emerging behemoth would exert a powerful influence on Taiwan, which would leave the island's residents deeply polarized.

The key precept guiding Deng as he steered China to economic strength was to let what was working continue to work. Peasants tilling their own land and keeping some of the produce were more productive than communes; self-tilled land and private gain, therefore, were to be allowed, even encouraged. Back when he had been subordinate to Mao, Deng had made an impassioned case for foreign trade: it was impossible, he had argued, to stand apart from the global economy. Now in power, he opened China up for business. Trade connections with the rest of the world flourished. Taiwan, which had been racing ahead as an Asian tiger, was an opportunity. An illicit trade had long enriched enterprising people across the strait. It was time to make that trade formal and open the riches to everybody. China proposed the famous three links—direct mail, direct transport, and direct trade—to deepen cross-strait economic exchange. The absence of direct connections was a major obstacle for Taiwanese business; surely it was time that they be established. It would take a long while before the links were actually forged, but there were already ties that bound the two economies together in Hong Kong and Southeast Asia. And some investment was making its way into the special economic zones Deng designated—places where the normal rules governing trade and investment in China relaxed into something more favorable to business.[26]

Ventures were small-scale to start with. Between 1983 and 1987, most of the Taiwanese businesspeople in China were focused on finishing products for the export market. There were only about eighty projects in all, worth about a $100 million. For a five year period, that seems pitifully small, and yet compared to what had been before, it was significant. It would grow. In 1987, KMT authorities finally relaxed regulations that had made travel to China difficult for most of Taiwan's residents. The PRC issued regulations to encourage Taiwanese investment. Between 1988 and 1991, there were over 3,700 projects, worth over $3 billion. The Tiananmen Square massacre, to these businesspeople, was an opportunity: as the rest of the world tried to distance itself from China, there was more room for Taiwanese to come in and make money. The course was set. Coastal China was booming, and Taiwan's businesspeople were going to cash in. Shared language and long experience of how the wider economic world worked made them an asset to the PRC. The consequent trade and investment would play a crucial role in the Chinese economic miracle.[27]

But even before those bonds drew tight, there was a certain excitement about China in Taiwan. In the 1980s, it was hard to sustain the position (as some old-school anti-Communists in the KMT wished to) that China was a moribund Communist country. The Japanese, the Americans, the South Koreans—everyone wanted a share of the China market. This made Deng's political message all the more tempting: he was willing to have unification based on the "one country, two systems" model that he was holding out for Hong Kong and Macao. "One country, two systems" was one of his little inventions that Deng was proudest of. It had its roots in his experiences crafting Chinese policy on Tibet, where he had realized that governing the region would be easiest if he allowed a certain amount of autonomy. China only really needed control of security and foreign relations; how Tibetans disposed of their land, worshipped, or lived their day-to-day lives was something that could be left to them. Their governance did not have to be identical to that of other parts of the PRC. This was the philosophy behind the 1951 Sino-Tibetan agreement, and, until 1959, the Tibet region was governed differently from China proper.[28]

The upheaval in Lhasa and the Dalai Lama's flight to India spelled an end to that system, but the idea stayed with Deng. When the time came to press for Hong Kong's return from Britain, it was "one country, two systems" that he pushed for. He had no desire to change Hong Kong's system, because it worked well. It had helped enrich China too; witness the Chinese entrepreneurs whose trade links with Hong Kong brought money to the mainland. There was no reason to homogenize governance. Hong Kong had to be part of China, but it could look different from other parts. Having spelled out these terms for Hong Kong, Deng was willing to offer them to Taiwan too. Margaret Thatcher was enlisted to seek Ronald Reagan's blessing for the deal.[29]

In one key respect, the terms for Taiwan were better than those offered to Hong Kong. In Hong Kong's case, the impending departure of British troops meant that PLA troops would come in to cater to defense. But Taiwan's troops could not be asked to go anywhere; they were Chinese, as the PRC saw it, and a part of China. Ye Jianying, chairman of the Standing Committee of the National People's Congress, declared that if Taiwan returned to the fold, it would be allowed to keep its own forces. Here was proof of China's benevolent intention of noninterference.[30] Taiwan could do whatever it wanted to. With the American troops departing and the ROC's diplomatic connections being steadily chipped away, there was no reason for the island to turn down the deal.

Beijing's message was reaching a Taiwan that could, for the first time in decades, have a genuine debate about how to deal with the mainland. Chiang Ching-kuo had succeeded his father as head of state of the ROC. The succession was gradual. The younger Chiang became premier in 1972. Upon the elder Chiang's death, C. K. Yen, the vice president, succeeded to the presidency. It was only in 1978 that Chiang Ching-kuo assumed the key post of the presidency. He was an enigma. As a youth in Moscow, he had been inspired by Communism; later, as spy chief in the ROC, it was his task to hunt down anyone with Communist sympathies. It was on his watch that the government once again moved to snuff out opposition when a demonstration in the southern city of Kaohsiung in 1979 ended in violence; it was on his watch, too, that martial law was finally lifted in 1987. Like his father, he felt the American rapprochement with China was pure treachery; unlike his father, he was willing to think seriously about what compromise with the mainland might look like. He was willing to contemplate unification, but, he claimed, it would have to be as a democracy—this even as his security forces murdered political dissidents.[31] Perhaps it was the realization that authoritarian rule was no longer sustainable, perhaps it was a son's vengeance on a father he had never really liked, perhaps it was a simple flicker of humanity. Whatever the reason, Chiang Ching-kuo's ROC was a somewhat less tyrannical state than Chiang Kai-shek's. It was no democracy, but it was something that had the potential—only the potential—to become one.

The pressure for change came from both within the KMT and without. Some of those changes had been crushed at the outset. Lei Zhen had been a KMT member and had served in a variety of positions both on the mainland and on Taiwan. But being a member of the party did not stop him from criticizing it. He had launched a journal called *Free China*. Lei was no Communist; he found the Soviet Union and its ideology antithetical to all he hoped to see in the world. But he was not sparing of the regime he served either. If his country was to be a proper democracy, it had to have a proper opposition. It needed functioning political parties that could compete and debate with the full protection of the law. This was not, it should be emphasized, a paean to Taiwanese independence; it was a Chinese democracy movement. Lei's goal was to transform the entire Republic of China into a Free China.[32] Chiang Kai-shek was having none of it. Lei was tried for sedition in 1960 and cast in jail.

But the idea of political opposition being necessary never quite died. With Chiang's death, it suddenly had room to breathe. Chiang Ching-kuo was far from seeing eye to eye with Lei on how Taiwan should be ruled, but he did feel his government needed to be more representative of those it governed. There had always been more than a whiff of Chinese settler colonialism to the government of Taiwan. The *waishengren* (those who had come from various parts of China) were ruling over the *benshengren* (the locals). Chiang Ching-kuo had sought to catalyze local Taiwanese participation in government (notable among those who benefited from this policy would be future president Lee Teng-hui). He had moved, too, to hold freer elections. There had been elections at the local and municipal levels, but at a national level elections had been suspended since the Chinese Civil War and its aftermath. The ROC was at war with the Communists. There would, therefore, be no elections. There would also be no new political parties, though the handful that had been in place before the emergency decree were not eliminated. The problem, of course, was that the emergency lasted longer than anyone had anticipated. The population grew. KMT officials elected long ago aged into infirmity. The authorities therefore held limited national elections from time to time, starting in 1969.[33]

These elections did not wrest government entities from KMT control. But they did spawn an opposition that was willing to venture onto treacherous ground. To not be of the KMT became a political identity in itself: *dangwai*, outside the party. The *Taiwan Political Review* circulated briefly, calling for an end to martial law before it was shut down. The Presbyterian Church preached the need for an independent Taiwan. A "Democracy Wall" popped up at National Taiwan University. In the run-up to the elections scheduled for December 23, 1978, different voices with different ideas of what Taiwan might look like were suddenly being heard.[34]

Chiang Ching-kuo postponed the elections. This was ostensibly because of the American decision to switch recognition to the PRC, but beneath that, one suspects, there lurked a fundamental unease about just where the elections might go. Democracy was all well and good, but Chiang Ching-kuo needed to keep control. So many different ideas at a time of such massive upheaval undermined that control, and that made the president deeply uncomfortable. When it came to political reform, his decision-making was marked by ambivalence and indecision. He wanted more Taiwanese voices, but he did not necessarily want to hear what they had to tell him. He had allowed the elections; now he wanted to postpone them.

Having given his people that small measure of liberty, Chiang Ching-kuo would be surprised by how far they would take their fight for it. A flood of publications emerged championing democracy. *Formosa*, started by Huang Hsin-jie, Yao Chiawen, and Lin I-Hsiung, would proudly proclaim that the moment called for letting democracy reign, and that this was the greatest contribution Taiwan's people could make. Done right, a political magazine is never just a publication. It is a cause, a community; its offices become the headquarters of a movement, which seeks to achieve the change the publication calls for. This would explain why, in defiance of government orders, Yao and another activist, Shih Ming-teh, decided to lead a demonstration in Kaohsiung on Human Rights Day. The results were predictable. Police surrounded the demonstrators. Fear and tension rose. At some point, the crowd was tear-gassed. Violence ensued. Nobody died and injuries were minimal. The regime, remarkably, considered its response for a couple of days. Only then were police sent out to round up suspects. Eight would be tried for sedition—and Lin I-Hsiung's mother and twin girls would be stabbed to death while he was in prison.[35]

Chiang Ching-kuo, like his former Moscow classmate Deng Xiaoping, prized stability over democracy. But unlike Deng, he was deeply conflicted about the choice—and it showed in what happened after Kaohsiung. Having ordered the arrests of the demonstrators, he would refuse to let the security forces take action against the illegal formation of the Democratic Progressive Party (DPP) in 1986. The next year he would finally end martial law.[36] It was as though there were two Chiang Ching-kuos at perpetual war with one another. The authoritarian, who could still be as rough as Dulles had once noted, was doing battle with a man flirting with the idea of a more liberal system. It was a jerky, bumpy transition from what Chiang's father had left, and there was no clarity on what that system would become in 1987. What was clear was that people on the island had different ideas about how their future should look. Was it best to go democratic or was a strong central government worth having? What form should Taiwan's relationship to the mainland take? The argument would rage for a long while.

There were those on Taiwan who felt that "one country, two systems" was indeed the best they could hope for. Wei Yung, a political scientist who was employed at the Executive Yuan, would think long and hard about "multi-system nations." The PRC and ROC, he would argue, were not a divided country but two systems within the same country. The "one country, two systems" model made intuitive sense to him, though he advocated for some measure of diplomatic autonomy for the different systems. (This might well have been acceptable to the PRC; Hong Kong, after all, continued to participate in certain international organizations long after its return to China.) To Wei Yung, the "one China" policy was gospel—a belief, as he pointed out, that was shared by the ROC's Mainland Affairs Council.[37] The question for some in Taiwan was not whether Taiwan was part of China but what particular mode of the "one country, two systems" model would work best.

For some, how unification was achieved was beside the point. Hu Qiuyuan, a septuagenarian KMT parliamentarian and public intellectual who had founded an unofficial organization called the China Unification League, would fly to China from the United States. In defiance of KMT policy, he met with CCP officials to discuss unification. The mainland, said Hu, had shown that China could be strong. Taiwan had shown that China could be rich. He was not sure about "one country, two systems"; he did not, he confessed, understand it very well. But whether one was capitalist or Communist mattered less now than it once had. The world was embracing mixed economies. If the mainland and Taiwan were to do that, the whole question of what kind of system they should employ might well be rendered moot. Unification was a goal all patriots should work toward. He hoped it would happen within the twentieth century; if it did, the next century would belong to China. The CCP, thrilled to have him as a visitor, was swift to remind him that it was open to Taiwan keeping its constitution and Sun Yat-sen's Three Principles (translated roughly as nationalism, people's authority, and livelihood) that the ROC leadership was so insistent on. Here was one more parliamentarian who could be peeled away. Hu was courting trouble at home, and he knew it. The KMT would expel him from the party (though it would let him keep his seat as legislator). Political opposition now had enough breathing room for a DPP legislator to say the KMT was "overreacting." And there were those who said that Hu had been right. Two hundred people from his China Unification League would show up to welcome him back to Taiwan.[38] It was, of course, a carefully choreographed performance. But the choreography itself showed both that there were people who supported Hu's cause and that they thought they could win more people over to it. Taiwan was changing, and talking to the Communists no longer meant automatic incarceration or worse.

But the old-school anti-Communists were still very much part of the polity too. Wang Sheng, who was head of the Liu Shaokang (an office set up to address policy toward the Communists), maintained that a Communist was always a Communist. Deng, as he saw it, was engaging in nothing other than a massive charade. The correct course for the ROC was not to fall for this "one country, two systems" plot but to double down on its opposition to the CCP. The state would have to root out Communist agents from the students and activists who seemed to be mushrooming overnight. The ROC security apparatus would murder Henry Liu, a writer, on American soil in October 1984. Liu's denunciations of Chiang Ching-kuo and the ROC, the regime felt, showed that he was treacherous and a Communist. The murderers were eventually tried and convicted, not least because of American ire at the killing, but their sentences were commuted. There was still a deep well of support for the old way of doing things. Madame Chiang, who symbolized that old order as much as anyone, would rail against anarchy let loose in the name of democracy. The Tiananmen Square massacre, proof of the CCP's moral bankruptcy, galvanized the KMT into organizing rallies of support for the murdered Chinese. Lee Huan, the premier, saw an opportunity to take back the mainland.[39] It was an old dream, but still alive and powerful.

There was, then, a cacophonous debate raging on Taiwan about how best to relate to China. Where Chiang Ching-kuo would have steered the country is uncertain. It is possible he would eventually have yielded to the blandishments of the mainland. Deep down, after all, however vehement his denunciations of the CCP, he did believe that Taiwan was part of China. Lee Kuan Yew, Singapore's prime minister, had been shuttling messages between Taipei and Beijing, and Chiang Ching-kuo felt a deep respect for Lee. That respect might have made unification easier. And yet, Chiang Ching-kuo knew too much of the Communists to trust his fate to them. The Tiananmen Square massacre, which he did not live to see, would have chilled any desire to reunify immediately. This was not because Chiang Ching-kuo would have had much sympathy for the butchered students (he might even have found himself envying Deng's ruthlessness), but because it would have reminded him, had he needed a reminder, of the difficulties of maintaining his own power in a world where he was a part of China. The maintenance of his power, after all, was what had kept those little shoots of freedom on Taiwan from blossoming into a genuine democracy. Ceding that power to the CCP would not be an improvement on ceding it to the people. Tiananmen had made clear that there were limits to just how much opposition Deng would brook. The one thing that might have overridden these considerations was the PRC's offer to allow Chiang Ching-kuo to keep his own forces. If one kept one's own forces, one still had power—and that was what mattered. But Chiang Ching-kuo died of a heart attack in 1988. Age had brought numerous health complications; he was bedridden most days, though he continued to govern.[40]

He never said where he wanted the island to go. There was no last testament, no set of instructions on democratization or the pursuit of "one country, two systems." The very absence of such instructions caused some angst in both Beijing and Washington. No one knew what was going to happen. Taiwan had been subject to dynastic rule for so long. That it was now to be governed by someone not named Chiang was nerve-racking in the way all great change can be. Taiwanese were, by and large, respectful at this time of mourning—the DPP decided to suspend political demonstrations—but that was to be expected. On Taiwan, it was understood that death demanded at least outward courtesy.[41] It was hard to believe that at least some of

Chiang Ching-kuo's former victims were not rejoicing. Taiwan was a wounded country. It remained to be seen if and how those wounds would heal.

Lee Teng-hui was native Taiwanese. He had come of age when Taiwan was still part of Japan and had served in the Japanese Imperial Army. The affinity for Japan would stay with him: decades later, he would own that most of his reading was still in Japanese. The feeling was mutual; the Friends of Lee Teng-hui association in Japan was a major contributor to his campaigns. He had, at one point, been a Communist, which was ironic given that, more than any other Taiwanese leader, he gloried in emphasizing what distinguished Taiwan from the PRC. But before those demonstrations of chutzpah, he would show guile and the capacity to conceal his intentions from some very sharp, very suspicious bureaucratic infighters. He had risen through the ranks of the KMT to become vice president. Chiang Ching-kuo, Lee would recall, had chosen him for the role precisely because he did not appear deeply engaged in politics. This was, of course, a politician's way of underlining his credentials as a man of the people rather than a high-end powerbroker, but there was some truth to it. Lee lacked the connections to the security apparatus and military that a Wang Sheng, for example, had. It made him less of a threat. And at a time when Chiang Ching-Kuo was eager to expand local Taiwanese participation in government, Lee was a solid choice.[42] He was willing to listen and eager for instruction, the perfect vice president.

There were those who had their doubts. Chiang Ching-kuo, Lee recalled, had not thought of him as a successor; succession had not been on the president's mind. Nor was Lee's succession as party head assured. Madame Chiang, among others, was suspicious of this Taiwanese upstart taking over the party and wanted the post of chairman left vacant. But Lee had been careful, upon assuming the presidency, to project continuity, a willingness to carry on with his predecessor's course. To do otherwise, at this time, would create too much instability. Party stalwarts felt the same way and granted him the chairmanship. When Chiang Ching-kuo died, Lee would muse later, there was no telling what Taiwan would become.[43] Here he was correct. The end of the Chiang dynasty could have seen the military call crisis and reassert its power in a coup. The ROC could have remained a moribund gerontocracy, with the KMT still claiming to rule all of China, still debating whether or not unification under "one country, two systems" was a viable path. There was nothing inevitable either about Lee's presidency or about his use of that office to democratize the country.

Standing in the way of political change were the "temporary provisions" that had been in place since 1948. Chiang Ching-kuo had terminated martial law in 1987, but the provisions had remained, a bulwark against democracy. They had been put in place to give the ROC sweeping powers to prosecute their war against the Communists; they meant, among other things, that nationwide elections had not been held regularly. Lee would have to bully, bribe, coax, and beg the members of the National Assembly to rescind the provisions—the same National Assembly members who owed their position in parliament to those very provisions. If they agreed to Lee's demands, they were making it possible for their own time in office to be terminated. "It was," Lee would say, "like asking them to dig their own graves, or, in any case, pave the road to that end." It helped that for all his protests to the contrary, Lee was a master politician. He managed—partly because they underestimated him—to outwit a number of KMT members who thought they could oust him. Prime Minister Lee Huan, for example, who had helped assure Lee Teng-hui's succession, had thought the new president would be pliable. Lee Teng-hui disillusioned him by bringing in Hau Pei-tsun as prime minister. Hau was a former general and had been chief of general staff for the ROC Army; he brought with him considerable support from the military. Hau himself would be subsequently sidelined.

In the intraparty squabbling that was a fact of life in the KMT, Lee Teng-hui was a grandmaster. But his true brain wave was taking the fight beyond the party. Crowds of students had surged into the Chiang Kai-shek Memorial Hall in the spring of 1990, clamoring for democracy and demanding an end to the temporary provisions. Lee met with the Wild Lily movement, as it was called, and where some would have been terrified, he saw opportunity. He called a National Affairs Conference. At first glance, it seemed a purely cosmetic move: an exercise in extended conversation with academics, opposition party members, businesspeople, and former political prisoners about constitutional reform. In another leader's hands, it might have been a ploy to pacify the Wild Lily movement without leading to genuine change. In Lee's, it was a tool for enacting political reform by threatening the KMT. Simply holding the conference was a threat to the party. If the KMT moved to block the change, there would be forces in the broader polity ranged against it. The mere act of having a wider conversation about change made it easier to push for and achieve. By April 1991, Lee had managed to prevail. The emergency order was finally lifted. There would be elections for the National Assembly and the Legislative Yuan. But the democratization did not stop there. Lee's own office would be up for direct elections starting in 1996.[44]

All this constitutional change raised two fundamental questions: Did suffrage apply to all of China, and what did that say about Taiwan's relationship to the PRC? The ROC, after all, claimed to represent the whole country, and the constitution—which had been promulgated in 1947—applied to China with Taiwan as part of it. Under that constitution, legislators purported to represent provinces of China, a place they no longer governed. Lee set out to change that, and his way of doing so seemed, as so much of his conduct did, deliberately calculated to bait the PRC. The elections could, naturally, be held only in the part of China that was free, and the members of the legislature would be elected from that free part (though there were some seats reserved for aboriginals and legislators at large). Democracy would be the key to unification with China; the ROC would not seek a military path. "We must earn the recognition and support of our compatriots in Mainland China," Lee declared, "by demonstrating what we can achieve in Taiwan in economic and especially political terms."[45] This was not a rejection of the "one China" principle. It was instead redefining that principle by preaching the gospel of democracy. If unification came (and Lee was saying it should), it would come because Taiwan had become a beacon of democracy and converted the PRC to its ways.

Some version of the "one China" principle did seem to animate Taipei's policy during Lee's early years in power. Beijing and Taipei were using semiofficial contacts to discuss matters like mail and future communication. The Chinese side had been quite insistent on the "one China" principle. Taiwan, rather than rejecting what it had itself claimed for so long, maintained that there were two different interpretations of the principle. Herein lay the origins of what would later be dubbed the '92 Consensus: Beijing insisted that Taiwan had agreed to the "one China" principle, and Taiwan would counter that it had done nothing that signaled agreement with Beijing. Lee was a believer in gradualism.[46] There was no point in rushing Taiwan to a place it was not yet ready to go; he knew that many of those he governed did think that Taiwan and China belonged together. Besides, an unprovoked declaration of independence would alienate the United States completely, and that was something Lee was too canny to do.

And yet, along with the pious reminders of what unification should look like, Lee issued the constant message that Taiwan was something different, apart from the mainland. He would, grandiloquently, compare himself to Moses leading his people from the clutches of a tyrant. If you followed that idea to its logical point, you could see the Taiwan he was creating as the promised land. There was a certain passion when he spoke of what made Taiwan Taiwanese. The old divisions between *waishengren* and *benshengren* should not matter, he argued when he accepted the nomination as the KMT's candidate for president in 1995:

I have upheld the idea of popular sovereignty. . . . We have just begun to practice democratic government. . . .

As you know, Taiwan is a society of immigrants. Most of its population, except the indigenous people who were here from ancient times, came from the continent. Whether early settlers or late arrivals, all of us cultivated this land by the sweat of our brows, throwing ourselves heart and soul into making Taiwan what it is today. It is meaningless and unnecessary to argue over who is Taiwanese and who is not, merely following the yardstick of who came when. Believing that Taiwan is ours, loving Taiwan and wholeheartedly devoting ourselves to its cause—these are the real significances of being Taiwanese.

Lee was seeking nothing less than the remaking of the Taiwanese nation. There had been no shortage of resentment between the locals and the mainland transplants, and it was a resentment that would outlast Lee. But Lee sought to overcome that division. It did not matter if you were a *benshengren* or a *waishengren*; what mattered was whether you were Taiwanese. And to be Taiwanese, you did not have to have a scripted origin story. You just had to believe in Taiwanese values: freedom, democracy, human rights. Believe in those values and this was your country. Believe in those values and Lee was your leader. Nor did he confine himself to speeches. Educational initiatives were launched. Taiwan's history was suddenly being taught as something distinct, with a set of currents and influences of which China was just one. The Taiwanese language was being taught in schools. Lee had not formally repudiated the "one China" principle, but he was schooling his people in the idea that they were a people apart. It was a political philosophy that underpinned his foreign policy too. He would lobby the UN to take Taiwan back as a member, and though he failed here, he did manage to make the case that some world organizations had room for both the PRC and Taiwan. Taiwan would participate in the Asia-Pacific Economic Cooperation (APEC) forum and win observer status at the World Trade Organization. States that had relations with the PRC were no longer barred from relations with the ROC. Lee no longer claimed to represent the mainland. But if you could have relations with this country he claimed to govern, then it might be something different from China after all.[47] He was dancing right up to the edge of two Chinas and raising Beijing's hackles as no one else had managed to.

Part of what galled Beijing was Lee's presumption of equality. Here he was, this upstart pretender on his defiant little island, lecturing them on the virtues of democracy and talking back to them as if he were a genuine world leader. When Jiang Zemin, who had become general secretary of the CCP and president of China, called for unification talks and declared China's willingness to visit Taiwan, Lee shot back demanding that China renounce the use of force as a means of unification. This, of course, was something Beijing would not do, for that would be countenancing interference in internal affairs (though, by Beijing's own admission, Lee was Chinese; his calling for a renunciation of force could have been construed as an internal demand).[48] It is interesting to speculate on how matters would have proceeded if Beijing had gone ahead and declared it would not use force. There was no way of holding it to such a commitment, of course, but the rhetorical agreement would, at the very least, have taken some of the wind out of Lee's sails. As it was, he could dismiss Beijing's overtures magnificently while Chinese leaders pouted. But worse was to come. Lee would inveigle a visit to the United States.

Several factors allowed him to do so. The first was his own skill at manipulating the levers of the American government. He had, on a visit to Costa Rica (at that time one of the ROC's dwindling number of diplomatic partners), sought a refueling stop at Hawaii. This was granted, but Washington, loath to offend Beijing, had sought to keep the event low-key. In a calculated huff, Lee decided not to disembark. The result was a flood of complaints about how

Lee had been denied the dignity of being allowed to set foot on American soil. For some in Congress, this was proof that America was being too soft on China. When Lee, therefore, was invited to Cornell University to give a speech as a distinguished alumnus in 1995, there were those on Capitol Hill who insisted that he be granted a visa to do so (it helped that he was willing to donate generously to their campaign coffers). They might have failed to carry the day but for the second factor: Beijing's utter incompetence at reading the mood in Washington. China was convinced that it had an understanding with the United States that Lee would not be granted a visa. But this understanding did not prevent China from hectoring the United States about Taiwan. China, Jiang declared, had not renounced the use of force, and foreign forces that backed Taiwan's independence would suffer. It was the worst possible message Beijing could have sent (though it was directed as much at Taiwan as at the United States), for it made the Americans feel that to deny Lee his visa would be to back down before a bully. President Bill Clinton, who had not previously been particularly sympathetic toward Lee, decided that enough was enough. There comes a point when a great power cannot be pushed around anymore.[49] Clinton was at that point. Lee got his visa.

Lee was not the man to be shy at a forum such as the one he had been granted. He would not repudiate the "one China" principle here, but he would give it his own distinctive twist. His own time at Cornell, he recalled, had coincided with the civil rights movement and protests against the Vietnam War; democracy, however, had endured. It was then, as Lee told it, that the virtues of democracy became clear to him, and he had returned home determined to promote it.

Today, the institutions of democracy are in place in the Republic of China; human rights are respected and protected to a very high degree. Democracy is thriving in my country.... The freedom of speech enjoyed by our people is in no way different from that enjoyed by the people in the United States.

I believe that the precept of democracy and the benchmark of human rights should never vary anywhere in the world, regardless of race or region. In fact, the Confucian belief that only the ruler who provides for the needs of his people is given the mandate to rule is consistent with the modern concept of democracy. This is also the basis for my philosophy of respect for individual free will and popular sovereignty....

I only hope that the leaders in the mainland are able one day to be similarly guided, since then our achievements in Taiwan can most certainly help the process of economic liberalization and the cause of democracy in mainland China.

I have repeatedly called on the mainland authorities to end ideological confrontation and to open up a new era of peaceful competition across the Taiwan Straits and reunification. . . . We believe that mutual respect will gradually lead to the peaceful reunification of China under a system of democracy, freedom and equitable distribution of wealth.

These were words that were calculated to appeal to an American audience. Here he was, this head of a foreign state, thanking the United States for teaching him about democracy so that he could go home and foster it there. They were also words that would antagonize a Chinese audience to the greatest degree possible. China had had its own struggles with democratization. It was still worried, especially in the wake of the collapse of Communist governments in 1989 and the subsequent fall of the Soviet Union, that the idea might infect its own party and bring it down. Here was Lee urging precisely that idea upon the CCP. Worse, who was Lee to tell the CCP how to govern? Lee noted piously that he was not ruling out a meeting with Jiang Zemin, but he knew that Jiang would never agree to be in the same room with him with these terms on offer. He had drawn attention to "the Taiwan experience" as something peculiar to the island and had laid out the thesis that China should emulate it.[50] No CCP leader would have tolerated the performance.

Jiang Zemin did not tolerate it. Beijing recalled its ambassador to the United States. Defense talks were canceled. Meanwhile, the PRC would also have to engage in that cliched display: a show of force. Thus began the third Taiwan Strait crisis, which unfolded in 1995–1996. From July 21 to July 28, 1995, the PLA engaged in military exercises on the Chinese coast and sent missiles flying in Taiwan's direction; they landed offshore.[51] Washington and Taipei would have to realize that there were consequences to defying Beijing.

This much was typical. What was bizarre, given what had gone before and what would come after, was the tepidity of the American response. Secretary of State Warren Christopher handed his counterpart, Qian Qichen, a note in which Clinton reassured Beijing that he had "resisted—and will continue to resist—calls for a 'two Chinas' or 'one China, one Taiwan' policy, for an independent Taiwan, or for separate UN admission for Taiwan." There was a statement of concern.[52] But there was no panic about the Chinese exercises or missiles, and no rush to counter with a similar display of America's own.

China's use of force came and went unanswered. Just why remains inexplicable. The likeliest explanation is that the Clinton administration was simply too occupied to do more.

To Beijing, this could only have signaled that the United States had come to its senses. Taipei's provocations no longer needed to be endured. So when the much despised Lee was running for president in 1996, Beijing decided that military intimidation was a safe and effective way of interfering in Taiwan's elections.

Reading history backward and taking a cue from Beijing's conduct, it is easy to mischaracterize the elections as hinging on the question of Taiwan's independence. But in political philosophy and general outlook, the two main candidates were practically kin. Peng Ming-min, now back from exile, was running as the DPP's candidate. He would insist on independence being part of his platform, but since Taiwan was functioning as an independent democracy, this failed to differentiate him significantly from Lee—at least, for an electorate focused on the here and now. Lee might not be calling for a referendum on declaring independence, but he was running as the man who had overseen Taiwan's transition to democracy. There was no doubting his commitment to "the Taiwan experience" he had celebrated at Cornell, nor were there any doubts of his willingness to stand up to Beijing.

Lee's tactics had caused his party to split. Two of his erstwhile fellow KMT members were running on tickets for independent parties, claiming that Lee was turning the country away from unification. They did not gain a significant portion of the vote; the tickets were never serious contenders. But the KMT would never wholly recover from the schism. Forever after, it would be a party with an identity crisis: Was it the party that would reunite with the mainland or would it compete among Taiwanese parties for the chance to lead Taiwan's democracy? For Lee, at least, the answer was the latter. In 1996, the choice between the KMT and DPP was emphatically not about how Taiwan would relate to China.[53] It was about something subtler: who voters felt could best be trusted to sustain a newborn democracy.

These nuances were lost on Beijing. To deter Taiwanese from voting for Lee, the PRC once again engaged in military exercises and launched missiles at Taiwan. On March 7, 1996, missiles flew toward the island, landing in the surrounding waters. This time, the Americans decided that something had to be done. The *Independence*, an aircraft carrier, was ordered to a point two hundred miles east of Taiwan; another aircraft carrier, the *Nimitz*, was asked to join it. Missile defense systems were placed off Taipei and Kaohsiung. The message was clear: America was willing to protect Taiwan. The carrier groups were there as Beijing tested more missiles and completed the scheduled military exercises. By the end of March, the exercises were over and the tension eased.[54]

If Beijing had hoped that its show of force would harm Lee's prospects, it failed miserably. The missiles served only to burnish Lee's credentials as a gutsy statesman who was unafraid of Communist thugs. On March 23, he was voted into office. Taiwan's voters were incensed rather than intimidated.

Matters did not have to go this way. Had the United States put the carriers in the Taiwan Strait during the crisis (as is commonly misremembered), Beijing might well have found itself unable to back down. The symbolism would have been too strong, the emotions too raw, for rational strategic calculation. Had the United States then decided not to back down, matters could have escalated all the way to general warfare. In a different political climate, with different political actors, there might even have been some who would have welcomed that catastrophe. It did not happen—but luck, as much as sensible decision-making at the eleventh hour, was responsible for the outcome.

"A look at US policy toward the mainland and Taiwan," Lee Teng-hui would remark, "shows differences in thinking between the administration and Congress, as well as among the various departments. This is only natural." It was an astute summary of why US policy on China and Taiwan was never clear. Lee understood American politics as well as Chiang ever had, and he knew how to exploit them. There was a part of America that wanted to normalize relations with China, but another part of it could not give up on an old ally—even if what it hoped to get from keeping that ally was left undefined. America believed the relationship with China was important, but China itself drove America crazy. Washington would affirm the "one China" principle, then twist itself into knots explaining how its tilt toward Taiwan was consistent with that affirmation. These basic conflicts permeated every level of government; they seemed, sometimes, to be raging in the mind of a single person. "I hate our China policy!" Bill Clinton exclaimed in a moment of frustration. "I wish I was running against our China policy."[55] In a way, he and every president since Nixon had been doing just that.

But there was ambivalence in Taiwan too. Democratization meant that that ambivalence would be reflected in policy. Beijing's economic growth and the proffer of "one country, two systems" had been tempting; absent Tiananmen Square or Lee's ascent to power, it might have been sufficient to bring about the peaceful unification Beijing so dearly wanted. The drama that Lee unleashed—the constitutional amendments, the internal political warfare, the setting of elections—meant that there would be room for different opinions on Taiwan's relationship with China to assert themselves. Lee's had carried the day, but there would be other days.

Had Beijing steered clear of threats and bluster, it might conceivably have achieved peaceful unification. The PRC had economic heft on its side. The debate that "one country, two systems" had generated in Taiwan was by no means settled. There were those on Taiwan who felt that their future did, in some way, involve a union with China. Lee was the face of the KMT for the moment, but the wing of that party that had argued for unification with China under "one country, two systems" was still active. The KMT would come to be defined as the party that favored some form of association with China. All else being equal, this might have been a shrewd political tack. The message of "one country, two systems" alone had the potential to convince Taiwanese voters that unification with China offered riches and a reasonable measure of autonomy. But the PRC was always its own worst enemy. Its sheer belligerence alienated Taiwanese and, in doing so, jeopardized the KMT's electoral prospects. The shelling and the military exercises simply confirmed that China was not a polity that Taiwanese wanted to be part of. If one cannot push a great power around, there comes a time when pushing a smaller one becomes hard too.

4

The Hardening Line

1996 to 2020

Now came the hurly-burly of democracy for Taiwan. The elections between 2000 and 2016 were truly fascinating, for the democracy was still too young for voters to have let their ideas harden into clear party lines. Both the KMT and the DPP were riven by factions. There was room, therefore, for political fluidity and shifts in allegiance. That room was all the greater because voters were still trying to figure out what they believed and wanted. The question of Taiwan's relationship with China had been subterranean for so long; now, all of a sudden, it had been dragged into open discussion. It would take some getting used to—and how Taiwan would answer the question would change over time.

That change was taking place against the backdrop of a Sino-American entente. The late 1990s and early 2000s saw a steady improvement in US-China relations. The United States genuinely believed that China could, in one official's phrase, become a "responsible stakeholder."[1] After the fireworks of 1996, Jiang Zemin and Bill Clinton met and reached an understanding that the Sino-American relationship was too important for Taiwan to get in the way. Clinton, George W. Bush, and Barack Obama would all seek a world in which Beijing and Washington could work together. Whether Taiwan could survive as a functionally independent entity in such a world was far from clear.

America's quest for an entente with China was made easier by the fact that both Jiang and his successor, Hu Jintao, were willing to act as responsible stakeholders. These were the dullest, least dramatic leaders the PRC had had, and that blandness did wonders for policy. There were too many benefits to cooperation with the Americans—participation in the WTO, investment opportunities, even the prestige of hosting the Olympics—for the PRC to sacrifice them by taking further military action against Taiwan. Beijing would make its red line clear: there could be no declaration of independence. The PRC was unable, too, to resist making counterproductive statements: reminding Taiwan that the "one China" principle was inviolable and letting it be known that the PRC retained the right to use force. But for the time being at least, Beijing saw no need to send missiles across the strait. In a way, the use of force seemed unnecessary. The growing economic strength that Beijing's cooperation with Washington had made possible meant that a powerful tug was being exerted on Taiwan. Cross-strait trade and investment were booming. Like other economies in the region, Taiwan's dependence on the PRC was deepening. In due course, that dependence should have allowed the PRC to bring the renegade island back under its control.

Economic incentives, then, were steadily bringing China closer to both Taiwan and the United States. Had the triangular relationship stayed on this trajectory, it might have ended with peaceful unification. Three distinct changes knocked it off course.

The first was the emergence of a powerful streak of separatism on Taiwan. Economic power can cut both ways. With deepening dependence comes deepening resentment, and it was this resentment that flashed out in the Sunflower Movement of 2014, when young Taiwanese, convinced that their futures were being sold out to China, occupied government buildings. A conviction took hold of much of the electorate that standing apart from the PRC was necessary. What had been built on the island was too valuable to be entrusted to Beijing.

If this had been the only change, Taiwan's fate might not have altered much. The United States had a powerful interest in getting along with China; sacrificing Taiwan would have been difficult but doable. But the second change to the triangular relationship came in Beijing. Xi Jinping, who succeeded Hu as general secretary of the CCP in 2012, was supposed to have been a calm, quiet personality who would not alter too much. Instead, he brought a kneejerk assertiveness to China's policy, both domestic and international. That assertiveness undermined his hopes for reaching a peaceful understanding with Taiwan. It also undermined American faith that a decent relationship with China was possible. The final change came with Donald Trump's surprise victory in the American presidential election of 2016, bringing a leader every bit as brash and belligerent as Xi to power in Washington. Between them, Xi and Trump presided over a return to Sino-American antagonism. And that antagonism created a climate in which Taiwan could assert itself as separate, even sovereign. It was still a risky adventure, but no longer one in which the island would be bereft of superpower support.

Washington moved swiftly to patch up its relationship with Beijing in the wake of the Taiwan Strait crisis of 1995–1996. Clinton assured Jiang that America intended to abide by the "one China" principle; he had been surprised by the intensity of Chinese emotion on the subject and was eager to allay concerns. Jiang, for his part, wanted the "one China" principle properly understood. "Sometimes," he told Clinton's vice president, Al Gore, in a pointed reference to Lee Teng-hui, "people state the One China principle when they are really advocating separatism." There would be no democratization of China, which was how Lee had cast the "one China" principle, but negotiations between Beijing and Taipei could proceed under that principle as the PRC defined it: Taiwan's unification with China under "one country, two systems." A Taiwanese delegation headed by businessperson and quasi diplomat C. F. Koo had recently met with Jiang. There had been no agreement. Koo's delegation had annoyed Beijing by insisting that unification would take place only once China democratized and that China and Taiwan were, in effect, two countries. Nevertheless, Jiang thought the talks were promising. It was "better to talk than not to talk," and Jiang hoped that the United States would do what it could to facilitate peaceful unification. Gore assured him that the White House was pleased with these developments and would hope to see "further constructive dialogue and cooperation across the Strait."[2] American policy on the Taiwan question was in synchrony with the PRC's. Washington and Beijing were eager to proclaim an end to their differences.

This did not faze the dynamic Lee Teng-hui. He was shrewd enough to realize that, whatever Clinton might say to Jiang, there was enough support for Lee's position in Congress to ensure Taiwan's survival. In the run-up to Clinton's 1998 visit to China, Congress had overwhelmingly supported a resolution calling upon the PRC to renounce the use of force against Taiwan. Diplomats had assured Taipei that there was no change in American policy, which Lee chose to interpret as support, however tacit, for Taiwan's continued existence as a democracy. He was confident enough to reject "one country, two systems" openly and to make clear that any communication had to proceed on the basis of "equality and mutual respect." Since equality and mutual respect were what Beijing invoked in its discussions of how states should relate to one another, this was tantamount to asking that the PRC treat Taiwan as it would any other state. By 1999, Lee was willing to be explicit. Relations between China and Taiwan were relations between "two countries." The outcome of the Taiwan Strait crisis in 1996 had shown that Lee could, in the final analysis, count on American support.[3] There was no need to defer to Beijing. Taiwan was a proud, democratic country and Lee was not afraid to say it.

Governing Taiwan in these years was a delicate balancing act in a world where the space for Taiwan to be Taiwan was limited. Lee's allies in the UN would lobby to get the ROC back in that organization. They would fail, but membership in the WTO meant that Taiwan could at least be part of some international forums. Meanwhile, there were the legacies of martial law to address. Lee had already apologized for the February 28 massacre on behalf of the government and moved to establish a compensation fund for victims. Now there would be a human rights monument on Green Island, where political prisoners had once been held.[4] Lee was presiding over a country coming to terms with its past, a process that would allow Taiwan to think of itself as a nation and possibly a nation-state.

Not that he would go too far. There would be no threatened referenda on independence, no unilateral changes of the country's name from Republic of China to Taiwan. What Lee had was a functionally independent state. Its international recognition was dwindling, but it could still govern itself as it saw fit. There was no point in jeopardizing that. To declare independence formally risked provoking China into destroying the freedom Taiwan already enjoyed.

This pragmatic calculus ran the gamut of political parties on the island. Given what was to come later, it is surprising to recall that the question of Taiwan's relationship to China was not an issue in the presidential elections of 2000. The DPP had not started out with independence as its goal, though it had written independence into its charter in 1991. The party was an odd mix of former political prisoners, young activists, and those who thought an opposition party was a good idea. Chen Shui-bian, the DPP's candidate for the presidency, was not raring to change the status quo. Chen was a local Taiwanese; he had gained fame as a lawyer defending political activists, been elected to the Legislative Yuan, and had served as mayor of Taipei. On the campaign trail, Chen had been clear that Taiwan was a separate country and should be treated as such, but this was no different from the position Lee Teng-hui had taken. For that matter, neither the KMT's candidate, Lien Chan, nor James Soong—who, miffed at losing the KMT nomination, was running as an independent— disagreed. Both held that the ROC was an independent country, albeit with some quibbling. (Soong would invoke the rather inexplicable concept of "relative sovereignty" to describe what the two sides of the strait had.) If anything, the DPP's Chen proposed policies that tilted more heavily toward the PRC. Where Lee had been cautious of China's growing economic pull, Chen wished to boost trade connections. One suspects that it was his idea of "normalizing relations" that provoked Beijing's ire.[5] To an outsider, it would have seemed a fairly innocuous concept. But to normalize relations is something only states can do with other states. So much emotion had been invested in the idea of Taiwan being an inalienable part of China that, to Beijing, even a hint that Taiwan was a state had become unacceptable. There were no missiles this time, but Chinese premier Zhu Rongji's fiery statement on the elections at a press conference on March 15, 2000, illustrated how intractable Beijing's policy had become.

Zhu had a well-earned reputation as one of the wiser, calmer heads in Beijing: a technocrat, a rational man. He earned plaudits for his stewardship of the Chinese economy in the 1990s. And yet when asked about the Taiwanese elections, that calm logic would desert him. It was a regional election, Zhu said, and the Taiwanese people's own business. Beijing would not interfere. But, Zhu continued, he wished to be clear: Taiwanese independence was not to be tolerated. He represented 1.25 billion Chinese in that sentiment, and they would not renounce the use of force. It was a remarkable performance. The normally astute Zhu seemed to miss both the lack of difference between the candidates on cross-strait ties and the fact that threats had never been shown to work with Taiwanese voters. There was a telling moment in his little rant. He swept on to tell the story of the Opium Wars, of China torn apart and invaded by foreigners, of how Japanese militarists had seized the island of Taiwan, of the need for heroic struggle. And he remembered being a boy of just nine, thrilling to the Chinese national anthem, with its call for all those who refused subjugation to stand up and fight. China had stood up now; it was unthinkable that it would tolerate Taiwan separating from the motherland.[6] Those childhood lessons had stuck. Taiwan, as Zhu was portraying it, was not a strategic problem to be dealt with rationally; it was a sacred cause, something that China could never give up. There was no grand strategy here, just blind nationalism. Propaganda aimed at a child had clouded the judgment of one of China's most intelligent statesmen. Like his fellow party members, Zhu had a blind spot. That Taiwan was no longer bent on attacking China was lost on him. That his rhetoric harmed the relationship was something he could not fathom. He had become, suddenly, that angry nine-year-old, intent on recovering what his motherland had lost.

As it was, the machinations within Taiwan's political parties wound up mattering more for the election than Zhu's rhetoric. James Soong's independent candidacy cost both him and the KMT candidate, Lien Chan, enough votes to win. Chen Shui-bian managed to just squeeze his way into the presidency.[7] It was a remarkable moment that showed how far Taiwan had come since Chiang's day. Here was a country that had been under martial law for decades. To create an opposition party had been to court charges of treason, with eventual imprisonment or execution the result. Now, here was an opposition party candidate triumphing in free and fair elections, taking office peacefully.

Given the drama that lay ahead, it is somewhat of a shock to remember that Chen sought to placate the PRC in his inauguration address. The Cold War was over, he told his listeners across the strait. It was time for Beijing and Taipei to cast aside their differences:

The people on the two sides of the Taiwan Strait share the same ancestral, cultural, and historical background. While upholding the principles of democracy and parity, building upon the existing foundations, and constructing conditions for cooperation through good will, we believe that the leaders on both sides possess enough wisdom and creativity to jointly deal with the question of a future "one China."

I fully understand that, as the popularly elected 10th-term president of the Republic of China, I must abide by the Constitution, maintain the sovereignty, dignity and security of our country, and ensure the well-being of all citizens. Therefore, as long as the CCP regime has no intention to use military force against Taiwan, I pledge that during my term in office, I will not declare independence, I will not change the national title, I will not push forth the inclusion of the so-called "state-to-state" description in the Constitution, and I will not promote a referendum to change the status quo in regard to the question of independence or unification.

This was a far more conciliatory note than Lee would have struck. Chen would sympathize with the "imperialist aggression" China had suffered. He would hail the economic miracle Deng and Jiang had presided over. The National Unification Council would, he promised, remain intact (a promise he would subsequently break).[8] He was renouncing any unilateral moves toward statehood, and he had expressed himself willing to talk to Beijing. It was not an acquiescence to "one country, two systems," and it demanded, once again, that Beijing renounce the use of force. But it was a line that, if stuck to, would allow Beijing to save face.

And yet, it was during Chen's time in office between 2000 and 2008 that the threat of a referendum suggesting Taiwan's independence became a regular feature of Taiwan's politics. In a popularly elected government, most politicians move with the voters, and voters are curious beings. Some can push hard for their positions; others change their minds. The DPP as a party encompassed many different factions, some of which—notably the New Tide faction—were pushing for a stronger stand on independence. There was, too, a contingent spearheaded by the dynamic Lee Teng-hui that set up the Taiwan Solidarity Union; they felt that the former leader's calls for state-to-state relations should be taken seriously.[9] Within the still evolving electorate, then, there was a force pushing for independence, and a savvy politician might be able to take advantage of it. It helped that this could be seen as standing up to China, which, as always, had refused to renounce the right to use force for unification. And it could also be seen as standing up to the United States, which had become far too cordial toward China for Taiwan's liking. It was this pro-independence strand in Taiwanese politics that Chen Shui-bian decided to follow.

George W. Bush was a president of blissful simplicity. If this served him badly in his Middle Eastern policy, it did make matters easier for him when it came to China and Taiwan. He had started off by saying the United States had a duty to defend Taiwan, though he promised, too, to make sure that Taiwan would not declare independence. The 9/11 attacks caused Bush to send troops to Afghanistan, where they would remain for two decades. But they also caused his administration to rethink US-China relations. China was suddenly important, a potential partner in the war against terror. The six-party talks aimed at denuclearizing North Korea—part of Bush's "axis of evil"—added to China's importance. Its growing economic clout did not hurt either. When Chen made a speech in 2002 declaring that there was one country on each side of the strait and that Taiwan should hold a referendum on its future, Bush came down on Beijing's side. The Bush administration made clear that it did not support Taiwan's independence.[10]

The president went a step further. Not being a "nuance guy," he explained to his diplomat representing America in Taipei, he did not differentiate between "do not support" and "oppose." But there was all the difference in the world. It was one thing for the United States to say it supported a peaceful outcome, without adjudicating the rights and wrongs of the dispute between Beijing and Taipei. That was "not supporting" Taiwanese independence. But to oppose it was something far more forceful; it was to endorse Beijing's claim that Taiwan had no right to independence. However lacking in nuance, Bush's position was one that his administration shared. In a television interview on October 25, 2004, Colin Powell, his secretary of state, would declare that Taiwan was "not independent" and did "not enjoy sovereignty." Powell would try to clarify his remarks and explain that he had only been hoping for a "peaceful resolution," an explanation that the Taiwanese government would cautiously accept. But the suspicion generated in Taipei would not dissipate easily.[11] A picture was emerging. The United States had ditched impartiality to take a stance on the dispute and had ranged itself with Beijing.

Chen's response was to double down on Taiwan's claims to independence. His main tactic—one he returned to time and time again during his presidency—was to threaten a referendum. A referendum is a dangerous tool. It can capture how a people feel at a given time, but its very starkness can compel action that those same people might later regret. But to Chen, the dangers were not worth worrying about, and between 2002 and 2004 his public proposals for referenda piled up. A referendum on Taiwan being independent. A referendum on nuclear power plants. A referendum on Taiwan joining the World Health Organization (WHO) under its own name (this one was triggered by the experience of SARS in 2003). None of these materialized, because the law did not allow for them to be called. And there were parties in the legislature—the KMT and the People First Party—who were intent on stymieing any changes to that law. Chen did eventually manage to get a bill passed that allowed him to call a "defensive referendum": if an outside power menaced Taiwan, the president could launch a referendum on "issues pertinent to national security." The bill took effect in January 2004, and Chen decided to hold defensive referenda at the same time as the upcoming elections in March 2004. Chen got reelected, but the referenda did not work out quite the way he had hoped. The questions the referenda posed were interesting, if loaded: If China kept threatening Taiwan with missiles, should the government get more antimissile weapons? Should the government negotiate with China to get a "peace and stability framework" within which to handle cross-strait relations? The bill had required that there be at least a 50 percent voter turnout for the referenda to be valid. Even formulated the way they were, these questions failed to elicit that turnout.[12] The problem was simple: the electorate was deeply divided.

It could have been worse for Chen. He was reelected, but it had been close. He was shot at during the campaign—some would say it was a staged shooting, designed to elicit sympathy—and after a very close race, Lien Chan and James Soong (finally on the same ticket) would file suit, alleging voting fraud. The suit was dismissed, but the narrowness of Chen's victory and the DPP's failure to take control of the legislature showed that this was a torn electorate and one that had a clear sense of the consequences of going too far.[13] There would be no referendum on independence just yet.

Broadly speaking, the results could be interpreted in two ways. One could see them as a rejection of the idea of independence. Lien Chan's subsequent conduct suggested that he at least saw it this way. He visited the PRC in 2005, where crowds of enthusiastic Chinese welcomed Grandpa Lien home. (Later, in 2014, Xi Jinping would meet with Lien to urge unification based on the '92 consensus.) Beijing was trying to win a chieftain who might deliver Taiwan to China someday.[14] The failed referendum and the DPP's electoral troubles—they lacked the votes in the legislature to set a lower threshold for the referendum—suggested that now was the time to make a show of CCP-KMT unity.

But there was another way of looking at the results. An intelligent analyst might delve into them and conclude that Taiwanese wanted a government that identified with them rather with than China. They just wanted a government that would do so in a practical manner. Rejecting a referendum was a far cry from rejecting the idea of independence altogether. Chen had won—against a ticket that united two bickering KMT members, no less—and he had done so while styling himself as a champion of independence. Lee Teng-hui had shown the KMT how to rebrand itself back in the 1998 Taipei mayoral election, when then mayor Chen was running against KMT challenger Ma Ying-jeou. Lee knew that Chen had won in large part because he was Taiwanese; there were local voters who felt that he spoke for them and the KMT did not. Those were the voters the KMT would have to win if it was to be a viable political force. It was Lee who went stumping for the KMT candidate, Ma Ying-jeou, in the 1998 mayoral election, Lee who dramatically asked Ma who he really was when they were sharing a stage, Lee who told Ma to answer as he did: "I am a new Taiwanese."[15] Those Taiwan values Lee had instilled still resonated with voters. If Ma said he was Taiwanese, if Ma said he loved Taiwan and was willing to govern that way, then they would vote for him—and they would do so again in 2008, when he ran for the highest office in the land. Grandpa Lien might get support over in China, but Ma was going to be president of Taiwan. Lee Teng-hui had homed in on a banal but often overlooked truth. In a representative system, voters will opt for a candidate they feel will represent them. Ma's flamboyant good looks and Harvard pedigree did not hurt.

Part of what hurt the DPP's chances was that it had come to be perceived as corrupt. Chen had forgotten that what had brought him to the presidency in the first place was not his stance on China but his vow that politics would be cleaned of graft. Allegations that his family had benefited from his office would dog him, and they were not partisan. Even before his presidency was over, there were calls to oust him. In 2006, Shih Ming-te, who had served as chair of the DPP, had organized a rally to protest against Chen's corruption. By 2009, Chen would stand convicted of embezzlement. Though he claimed it was Ma's attempt to punish him for his anti-Beijing stance, the denials failed to ward off a jail sentence.[16] Voters did not like a party that had tolerated corruption, even if it was a party they had hitherto supported. Chen's crimes would sink the DPP's electoral prospects for a long, long time to come.

For both Washington and Beijing, the new president, Ma Ying-jeou, was a far more congenial leader than his predecessor. His goal, as he recalled it, was to rebuild the trust between Washington and Taipei that Chen's antics had shattered. Ma had visited America in 2006 in his capacity as chairman of the KMT. There he met, among others, Robert Zoellick, the deputy secretary of state who had announced that the United States hoped to see China become a "responsible stakeholder." The experience left Ma convinced that what the Americans wanted was a conciliatory Taipei that showed itself eager to reach a modus vivendi with the PRC. It was clear that the Americans would put their own interests first. It was clear, too, that they were hoping for an amicable relationship with the PRC. It was pointless for Taiwan's leader to provoke China and then count on the Americans for help. Ma, therefore, would set out to be "low-key, surprise-free," a "peacemaker."[17] In a world where America was trying to cultivate China as a "responsible stakeholder," the best Taiwan could do was placate both powers.

Ma's first step on this road was to reaffirm the "one China" principle as espoused by the '92 consensus. This was treacherous ground. Many Taiwanese held that there was no such consensus—the two sides of the strait disagreed about what they meant by "one China," and that meant no consensus had been reached. And among them was the man who had helped Ma in 1998, Lee Teng-hui. Ma would reach out to Lee and try to reason with him; the consensus had emerged at a time when Lee himself had been in power. In this effort, Ma failed. But the broader goal of improving relations with China was served. Hu Jintao took note of Ma's affirmation. In a conversation with Bush, the Chinese leader expressed his hopes that the Chinese mainland and Taiwan could start talking again on the basis of the '92 consensus. Cross-strait relations were suddenly functional again. In July 2008, tourists were allowed to fly directly across the strait for the first time. The "three mini-links" had created direct postal, transport, and trade connections between China and the offshore islands of Kinmen and Matsu in 2001. Now, Taiwan would enjoy the benefits of those three links to the mainland. Trade agreements with China were inked. The jewel in that particular crown was the Economic Cooperation Framework Agreement, a pact aimed at liberalizing trade and investment across the strait. It would, so Ma promised, bring riches to Taiwan and tie the island more securely to the global economy.[18]

But there were limits to how far Ma was prepared to go. He would admit Chinese tourists; he would allow direct flights across the strait; he would allow Chinese leaders to visit Taiwan. But he would not rush to unify with the PRC. His avowed policy when it came to dealing with China was simple: no talk of unification, no declaration of independence, and no use of force.[19] In a democracy, one has to find a way of winning votes. Ma's was to portray his party as a responsible custodian of the will of the people. Chen might seek to provoke China with threats of a referendum, even if American support was not forthcoming. It was the KMT that cared about the people enough to maintain the status quo by managing China carefully. The DPP had slogans; the KMT understood national security.

The new moderation Taiwan was showing won the desired plaudits from Washington too. The United States declared itself enthused by the developments in cross-strait relations. At least initially, Barack Obama's China policy was much the same as that of his predecessor, George W. Bush. A reasonable Taiwan was something Obama welcomed. Taiwan was dubbed a "security and economic partner." According to no less a person than Secretary of State John Kerry, it was crucial to America's position in East Asia. Gina McCarthy, head of the Environmental Protection Agency, would visit the island. Taiwan won the rare distinction of getting a visa waiver for its citizens who wished to travel to the United States. As former deputy secretary of state William Burns enthused, relations between Washington and Taipei had "never been better."[20] Ma was achieving that rarest of feats for a Taiwanese leader: keeping both Beijing and Washington satisfied.

There was, however, a massive gap between the smooth functioning of Taiwan's internal politics and its conduct on the international stage. Democracy was working as it was supposed to in Taiwan. Fledgling democracies can crumble, and it is in the transitions of power that the stiffest tests for them lie. Lee could have decided that he would rather the KMT stay in power, perhaps even selling it as an attempt to make sure that democracy took firm root before giving up authority. He resigned as the head of the party in 2000, and the opposition came in. When Chen's electoral victory was contested in 2004, the matter was referred to the judicial system. The courts gave a verdict and the verdict was respected. The winning party governed. When the KMT under Ma came back to power, Chen could have insisted that the charges against him were part of a plot by old-school tyrants to kill Taiwan's democracy and that he was not going to leave office, that he had to save democracy by keeping power. There would have been those among the DPP faithful who would have agreed with him; they had suffered too much at the KMT's hands to willingly give authority back to that party. The KMT, once it had succeeded in removing Chen, could have maintained that the whole experience showed how corrupt the opposition was. Continued KMT rule, rather than these experiments with elections, was what Taiwan needed. None of this happened. Chen was tried for pilfering funds, convicted, and jailed. Ma proceeded to govern. There were allegations; there were crimes; there was drama.

Allegations were investigated; crimes were punished; elected parties came to power. This was exactly how things were supposed to work.[21] That Taiwan had managed this, given all the baggage of the past, was no mean feat. It had become, within a few swift years, a functioning democracy.

But being a sound democracy did not make Taiwan a decent international citizen. Many countries would resent the conduct of its fishing vessels. In 2007, to take one example, Costa Rica terminated its diplomatic relations with the Republic of China. The ROC had, for a long time, offered aid to Costa Rica. In exchange, it got Costa Rica's recognition and fishing rights in Costa Rica's waters. As they did elsewhere, Taiwanese fishermen overfished the waters completely. They did not see a problem here; as far as they were concerned, it showed their prowess at harvesting fish. But local resentment was intense. It flared to its highest point in May 2003, when a Taiwanese vessel was caught shark finning: chopping fins off sharks and tossing the maimed fish back into the water. The practice was prohibited by Costa Rican law. The discovery that a Taiwanese ship was engaging in a massive shark-finning operation off Puntarenas created genuine anger among Costa Ricans, particularly those who made a living along the coast. When the PRC came along and offered more money, San José was happy to switch recognition. The switch caused no backlash from the populace about ditching a democratic ally, because the populace had never felt that the ROC had treated them decently. The Chinese, as far as they were concerned, were essentially the same, and Costa Rica might as well go with the Chinese who paid the most.[22] Such feelings were not confined to Costa Rica. A great power can sometimes afford to be callous about those it deals with. A small island, dependent on goodwill for its continued international survival, cannot. The result might well have been the same in the end, but Taiwan had inspired no affection to counter the lure of the PRC's largesse.

There was one major problem with Ma's cross-strait policy: the suspicion it engendered among Taiwanese. His campaign had capitalized on the existence of a Taiwanese identity. For those who truly believed in that identity as something distinct, the economic ties to China felt too constricting. Its greatest chronicler would call it "Taiwan's China dilemma": even as the number of people identifying as Taiwanese increased, so, too, did Taiwan's economic dependence on the PRC.[23] This went beyond the usual worries caused by trade liberalization. Other countries would also worry about China's economic power, but what set Taiwan apart from those countries was that China claimed to own it. How could Taiwan forge an independent identity if it was economically dependent on a country that sought to stamp that identity out? The issue was not new—Lee Teng-hui had worried about it and had tried to shift some of Taiwan's economic relationships to Southeast Asia—but with the growth of China's economy, it had become bigger. Ma's headlong embrace of the riches China had to offer made it all the more terrifying.

The DPP did seek to exploit that fear in the presidential elections of 2012. Lee Teng-hui, worried by the direction his onetime protégé was taking the country in, would actually campaign for the DPP's candidate, Tsai Ing-wen. Lee's criticism of Ma cut to the heart of the president's economic policies. In Lee's telling, Ma was a man who worked only for "big conglomerates," not for the farmers or the young. The time had come, he said, for voters "to abandon Ma Ying-jeou in order to save Taiwan." An annoyed KMT spokesperson suggested that the former president was too old to be interfering in politics.[24] Lee's efforts notwithstanding, Ma was reelected. He had the advantages of incumbency and the public's unwillingness to forgive corruption scandals too easily. But the discontent Tsai had sought to tap into was still there, and two major developments would soon lay waste to Ma's China policy.

The first came in the spring of 2014, when young activists launched the Sunflower Movement. The movement was sparked by Ma's wish to follow up on the Economic Cooperation Framework Agreement with a Cross-Strait Service Trade Agreement, opening new sectors in Taiwan to Chinese investors and workers. A trade agreement is supposed to improve efficiency and boost the economy. But bureaucrats touting such agreements often forget that the "economy" is composed of people and that people are individuals with different agendas and different needs. To those who lose out or feel threatened by improved efficiency and greater competition, a trade agreement can be evidence of their government's indifference to their fates. Cross-strait trade and tourism had provided jobs, but not for everyone. Inequality was widening, and amid the growing wealth, the economy seemed to have diminishing space in which the young could make a living. These concerns had been registered by both the KMT and the DPP, but the former still had enough members who were keen on ratifying the act. Ma had not bothered to consult widely among his people when he pushed for the agreement, and now they spoke with a vengeance. The students decided to take matters into their own hands. On March 18, 2014, they burst into the

Legislative Yuan. They would occupy the building for twenty-four days. The sunflowers they bore signaled hope.[25]

There were several remarkable features to the protest, but what stood out most, perhaps, was the cool moderation the students showed. It was hard to portray them as wild-eyed anti-capitalists who wanted to overthrow the government. Their demands boiled down to transparency when it came to business deals with China and a mechanism to ensure that such deals could be monitored. The protesters made clear that they were in this for Taiwan, and the professionalism with which they cleaned the building and made sure medical needs were met made it hard to disagree. Their calls won support from older people too, veterans of protest who found the youthful idealism on display inspiring. "Never trust anyone over thirty," one such elder encouraged them, "including me."[26] The Sunflowers were Taiwan's future, inheritors of its past protests. The Ma administration had forgotten them; for that, there would be consequences.

There were those in the KMT who thought Ma's intransigence was proving politically costly. One such person was Wang Jin-pyng, a KMT member and speaker of the Legislative Yuan. Meeting with the protesters on April 6, 2014, Wang made a crucial concession. The legislature, he vowed, would give full consideration to a bill on how to monitor such cross-strait agreements before proceeding any further with its deliberations on the Cross-Strait Service Trade Agreement. To put it simply, the legislature would seek to devise a supervisory mechanism (and it did eventually do so) before ratifying Ma's pet agreement. This was a concession, but not complete surrender, and it caused some debate among the protesters. Nevertheless, the Sunflowers eventually decided that they had achieved what they could. On April 10, 2014, they went home.[27]

They left behind a transformed political scene. Ma had failed to understand the protests. To him, the students were little better than criminals. His policies made economic sense, and the DPP was scoring political points at the expense of the national interest. He would recollect all the foreign experts supporting his position. No less august an entity than the *Wall Street Journal* had called for the ratification of trade agreements with China. How could the Sunflowers then possibly object to his economic plans?[28] But if Ma was misreading his own society, the DPP was not. The Sunflowers spelled hope for the opposition party. Here was evidence that the connections with China that Tsai had objected to in 2012 could galvanize Taiwanese into action. That could translate into votes in 2016.

Taiwanese suspicion of China was fueled by a second factor: Xi Jinping's assumption of power in Beijing in 2012. When Deng Xiaoping had first offered the possibility of unification under "one country, two systems" to Taiwan, it was possible to genuinely believe that the second system might involve a fair amount of autonomy. To Deng, there would have been no point in destroying what made Taiwan function. Jiang Zemin might have presided over the 1995–1996 Taiwan Strait crisis, but he seemed, by and large, a man who could live with the status quo; so, too, did Hu Jintao. There were problems in China during the Jiang and Hu years, to be sure, but Hong Kong remained a place where one could commemorate the Tiananmen Square massacre. Even within China proper, there were spaces in civil society where one could discuss matters like Tibet and the Korean War without fear of authoritarian intervention. In those years, it was possible to argue (albeit not incontestably) that Chinese sovereignty might not mean the end of Taiwan as Taiwanese knew it.

Xi's advent changed all that. The expectations of him had been that he would be passive, quiet; instead, he brought a bristling, insecure assertiveness to his role that created immense fear both in China and abroad. In China proper, those whose views differed from Xi's—and not just dissidents but party members, businesspeople, and academics—found themselves bullied into silence or incarcerated. Tibet and Xinjiang were transformed into gulags. And Hong Kong, that erstwhile poster child for "one country, two systems," found its autonomy dismantled completely. Far from the universal suffrage it had once aimed for, Hong Kong found Beijing seeking to pick candidates for the position of chief executive on its behalf. Pro-democracy protests broke out, inspired in part by what had happened in Taiwan. The protesters were jailed.[29] Xi's China was becoming an advertisement for everything Taiwan did not want to be.

When Tsai ran for the presidency in 2016, therefore, it was a very different race from the one she had lost in 2012. This time, her criticisms of Ma's China policy were landing with an electorate that was increasingly wary of the PRC's influence over their home. The KMT was once again at war with itself. Its initial nominee, Hung Hsiu-chu, had to be replaced by Eric Chu because her support for unification was seen as a liability. James Soong was running again, this time for the People First Party, taking voters who would have supported the KMT candidate with him. There were still KMT members hearkening back to their past with China and seeing in it a path for the future. It was a path that most voters had no interest in taking.[30] Ma Ying-jeou proceeded to make matters worse. He decided to meet with Xi Jinping in Singapore.

So here they were, the two top leaders of China and Taiwan (they dodged the one-or-two-state problem by referring to one another

as "mister" rather than "president") meeting in Singapore to cele-
brate the '92 consensus and proclaim a desire for further exchange.
They talked of World War II, of how the Americans had bombed
Taiwan and killed thousands of people. Xi broached the topic of the
Sunflowers. He asked about Lee Teng-hui and Tsai Ing-wen: What
did they really think? Amid the polite exchanges on the potency of
mao-tai and their astrological signs, there was a sinister note. Xi represented a country that was bent on the annexation of Taiwan. Ma,
Taiwan's leader, was giving Xi information on the people who might
possibly lead that island. The head of the PRC was using the custodian of Taiwan's democracy to spy on Taiwanese citizens—the very
citizens who were ranging themselves against Chinese attempts to
quash their independence. Ma would sound more than a little dis-
ingenuous when he proclaimed that it was not altogether inconceiv-
able that Xi might bring political reform to China.[31]

What the meeting made clear was how completely both Ma and
Xi had misjudged the Taiwanese electorate. For citizens who were
already suspicious of the KMT's ties to China, the meeting was con-
firmation of all their worst fears. Ma really did seem to be selling
them out to the PRC. The Taiwanese president had become deeply
isolated from his people; only such isolation could have allowed him
to think that the meeting would help the KMT at the polls. And Xi,
like almost every Chinese leader before him, had no understanding
of Taiwan. He was playing the benevolent emperor, whose deigning
to meet with a favored subordinate would elevate that subordinate's
status. Surely the Taiwanese would respect Ma's party all the more
for Ma having met with China's great leader. That there were large
numbers of Taiwanese who liked being distant from China, that
Ma's meeting with Xi was not an honor but a threat, that they would

move to distance themselves from China because of Xi's grandiloquent display—all this was lost on the Chinese president. He was, in a way, still following the old CCP policy of picking off KMT leaders. It was the same thinking that had motivated the CCP outreach to Li Zongren back in the Mao era. Once upon a time, it might have worked. But Taiwan had changed. It was no longer an authoritarian state where the defection of a few key leaders could bring about the conquest of the island. It was a democracy; people might disagree with their leaders and punish them for policies that they found unacceptable. Winning Ma for China was not going to win Taiwan; it would do the exact opposite. The DPP won a majority in the legislature and Tsai Ing-wen was voted into the presidency.

Tsai Ing-wen had not been popular with the American establishment when she visited Washington in 2011. Like Lee, she had attended Cornell, but there the similarities between them ended. Hers was a studiously dull public manner. She chose her words with the precise caution of the lawyer that she was and delivered them with all the enthusiasm of a robot. In another life, she might have been happy staying in academia. Instead, she wound up helping negotiate Taiwan's admission to the WTO and then serving on the Mainland Affairs Council, which was charged with attending to Taiwan's relations with China. She never made much of a fuss in any of those roles; hers was a quiet, technocratic approach to governance. Get the job done, move on to the next task—that was Tsai. She had vowed not to be a radical when she talked to officials in Washington. And yet, this shy, bland personality had the Americans terrified that she would somehow destabilize the strait. That favorite character of both journalists and government, an anonymous official, informed the *Financial Times* that Tsai had "left us with distinct doubts about whether she is both willing and able to continue the stability in cross-Strait relations the region has enjoyed in recent years." It was, the official continued, "far from clear . . . that she and her advisers fully appreciate the depth of [Chinese] mistrust of her motives and DPP aspirations."[32]

This was as condescending as it was untrue. Tsai was no fool. She knew exactly how the Chinese felt about her motives and aspirations. She knew, too, that if and when she came to power, handling those feelings without surrendering to China completely would demand all her considerable ingenuity. (To call it "mistrust," as the anonymous official did, was to miss its true depth. It was not that China did not trust Taiwanese leaders but that it found the very concept of Taiwanese leaders unacceptable, something that had to be stamped out.) Washington's reception would have shown her how deep American suspicion of Taiwan's democracy ran. For all its praise of democratic processes, Washington did not want those processes to undermine its entente with Beijing. Tsai had not forgotten this when she won the presidency in 2016. But she had her own citizens to deal with too. There were those in Taiwan who were chafing for greater clarity on who they were. The "Republic of China" had been a colonizing regime, its brutality and oppression now consigned to the past. Surely it was time to change the country's name to Taiwan, perhaps even to declare independence. Between Washington's calls for prudence, Taiwanese demands for assertiveness, and Beijing's growing belligerence, Tsai's presidency looked like it would be off to a tough start indeed.

Tsai had an unexpected bit of luck: a massive change in America's China policy. The cliché about historical change applied to this one: it came incredibly slow and then incredibly fast. Concerns about China's conduct had been growing even in the last years of the Obama administration. From disputes over intellectual property theft to aggressive Chinese military conduct in the East and South China Seas, there was a growing sense that China was not turning out to be a "responsible stakeholder" after all. Obama's much vaunted "pivot to Asia" was, in some respects, a response to these worries; it was touted as a way of showing China that the United States was set to play a definitive role in the region. The hinge of that pivot was the Trans-Pacific Partnership (TPP), a trade agreement that would link Asia-Pacific economies in a free trade area that excluded China. In seeking support for ratifying the pact, the White House portrayed it as crucial to countering Chinese influence in Asia. If the United States did not step up and show it meant business in Asia, that vast region would come under China's sway. But this line of argument had little impact on American voters. As in Taiwan, there were significant numbers among the electorate who had felt left behind by trade deals.[33] The contenders for the presidency recognized this. Donald Trump, Bernie Sanders, and Hillary Clinton (who had served as secretary of state in the administration that had devised the TPP) would all denounce the pact in their campaigns.

At first glance, this call for inertia would have seemed incompatible with getting tough on China. The rejection of the TPP was an explicit abdication of America's role in Asia. This was exactly what Beijing—long concerned about being hemmed in by US allies—would have wanted. It took Donald Trump to show that the spirit of what he branded "America first" could go hand in hand with a crude, self-defeating thuggishness. Trump had neither principle nor genius, but he did have a low cunning; he saw and exploited the worst feelings in his electorate. He understood that the anger generated by the TPP and other deals like it could be channeled into anti-China sentiment, and that getting tough on China would strengthen his political position. For all the shock and disgust his victory in the 2016 election caused, his administration's China policy would outlive his presidency.

The first indication that Trump's presidency might open a new opportunity for Taiwan came with a phone call. Tsai became the first Taiwanese leader since 1979 to call an American president-elect or president. For Trump, the main significance was personal. "The President of Taiwan CALLED ME today to wish me congratulations [sic] on winning the presidency," he tweeted. "Thank you!" But if it was all about Trump to the president-elect, to Beijing it was dangerous. Authorities initially tried to play it down. Chinese foreign minister Wang Yi blamed it on Taiwan's pettiness and proclaimed that it would not alter the "one China" principle. Trump promptly followed up by saying that he saw no reason why that principle could not be altered. "I don't know why we have to be bound by a 'one China' policy unless we make a deal with China having to do with other things, including trade," he said in an interview with Fox News.[34]

It was a remarkable move. Whatever one thought of it, America's agreement not to dispute the "one China" principle had been the foundation of US-China relations. Now, all of a sudden, it was being called into question. Not since Reagan had a president-elect threatened the very basis of America's relationship with the PRC this directly. Trump was saying that the principle was not set in stone but rather up for haggling. China might have it, but it would have to give him something—concessions in the trade war he had promised to wage, for example—in return. It was a transactional approach to the principle.

Trump being Trump, it was unclear whether this was a genuine reconsideration of American policy or just an impulse articulated that would be abandoned with his next breath. But to China, it was beyond provocation. Here was a country that had had its sovereignty dismantled so that foreign powers could wrest the trade concessions they wanted. That trauma had been woven into the national fabric, and it was precisely what Trump's businesslike approach to the matter would reawaken. Nevertheless, Beijing did show some restraint. It sent warships through the Taiwan Strait, causing Taiwan to scramble its forces, but there was no repetition of the drama of 1996. America was told politely but firmly that the "one China" principle was inviolable. There could be no deal that involved compromises on sovereignty. Beijing was hoping that Trump, like Reagan before him, would understand the stakes of the US-China relationship. If reasoned with properly, he might be more agreeable once he was in office. Initially at least, that expectation seemed justified. Trump and Xi had their own telephone call on February 9. The ever mercurial American president confirmed that the United States would abide by the "one China" policy.[35]

Just what Trump would have done on the "one China" policy if left entirely to his own devices is unclear. There was a curious whiplash to his moves on China. Having threatened a trade war, he declared a deal had been reached, only to slap tariffs on Beijing and initiate a tit-for-tat battle. He hosted Xi at Mar-a-Lago and tweeted his praise for the "King of China," but he launched a hunt for spies among Chinese students studying in the United States. He would champion the campaign against Huawei: the Chinese telecom company was out to steal people's data, Trump argued, and had to be driven out of the Western market. Meng Wanzhou, a Huawei official, was arrested in

Canada at America's behest. She was charged with fraud and violating the sanctions on Iran. When the Canadians explained that they were just following the law, that there was nothing political about the arrest, Trump dismissed that by suggesting that Meng might be released if China made a trade deal. But for all the pressure on Huawei, it was Trump who was willing to weaken the penalties Congress imposed on ZTE, another Chinese telecommunications company, if it helped with his trade deal.[36] It was a bizarre, inexplicable mix of all-out attack and saccharine fawning. Future historians will work long and hard to figure out the calculus underpinning these moves. One suspects that the president himself did not have a China policy. He operated on ego and political instinct: China policy was whatever happened to please him and his base at a given moment. Depending on his mood, he might have been as willing to provide Taiwan with nuclear weapons as to sell it to China for a trade deal. He might even have tried to do both in quick succession.

But the anti-China sentiment he had set loose went far further than he might have intended. As a strategy for getting votes, China bashing worked. This meant that the message was quickly adopted by other politicians. An odd alliance in the Senate—Republicans Marco Rubio and Tom Cotton joining forces with Democrats Elizabeth Warren and Chuck Schumer—would be outraged when their proposed sanctions on ZTE were watered down by the president.[37] Trump might talk a tough game on China; here were senators actually willing to play tough too.

What was emerging was a bipartisan consensus in an age where bipartisanship was a rarity: China was a threat, and America needed to respond. The basic view of China that both Republicans and Democrats would take was set out by the Trump national security strategy:

China and Russia want to shape a world antithetical to U.S. values and interests. China seeks to displace the United States in the Indo-Pacific region, expand the reaches of its state-driven economic model, and reorder the region in its favor. . . .

For decades, U.S. policy was rooted in the belief that support for China's rise and its integration in the post-war international order would liberalize China. Contrary to our hopes, China expanded its power at the expense of the sovereignty of others. China gathers and exploits data on an unrivaled scale and spreads features of its authoritarian system, including corruption and the use of surveillance. It is building the most capable and well-funded military in the world, after our own. Its nuclear arsenal is growing and diversifying. Part of China's military modernization and economic expansion is due to its access to the U.S. innovation economy, including America's world-class universities.[38]

This conception of China was as far removed from the "responsible stakeholder" as one could get. It was an odd mix of truth and inaccuracy. China had indeed been growing as an economic and military power. It had, like many a great power before it, made its weight felt in the region around it. What the Trump team's analysis left out was the fact that the United States had China's coast surrounded by military bases, that it had balked China's wishes on Taiwan for as long as the PRC had existed, and that American talk of democracy coming to Beijing sounded suspiciously like a call for regime change. China had altered the balance of power in the South China Sea. It had menaced, albeit less successfully, both the Senkaku

Islands and Taiwan. But official US policy was to take no position on the territorial disputes in the South and East China Seas, nor to consider Taiwan sovereign. Suggesting that China's rise had come at the expense of the sovereignty of others was a difficult position to sustain. China's conduct was a product of a vituperative nationalism and genuine security concerns. Condemnation of the former need not preclude understanding of the latter.

Such nuance, however, was lost upon the American body politic. Bit by bit, Trump had normalized the idea of a China threat that had to be addressed by getting tough. The response among the American foreign policy cognoscenti when Trump first broached the idea of scrapping the "one China" policy had been shock and horror; here was proof of just how foolish this president was. Yet by 2020, respectable commentators were suggesting that the United States offer Taiwan a defense guarantee—a revival, in effect, of the mutual defense treaty that normalization had terminated. When Democrats criticized the president's China policy, it was not a disagreement with the diagnosis of China as a threat. They argued that one could be tougher if one cooperated with allies better than the Trump team had been doing. Trump was not tough enough.[39]

In the black-and-white thinking of the US government, being tough on China meant being nice to Taiwan. New weapons deals were inked, including for F-16s and surface-to-air missiles. The number of American ships sailing through the Taiwan Strait went up. The secretary of health and human services would travel to Taipei and meet with Tsai. When Tsai suggested a free trade agreement, the United States seemed receptive. At least some members of the National Security Council were intent on defending Taiwan; it was part of the first-island chain, and as such key to countering China in a war. They also sought to boost Taiwan's own defense capabilities, so that it could "engage China on its own terms." The Trump administration's statement of Indo-Pacific strategy proudly declared that "we are also strengthening and deepening our relationship with Taiwan. We have repeatedly expressed our concern over Beijing's actions to bully Taiwan through military maneuvers, economic pressure, constraints on its international space, and poaching of its diplomatic partners." Lost in this telling was the reminder that America had abjured a diplomatic partnership with Taiwan itself. That same blind spot was evident in the creatively named Taiwan Allies International Protection and Enhancement Initiative (TAIPEI) Act of 2019, which would be approved in 2020. The act took cognizance of Taiwan's recent loss of diplomatic partners: Burkina Faso, the Dominican Republic, El Salvador, the Gambia, Kiribati, Panama, São Tomé and Príncipe, and the Solomon Islands, it noted, had all recently switched recognition to the PRC. Congress therefore asked that the US government:

1. support Taiwan in strengthening its official diplomatic relationships as well as other partnerships with countries in the Indo-Pacific region and around the world;

2. consider, in certain cases as appropriate and in alignment with United States interests, increasing its economic, security, and diplomatic engagement with nations that have demonstrably strengthened, enhanced, or upgraded relations with Taiwan; and

3. consider, in certain cases as appropriate, in alignment with United States foreign policy interests and in consultation with

Congress, altering its economic, security, and diplomatic engagement with nations that take serious or significant actions to undermine the security or prosperity of Taiwan.

This was quite an act. Though it noted that Taiwan had a "unique [*sic*] relationship with the United States, Australia, India, Japan, and other countries," it did not call for the United States to restore diplomatic relations with Taiwan.[40] But it wanted other countries to have diplomatic relations with Taiwan, and it was willing to bribe, coax, and bully those relationships into being. The logical inconsistency was immaterial. The point was that Trump's America was going to stand up to China, and Taiwan was going to play its part in making that happen. America's most fervent support for Taiwan's democracy emerged under an administration that was bent on wrecking liberal democracy at home.

This was precisely the sort of environment in which a move for Taiwanese independence could flourish. Another leader—Chen Shui-bian, with his love of referenda, comes to mind—might well have pushed for a referendum as US-China tensions rose. It was a measure of Tsai's prudence that she did not risk this. Tough talk was one thing. Whether the United States would follow through on that talk was something no one—not even the Americans—really knew. Besides, Tsai Ing-wen did not do flash. There were no vows to hold a referendum, no threats of a name change, just quiet technocratic governance and a search for the fine line between annoying China too much and caving to it entirely.

If Taiwan was going to walk that line, it needed to look to its defenses. The DPP had been critical of the KMT's defense policy. Abandoning the means to defend oneself, it argued, was no way of ensuring peace. The PRC had not abandoned the right to use force against Taiwan; Taiwanese knew what it was like to live under constant threat. Given the military transformation being seen across the strait, Taiwan, which had seen its military spending languish, would have to catch up. This was the only way of ensuring that the rest of what the country enjoyed—trading connections to the outside world, political stability—endured. Tsai's tenure, therefore, saw a steady rise in the military budget, from about $10 billion in 2016 to about $24 billion in 2023. And while Taiwan would continue to purchase arms from the United States, Tsai would spearhead an attempt to manufacture weaponry at home. Why should Taiwan, with its superb companies and scientists, not be able to build its own submarines and aircraft? The Americans were sometimes loath to deliver more sophisticated weapons systems. Taiwan would need to look after itself. It was an ambitious plan—and there was some criticism of its cost-effectiveness—but by 2023, the island would launch its first, somewhat garish submarine.[41]

There was also the question of how to counter China's economic influence. The DPP had come to power, after all, riding a wave of anxiety about how dependent Taiwan had become on China economically. Allaying that anxiety was hard. China was Taiwan's largest source of imports and a prime destination for outbound investment. These links had built up over decades; one could not just sever them overnight. Tsai's response was the "new Southbound policy." She would seek to diversify Taiwan's economic partnerships. Southeast Asia, India, Australia, and New Zealand—here were potential markets that Taiwan could tap into more than it had. This idea was by no means exclusively the DPP's. Lee Teng-hui had had a similar plan, and it had seen increased foreign direct investment in Southeast Asia. Japanese companies were talking quite seriously about the need to find sources of revenue other than China. They, too, were looking south.[42] The search for ways of curtailing Chinese power was on.

The policy did bear some fruit. There were new trade deals with the countries Tsai had targeted. Investment in Taiwan grew. "People to people" exchanges had been something the new plan emphasized. The success of such exchanges is hard to evaluate. Wandering around the streets of Taichung, one could see a growing number of workers from Southeast Asia, but one could not help wondering just what place they would take in society. Those age-old barriers of language and class seemed as insuperable as ever. But regardless of the successes, one problem remained. China was still indispensable. Beijing might be outraged by the southbound policy's effects—an investment agreement between the Philippines and Taiwan, for example, brought yet another finger wagging about the "one China" principle—but its own economic relations with Taiwan continued to burgeon. China remained Taiwan's largest trade partner.[43] In a capitalist world, trade and investment tend to follow profit. Concerns about identity and political independence are secondary. Money chases money. Taiwan could talk about lessening reliance on China, but China was where the money was.

If facing China in the present was difficult, it was perhaps even harder to come to terms with the past. The years of the White Terror had brought so much suffering to so many and had left so much trauma that was still unaddressed. Tsai would launch a transitional justice initiative. There would be a historical fact-finding commission that would document the arrests, the killings, the torture. The victims would be acknowledged. The national archives would slowly, very slowly, open further files on the 228 incident and its aftermath.

Only thus could the past cease to be a source of division among Taiwanese; only thus could Taiwan move forward. It was a painfully slow process (in part, one suspects, because some of the perpetrators of violence are still alive and well-connected). The details are still trickling out. But it was a start. And the historical reckoning would not be confined to the familiar ground of ROC forces against Taiwanese or democracy advocates. Tsai would apologize for the harm done to the indigenous peoples too. A commission was formed to ensure, among other things, that their languages were protected and that they were no longer dispossessed of land. There was no undoing the past. But understanding its wrongs could build a better future. The indigenous people, too, were part of Taiwan. If Taiwan was to thrive, it had to make sure it was doing well by them.[44]

Even here, Tsai was moderate. In other hands, this might have become an all-out assault on the KMT and what it stood for. Such an assault would have destroyed trust in politics and undone Taiwan's still young democracy. Tsai did not make that mistake. When a park commemorating Chiang Ching-kuo was opened on January 22, 2022, it was Tsai who stood at the inauguration ceremony. The Taiwanese, she said, would reach a verdict on where their leaders had stood. She hoped that the library situated in the park would help provide the sources and information that would ensure a fair verdict. The historical record, she maintained, would reflect that Chiang Ching-kuo had presided over a period of extraordinary economic growth. To a historian, this was as close to a dispassionate assessment as one could get; for a politician to offer it was quite remarkable. Chiang Ching-kuo had been cruel and despotic. He had also managed to keep Taiwan both prosperous and separate from the PRC. Dispassionate analysis, however, could be galling to victims.

For people who had experienced the brutality of Chiang Ching-kuo's policing methods, this felt like a betrayal by their president. They were not shy about making their displeasure known. But Tsai knew that there were many Taiwanese united in the belief that Chiang Ching-kuo had stood up to the CCP (and in that belief, they were perfectly correct).[45] She was their president too.

Inevitable as it seems in retrospect, Tsai's reelection to the presidency in 2020 was far from assured. There was deep discontent with her pension reform scheme. Her very moderation had caused members of her own party to turn against her. There were those within the DPP who were tired of the notion that Taiwan had best keep its head down and go quietly about its business. It was time, they said, to hold a referendum and declare independence. The DPP's losses in local elections were ascribed to her. She was the reason, her critics claimed, that there were now mayors proclaiming the '92 consensus, with its assertion that both sides of the strait agreed on the "one China" principle. The premier, William Lai, challenged Tsai in the DPP primary for presidential candidate.[46] Lai failed—he was put on the ticket as vice president as compensation—but the challenge had made clear that Tsai's position was far from unassailable.

Tsai's opponent was tricky too. Han Kuo-yu, the KMT's candidate, was a true populist in the Trump mold. He was far too savvy to proclaim allegiance to China and far too savvy to take a definitive stance on policy. Han had an unerring sense for the gap between rich and poor and the resentment that gap could create. He was unafraid of activating the misogyny and racism that lay buried in the electorate, for those forces could translate into votes. In dealing with such a candidate, making the election about the relationship with China would be hard. And yet, this was precisely what Tsai managed to do. The question she posed to voters was simple. Did they want to become part of China, given what had happened in Hong Kong?[47] If the answer was no, they needed to vote for the DPP.

The person who made it possible for Tsai to take this tack was none other than Xi Jinping. Under Xi's heavy-handed rule, Hong Kong had been realizing just how brittle the "one country, two systems" agreement could be. Concerns about "mainlandization" had been simmering. Then, a bill allowing for Hong Kong citizens abroad to be extradited to Beijing was proposed by the territory's leader, Carrie Lam. The legal systems of the two territories were wildly different, and Hong Kongers decided to protest. A violent police crackdown ensued. (The bill died, but a new national security law—which, among other things, made "secession," "subversion," "terrorism," and "collusion with foreign forces" punishable by life imprisonment—proved the protesters' point.) Hong Kong had once upon a time been a place where one could, without any fear, say what one wanted, criticize whomever one wanted, and hold vigils to commemorate Tiananmen.[48] Xi made that impossible. Hong Kong as it once was had ceased to exist. The model of governance was no longer "one country, two systems"; it was just one country, and a rather miserable one at that.

If you were a voter sitting in Taiwan, it was impossible not to take notice of what was happening in Hong Kong and ask if this was what Taiwan would become. Like Hong Kong, Taiwan was a young democracy; like Hong Kong, it had people who relished their political freedoms and were loath to give them up. China had never renounced the right to use force to compel unification. Asking whether Taiwan would be the next Hong Kong was therefore a perfectly logical question. Tsai, with her defense budgets and avowed determination to keep Taiwan's democracy free, was the candidate who addressed that worry head on.

Beijing proceeded to alienate Taiwanese voters further. Had it used past experience to try to understand Taiwan's democracy, it would have come to the realization that interference usually backfired. But it could not bring itself to steer clear of the election, and this time the interference came in the form of disinformation. The PRC's United Front Work Department—a government agency tasked with propaganda—and other government agents flooded social media with denunciations of democracy and the DPP. Tsai was a US agent; the United States was intent on blocking China's rise. Very often, the PRC operatives outsourced the content creation to Taiwanese. The content spread like wildfire. It also proved completely ineffectual. Taiwanese voters were aware of disinformation. They had had previous experience with it, which, as with a virus, served as an inoculation. DPP voters were indignant about this latest Chinese attempt to interfere in their elections. Enough of them were suspicious of Han and the absence of a clear policy platform to make his victory untenable. And there was a simple realization that whatever her perceived faults—her almost deliberate lack of charisma, her refusal to call a referendum on independence or changing the island's name—in this particular electoral contest, Tsai offered the only credible path to keeping Taiwan safe and free. On January 11, 2020, she was reelected president by a comfortable margin.[49]

By 2020, Taiwan had come of age as a democracy. It had experienced peaceful passages of power from one party to another. Voters had punished corruption and rewarded competence. They held that their government was answerable to them. It was their fate to achieve all this while being claimed by another country that insisted Taiwan had no right to exist as an independent state.

It had been possible to ignore the China question in Taiwan's initial years as a democracy. Indeed, the US-China entente made it necessary to do so; one could not make an issue of independence for fear of losing such defense as the Americans might provide. By 2016, however, the China question could no longer be dodged. A combination of economic dependence on China and Xi Jinping's assertiveness had made studied avoidance of the matter impossible. Prospective governments would have to make their case to the people based in large part on how they proposed to deal with China.

For all the flack she caught from her party—there would remain those who felt she should have come out more strongly in favor of independence and there would remain some die-hard misogynists who could not forgive her for being a woman in power—Tsai had played a bad hand with considerable skill. A declaration of independence, such as her detractors demanded, might well have triggered a Chinese invasion, and there was no guarantee that America would have done anything. That she managed to keep Taiwan functionally independent during the Xi Jinping era was no small achievement. That she managed to do so without yielding to the temptation of going even further showed a sound understanding of her superpower patron. Trump's America might have come through on defending Taiwan, but it was equally possible that it might not. There was no way of knowing and no point in courting unnecessary risks.

The vagaries of American democracy, meanwhile, had led the country into one of those periodic outbreaks of anti-China sentiment

THE STRUGGLE FOR TAIWAN

that seem to be a recurring feature of US foreign policy. This is not to say that China had not provided grounds for action. Its conduct in the South and East China Seas should have jolted Washington out of complacency. What was happening in Tibet, Xinjiang, and Hong Kong, to say nothing of China proper, was a travesty. On all these, America would have had even sounder grounds for complaint if it had had a better track record of abiding by international law. Had the United States ratified the UN Convention on the Law of the Sea, for example, its support for the Philippines when The Hague ruled against China on one of the many South China Sea disputes would not have rung quite so oddly. It was hard to demand that China abide by a treaty it had signed when America itself was not party to the treaty. (The United States had initially objected to the treaty because it sought to create an international mechanism for marine technology transfer, but over time those objections had morphed into a simple dislike of being bound by international treaties.)[50] Regardless of America's own position on this and other issues, a rethink of its China policy was necessary, for China itself had changed. But Washington could not calibrate policy to nuance. It had decided China was a threat, and it was intent on showing China just how tough it could be.

All else being equal, it is interesting to wonder how long that would have lasted. Trump's policies had done little to alter Chinese behavior and had, arguably, upped the risk of Sino-American conflict. The intelligent thing to do would have been to jettison them quietly and come up with a policy that protected core interests without being needlessly belligerent. One could continue to defend the Senkakus and the South China Sea without the rhetorical flights the Trump team engaged in. One could quietly work with allies to push for WTO reform without threatening a trade war. If one sincerely wanted to defend Taiwan, the public strutting was counterproductive. It was far better to arm the island effectively without challenging Beijing to respond in public. But such moderation would have been politically difficult, to say the least. Trump had not occurred in a vacuum. His China policy had enjoyed broad bipartisan support. There was a nationalistic fury targeting China that had taken hold of the American body politic. Reasoning with such fury is hard, and it might well have proven beyond even the most skillful politician on the scene.

As it was, the question was never put to the test. A mysterious virus going around southern China around the time Tsai was winning reelection would soon burst upon an unprepared world. That virus would lay waste to US-China relations—and in doing so, bring both danger and opportunity to Taiwan.

5

After Covid

While Tsai and Han were on the campaign trail, the virus that would shut the world down was making its way around Wuhan. It moved as easily as breath and its symptoms varied dramatically. You would not necessarily pause to worry at a throat tickle or fatigue in Wuhan. These things happened, and besides, it was the season for coughs and sniffles. But the virus was far rougher on some, and Wuhan doctors began seeing patients with mysterious respiratory conditions coming to ask for help.

Some of Wuhan's medical practitioners were already worried in late 2019. On December 30, 2019, two doctors, Ai Fen (who was the first to sound the alarm) and Li Wenliang, would warn their colleagues that the virus seemed suspiciously similar to the one that had caused the SARS epidemic and that authorities needed to take it seriously. But in China, bad things happen to bearers of bad news. Both were told by hospital management to shut up about the virus. Ai Fen was reprimanded. Li Wenliang would lose his life to the virus he had been trying to sound the alarm about. It was only on January

7, 2020, as far as we know, that Xi seriously took up the question of how to deal with the problem. Even then, no hint of the full scale of danger was given to the general public for weeks. On January 28, the head of the World Health Organization, Tedros Adhanom Ghebreyesus, beamed reassurance. "We appreciate the seriousness with which China is taking this outbreak, especially the commitment from top leadership, and the transparency they have demonstrated, including sharing data and genetic sequence of the virus," he declared. "WHO is working closely with the government on measures to understand the virus and limit transmission. WHO will keep working side-by-side with China and all other countries to protect health and keep people safe."[1] The world could rest assured that the virus was contained in Wuhan. Beijing and the WHO were working on it. All was well. There was nothing to worry about.

The problem, for the WHO, was that working with Beijing made it harder to work with Taipei. Taiwan, like many countries near China, had been scarred by the SARS experience in 2003. With the benefit of hindsight, the SARS numbers in Taiwan seem small—668 cases, with 181 deaths—but the contagiousness of the disease had been terrifying. So, too, was the knowledge that if the disease had persisted, the hospital system would have been overwhelmed. If SARS came back, two facts were clear: China was not to be trusted when it came to communicating information about diseases, and Taiwan would be on the front lines. So Taiwan had moved to develop its own sources of intelligence on epidemiology. When the Covid-19 pandemic hit, Tsai's vice president, Chen Chien-Jen, was an epidemiologist. He would help chart Taiwan's response to the pandemic even after he was replaced by William Lai as vice president. On December 31, 2019, the Taiwan Centers for Disease Control (modeled, ironically, on an American counterpart that would prove hapless) shared its intelligence with the WHO. The phrasing was cautious; it shared facts, not hypotheses. But it made clear that China was keeping patients in isolation.[2] Patient isolation meant that the possibility of human-to-human transmission was very real. That was a possibility the world needed to know about, so Taiwan was telling the WHO. It was a smooth, technocratic performance.

The WHO decided to sit on the information. Later, on April 20, 2020, when press conferences had gone virtual, Tedros, the head of the WHO, would claim that Taiwan had never said anything about human-to-human transmission. (This was true as far as it went, but neglected to address why Taiwan's report of patient isolation had not caused the WHO to investigate the possibility of human-to-human transmission. Taiwan could report on what it had found; it was for the WHO to interpret those findings and devise a plan for delving further into what they might mean.) He would proceed, on April 8, 2020, to claim that Taiwan was launching a racist campaign against him, which Taiwan promptly denied. Tsai took to Facebook to invite the WHO to resist pressure from China and come visit Taiwan to see how the island was handling the pandemic. Just why the WHO did not follow up on Taiwan's warning of December 31, 2019, awaits a full reckoning. But at the end of the day, China was a member of that august organization and one that provided substantial funding.[3] China could help advance the careers of senior WHO officials. Taiwan was just an island left out of the international system. Why pay attention to anything it had to say? So the virus surged beyond China's borders. A global pandemic that killed millions and shut down the world ensued.

Two broad lessons that emerged from all this were taken to heart in the United States. The first was that China had lied. It had covered up just how serious the virus was and it had used its influence in international organizations to do so. Its deceit had harmed the world. This was not to be tolerated, and America should show as much. The anger here, it is worth noting, went beyond the United States. Countries like Australia, Germany, and Pakistan, hitherto quite amicable in their relations with China, would be sharply critical of Beijing. China's response—a vehement denunciation of all critics and the spreading of truly wild conspiracy theories—did little to help Beijing's cause.[4]

The second lesson was that Taiwan had done the right thing. It had raised the alarm early; it was only its unfortunate exclusion from international organizations that had kept that alarm from sounding across the globe. Taiwan was a good actor and deserved to be rewarded—not least because such reward would be punishment to China. The superb public health system that had been strengthened after SARS burnished Taiwan's credentials. Contact tracing, quarantining, pinpointing potential outbreaks—all these were things Taiwan was doing with ease while much of the rest of the world was still figuring out what they meant. Inasmuch as a country could carry on as normal during the pandemic, Taiwan did, albeit at the cost of shutting itself off from the world. Here was further proof of Taiwan's virtue compared to China's vice. Senator Chuck Grassley spoke for many when he fired off an angry letter to the WHO's Tedros:

Like many of my colleagues in the United States Senate, I question Communist China's ability and willingness to coordinate in a transparent manner with international bodies when it comes to combating the threat of the coronavirus.

Additionally, numerous reports suggest that Taiwan has been largely shut out of global health discussions. . . . Taiwan has been allowed to participate in WHO meetings in the past, with observer status, but as of 2016 Taiwan's requests to participate have all been denied due to political objections from Beijing. While WHO includes Taiwan's statistics with those of China, Taiwan's responses to the coronavirus appear to have been completely different from China's and it is vital for public health decision-making that the data and information on Taiwan's public health practices be accurately disaggregated and made available to the world. According to reports, as of March 18, 2020, Taiwan had seen only 100 cases compared to the more than 80,000 in China.[5]

It was impossible not to draw this contrast between the two sides of the strait. China's influence had hurt the world; Taiwan's absence of influence had hurt too. In asking that the statistics be disaggregated, in lamenting Taiwan's absence from global health discussions, Grassley was asking for a world in which Taiwan be considered separate from China.

In another world, where the pandemic had not happened, the deterioration in US-China relations just might have been arrested. The trade war was hurting Americans; the risks of blundering into a wider war with China had become more sharply defined. A cautious president might have had a chance—albeit a very small one—of quietly resetting the relationship closer to neutral. (But then, had the pandemic not happened, Trump might well have returned to office, and his presidency was anything but cautious.) As it was, the virus killed any chance of an improvement in US-China relations in the near future. The American policy of getting tough on China would now be pursued with even greater gusto. That policy would exacerbate the nationalistic resentment that had taken hold in Beijing. It was in this world of entrenched Sino-American competition that Tsai Ing-wen would have to find that elusive balance between keeping Taiwan independent and provoking China to the point where it might risk an attack on the island. For all three actors, the room for error had shrunk to virtually nil. The accumulated weight of the past had brought them to the edge of chaos, where a single misstep could take them from the fragile, barely intact order they were in existing in to catastrophe.

Donald Trump took to the task of blaming China for Covid-19 with characteristic gusto. It was the "Chinese virus," the "kung flu," and China needed to be punished. Perhaps, he mused, one could sever relations altogether and save $500 billion in the process. At his address to the UN General Assembly on September 22, 2020, he demanded that China be held accountable for the "China virus" and added a long litany of Chinese crimes: overfishing, pollution, trade practices. Given that America wanted China punished, it made sense to support Taiwan even more loudly than the Trump administration already had. When Tsai was inaugurated for her second term in May, Secretary of State Mike Pompeo released a statement of congratulations that hailed Taiwan as "a force for good." He followed up with a blunt declaration in a radio interview: Taiwan "has not been a part of China." Taiwan's separation, he argued, had been accomplished by the work of the Reagan administration. This was completely untrue. Reagan had indeed given Taiwan six assurances, but these had carefully steered clear of formalizing a separation from the PRC.

Reagan himself had, once in office, been meticulous about abiding by the "one China" policy. To come out and say explicitly that Taiwan was not a part of China was new. But historical accuracy did not matter; what mattered was how the politics of supporting Taiwan played in public. And Pompeo did not stop here. Before he left office, he eliminated the restrictions that had governed American officials' meetings with their Taiwanese counterparts.[6] He was chipping away at the obstacles that kept Taiwan from being a full country.

There was one thing Pompeo had been correct about: American feelings toward Taiwan were bipartisan. The Covid pandemic was one of the things that cost Trump reelection, but there was broad-based public support for the tack he was taking with China. Joe Biden's arrival in the White House brought no change to China policy, except to make it even tougher. Biden was, in many ways, precisely the sort of president who could, in another life, have overseen an improvement in US-China relations. Back in 1979, when the Senate Foreign Relations Committee was furiously debating what sort of legislation it should come up with to protect Taiwan if US-China relations were normalized, Biden was one of two senators who felt that a congressional statement on Taiwan's security was unnecessary. As Obama's vice president, he had shown a clear understanding of the limits of American power, notably in being the lone senior voice to insist that it was time to withdraw from Afghanistan. Confrontation had its place, in Biden's world view, but there was only so much confrontation could do to change geopolitical realities. Personal relationships, careful diplomacy—this was how one could best protect American interests.[7] But against this practical streak on foreign policy, Biden had to set the realities of domestic politics. Easing policy on China as he took office was simply not a viable political option. The Indo-Pacific strategy the Biden administration put forth in February 2022 diagnosed the China threat in language that could almost have come from its predecessor:

> The PRC is combining its economic, diplomatic, military, and technological might as it pursues a sphere of influence in the Indo-Pacific and seeks to become the world's most influential power. From the economic coercion of Australia . . . to the growing pressure on Taiwan and bullying of neighbors in the East and South China Seas, our allies and partners in the region bear much of the cost of the PRC's harmful behavior. In the process, the PRC is also undermining human rights and international law, including freedom of navigation, as well as other principles that have brought stability and prosperity to the Indo-Pacific.

The concept of China as a key threat was still intact. The Biden team placed a slightly greater emphasis on allies and partners than Trump's administration had, but it was clear in its portrayal of a China that was out to take over the world. That China was "harmful," "bullying." The change Trump had wrought had solidified, and it was accepted across the American political spectrum. The statement made clear that American support for Taiwan was still at the new normal: "We will also work with partners inside and outside the region to maintain peace and stability in the Taiwan Strait, including by supporting Taiwan's self-defense capabilities, to ensure an environment in which Taiwan's future is determined peacefully in accordance with the wishes and best interests of Taiwan's people."[8] This was a marked departure from the mere wish that the question of Taiwan be resolved peacefully. It was, in essence, a guarantee of protection for self-determination. Taiwan's people would have to decide on their future. The Biden administration claimed that this was consistent with the "one China" policy, but it was hard to see how. American agreement to the "one China" principle had come down to not disputing the idea that there was "one China." In the Biden team's formulation, if Taiwan's people did wind up disputing that idea, they would still be protected. It was a nuance, but nuance mattered. Biden's approach to Taiwan had more in common with Trump's than Obama's or Bush's.

Biden's national security strategy would go on to clarify that his administration did not support Taiwan's independence and that, where China and the United States needed to work together—climate change being the obvious, most touted example—his administration would seek to do so. But a raft of policies aimed at countering Chinese influence was being put into practice. The key difference between Biden and Trump was that the new president believed in multilateralism. Allies had to be brought on board. The unfortunately named AUKUS was formed: a trilateral military pact between Australia, the United Kingdom, and the United States, which would work to secure a "free and open Indo-Pacific" against America's key competitor, China. The Quad—a loose group comprising Australia, India, Japan, and the United States—convened to announce that it would work for a "free and open Indo-Pacific." Lest there be any doubt that this was a jab at China, the Quad made clear that it would "champion adherence to international law, particularly as reflected in the UN Convention on the Law of the Sea (UNCLOS), to meet challenges to the maritime rules-based order, including in the East and South China Seas." (That the United States had not ratified

UNCLOS was left carefully unremarked.) The Quad would also take on vaccine distribution. A chorus of voices rose demanding that America compete with China at "vaccine diplomacy"; otherwise, the future would be lost to Beijing.[9] The question was no longer how to get vaccines into as many people as possible. It was who would win in the US-China competition.

The adamant opposition to China meant adamant support for Taiwan. The first hint of just how staunch Biden could get in that support came when he gave an interview after pulling American troops out of Afghanistan. The hint was lost in the angst, horror, and soul-searching the withdrawal from Afghanistan provoked, but it was there. "You already see China telling Taiwan, 'See? You can't count on the Americans,'" an interviewer pointed out to Biden. The president's response was that Afghanistan was fundamentally different from Taiwan. The category he proceeded to put Taiwan in was telling: "We made a sacred commitment to Article Five that if in fact anyone were to invade or take action against our NATO allies, we would respond. Same with Japan, same with South Korea, same with—Taiwan."[10]

Taiwan, as the president had it, was in the same category as Japan, South Korea, and NATO allies—all parties that had mutual defense treaties with the United States. If Biden was serious about treating Taiwan just as he did those other countries, it was as though the defense treaty of 1954 had come alive again. Never mind the Sino-American rapprochement and the painful work of achieving normalized relations between the United States and the PRC. America was once again committed to intervening if Taiwan was attacked. And this was no ill-judged remark made in haste, trying to fend off tough questions about an unpopular decision on Afghanistan.

Biden would repeat that the United States would defend Taiwan several times. The Russian invasion of Ukraine sharpened his insistence. American troops had not intervened in Ukraine; there had been no treaty obligation. But the United States would defend Taiwan. He would go further and reiterate his belief in Taiwan's right to self-determination. It was not for the United States to support independence, but "Taiwan makes their own judgments about their independence . . . that's their decision." This was—regardless of what the White House claimed—a shift in policy.[11]

Nor was support for Taiwan confined to the White House. Congress decided to take up the Taiwan Policy Act (TPA), despite the White House thinking that this was going a step too far. The purpose of the TPA was "to support the security of Taiwan and its right of self-determination." The bill, as written, did not pass, but it showed just how powerfully suspicion of China had taken hold of the American legislature. There was a line designating Taiwan a non-NATO ally, another demanding that the United States clap sanctions on Chinese officials right up to the rank of president if they escalated hostilities against Taiwan, yet another that called on the US government to "treat the democratically elected government of Taiwan as the legitimate representative of the people of Taiwan." These provisions did not make it into the modified version called the Taiwan Enhanced Resilience Act, which Senator Bob Menendez of New Jersey (this was before corruption charges marred his profile) cleverly attached to the National Defense Authorization Act. Ten billion dollars' worth of security assistance was to be provided to Taiwan. There was, Menendez vowed, more to come: "I am committed to continue pursuing legislation next Congress to mobilize all the tools in the US strategic, economic, and diplomatic toolkit so our nation can fully confront the challenges China poses to our national and economic security."[12] Menendez made due acknowledgment of Taiwan's democracy, but it was clear that Taiwan was being supported not because it was a democracy but because supporting it antagonized China.

American politicians were now vying to get tough on China. Since nothing showed toughness as much as a visit to Taiwan, those trips became something the politically ambitious had to make. Mike Pompeo's performance in March 2022 triggered a series of high-profile pilgrimages, which culminated in Nancy Pelosi's trip to Taiwan. Her visit did as much as anything since 1996 to send China into conniptions. The episode was the perfect illustration of how the logic of deterrence, the need to appear tough, and the corresponding need for escalation locked together in a self-reinforcing cycle. Pelosi had unimpeachable credentials as a China hawk. Like most American politicians, she also had a fine record of adoring limelight. She had held her own protest at Tiananmen Square when she visited China in 1991, which had resulted in a wearying detention for an American journalist. To see the Mike Pompeos and Mike Mullens of the world getting grand receptions in Taipei as they spoke of American support for Taiwan's democracy, while she, Nancy Pelosi, stayed at home was not to be borne. Pelosi therefore announced that she would be visiting Taiwan too. Once the announcement was made, it was impossible to back down. Biden suggested that the military thought it was not the best moment for such a visit. This was a sensitive time in China, with a party congress scheduled in the fall. But this in itself made the visit necessary. America had to show that it would not be cowed by military threats or by sensitivities. It was going to support democracy, whatever China might do or say. The

PRC did not help its cause with its usual incomprehension of the United States. When Xi Jinping warned that those who "play with fire will perish by it," he rendered the trip inevitable. Washington could not appear as though it lacked the courage to stand up when such remarks went public. Hu Xijin, editor of the prominent nationalistic paper *Global Times*, helpfully suggested that Pelosi's plane be shot down.[13] For Pelosi, this was gold. She was the heroic leader who would fly to democracy's support at the risk of being shot down. For America as a whole, Chinese remarks had made this a matter of face and credibility. Pelosi now had to go to Taiwan.

The trip could have gone tragically wrong. For China, the provocation was immense. The nationalistic fury that had taken hold of the government and people could have led Beijing into dangerous territory. PLA planes flying close to Taiwan had become a more regular feature of cross-strait life. Xi might well have resisted the calls to shoot Pelosi's plane down, but what if a young pilot had decided to buzz the Speaker's plane to give it a scare, or if a small squadron had been ordered to dog the plane until it landed? What if, in carrying out these orders, the PLA aircraft had got too close and an accident had occurred?

This was precisely what had happened on April 1, 2001. A Chinese fighter pilot, Wang Wei, had flown too close to an American spy plane in international airspace. The resulting collision cost Wang his life and forced the Americans to make an emergency landing on Hainan Island. Tempers had run high on both sides. Had the PRC harmed the American crew or had the United States insisted that the collision was an act of war, the situation might well have got out of control. But in 2001, both Washington and Beijing were willing to dial tensions down and find an amicable solution to the matter. The

United States refused to apologize, but it did choose to express sorrow at Wang's death and regret that the spy plane's call for an emergency landing had gone unregistered. The PRC decided that this was a sufficient apology, though the Americans refused to call it that. The possibility of conflict was snuffed out because the general mood favored getting along. This was emphatically not the mood in 2022. Had an aerial accident occurred and claimed a PLA soldier or Speaker Pelosi, two countries that were increasingly suspicious of one another would have been charged with preventing the outbreak of World War III. American forces in the vicinity were on the alert to ensure safe travels for their Speaker.[14] But their very presence both spoke volumes about the threat and increased the possibilities of a clash.

In the event, the visit went safely. On August 2, Pelosi became the highest ranking American official to visit the island in twenty-five years. In her wake, more officials would come thronging to Taiwan to show support. But just because the visit went off safely does not mean that it had to. America and China had been lucky.

Potential risk aside, there were three problems with the Pelosi visit. The first was that, barring the symbolism, there was not much to show for it. Pelosi had given a rousing set of speeches in praise of Taiwan's democracy, but this did not amount to a defense guarantee. The symbolism could of course make a commitment harder to evade in the future, especially if enough American politicians partook in it, but that was an uncertain gamble at best. The second problem was that there was a faint whiff of nepotism to Pelosi's son accompanying her on the trip. Paul Pelosi Jr. was a tech investor; he had a chance to chat with Morris Chang, founder of the Taiwan Semiconductor Manufacturing Company. Pelosi might have been telling the truth when she said that her son did no business, but it was not a good look for someone who had come solely to champion democracy.[15] Taiwanese could be forgiven for wondering if the cost of American support was a few quiet business deals for America's political elite.

The third problem was the display of force that China undertook in response to the announcement of the visit. Military exercises were launched. The PLA simulated a blockade of Taiwan. The median line—an informal boundary that China had passed before and now made a point of dismissing as nonexistent—between the PRC and Taiwan was crossed by both aircraft and ships. Missiles went scudding over Taiwan, with some landing in Japan's exclusive economic zone. This last might well have been a signal to Japan. Tokyo had warned Beijing against changing the status quo by force, and its coastguard had shown itself perfectly capable of defending the Senkaku Islands, despite being regularly harassed by Chinese fishing militias. To officials in Beijing, it would have made sense to show Japan, as well as the United States and Taiwan, just how tough an opponent the PRC was. It is perfectly possible that the PRC might sooner or later have demonstrated such capabilities regardless of the Pelosi visit. But the visit did give it a pretext for normalizing such a massive display of force. Not content with this, Beijing also suspended talks with the United States on everything from climate change to defense.[16] Cutting off communication while rival ships and aircraft swarmed around one another—this was truly playing with fire.

If Taiwanese shrugged it off as just another day living in Beijing's shadow, Americans took to a tricky guessing game: When would China actually invade the island? A series of guesses were set forth. American intelligence said that Xi had asked his forces to be ready to take Taiwan by 2027. Air Force general Mike Minihan's "gut" warned the fight was coming in 2025. Philip Davidson, the admiral leading Indo-Pacific Command, suggested sometime within the next six years. The truth was nobody knew. China's intentions could only be guessed at—and even if they were guessed at accurately, they were subject to change. Xi could have miscalculated and invaded right after the Pelosi visit. He could wait six years or sixteen. It fell to John Aquilino, Davidson's successor, to make the obvious point. "I think everybody is guessing," he said simply. "I'm responsible to prevent this conflict today and if deterrence were to fail to be able to fight and win."[17]

Forecasting Chinese behavior was made all the more difficult by the fact that China itself was being torn in several different directions. The regular knee-jerk reaction to anything that deepened the cross-strait divide was still there. But added to this was a new phenomenon: wolf warrior diplomacy. The name came from a series of films celebrating the exploits of Chinese action heroes out to protect the PRC's interests. A new type of Chinese diplomat claimed that their tough diplomacy was doing the same. What set the wolf warriors apart from traditional Chinese nationalists was that there seemed to be no object to their belligerence. These diplomats extended the blind hurt that Beijing usually brought to discussions of particularly sore spots to anything and everything—and did so without any calculation of the pros and cons of a nationalistic tantrum. When Trump slammed China for the pandemic at the UN General Assembly, the Chinese ambassador to the UN, Zhang Jun, accused the United States of "abusing the platform of the United Nations to provoke confrontation and create division." This was standard Chinese diplomacy:

hitting back when hit, to show that China would not compromise on being treated with respect. What was not standard was the wolf warriors' decision to tweet conspiracy theories about the American creation of Covid. When Australia called for an investigation into the origins of the pandemic, an old-school Chinese diplomat would have either warned against politicizing the pandemic or, at worst, added a tirade about interfering in China's internal affairs and the hurt done to the feelings of the Chinese people. The wolf warriors, by contrast, clapped sanctions on Australia and compiled a list of grievances against a country that had previously enjoyed fairly amicable relations with the PRC.[18] The result was to alienate Australia completely. It was as though the older, more contained nationalism had gone cancerous and now threatened to take over the PRC.

The risk of angering other countries in this fashion did seem to resonate with Xi Jinping. He himself had done as much as anyone to use Taiwan as an ignition switch for Chinese nationalism. Where Mao and Deng had emphasized that the problem could be left to the future, Xi had repeatedly made clear, both to an envoy from Taiwan and to his own public, that his patience was not infinite. He did not wish to keep punting the problem from "generation to generation." But now, though his own nationalism would continue to flash out, Xi called for a more "lovable China" in what seemed to be a subtle condemnation of wolf warrior diplomacy. (Perhaps, too, he feared what such nationalism might mean for China's own internal stability. He had suffered through the Cultural Revolution. If there was a clash within the party about just how aggressive to get with the outside world, it was perfectly possible for that clash to develop into furious infighting—the kind that would sap the CCP of political strength.) Xi's call did little to muzzle the wolf warriors. Perhaps Xi, like Biden, was in the uncomfortable position of trying to handle forces that had outstripped even his considerable authority. Nevertheless, at the national party congress in October 2022, Xi seemed to be at the zenith of his power. He was awarded a third term as president as the party dropped the idea of term limits; the politburo standing committee was stacked with his cronies. Opening the twentieth party congress, Xi sounded the same note on Taiwan that Chinese leaders since Mao had. China hoped unification would be peaceful, but it would not forswear the use of force. Unification was nonnegotiable.[19]

Taiwan's response was a bipartisan dismissal of Xi's speech. The DPP vowed to protect Taiwan's sovereignty. The KMT said it would safeguard the Republic of China, citing public opposition to the "one country, two systems" model that Xi had once again touted. The DPP's opposition was to be taken for granted, but to have turned the KMT so thoroughly against Beijing—that was the product of years of miscalculation about Taiwan.

Miscalculations at home would confront Xi with a larger problem when Chinese burst into protest. Having refused to acknowledge the virus's power at first, the CCP had decided to enact a zero-Covid policy. In essence, this involved shutting down neighborhoods or cities at the faintest hint of the possibility of infection and keeping them shut down until the threat was deemed to have passed. Wuhan was the first city to see such a lockdown in early 2020, but they would be replicated across the country, from Xinjiang to Shanghai. There was no predictability to the lockdowns, no room for citizens to plan how to work or reach loved ones. No one knew when they might start, and, once started, no one knew when they might end. The policy had caused discontent, not least because it was still in place in 2022, when other countries, having boosted their vaccination rates, were beginning to return to normal. In a way, the surprising thing was how long the shift from simmering discontent to mass protest took. On October 13, 2022, banners of protest unfurled on Sitong Bridge in Beijing, and they struck a chord among Chinese. By December, mass protests against the zero-Covid policy were breaking out across the country. People had been burned to death in an apartment in Ürümqi because they were not allowed out. This was no way to live. For the first time, citizens dared to call for the removal of Xi Jinping.[20] It was the most dramatic outburst of dissent since Tiananmen.

Xi's response was to surrender. The zero-Covid policy was terminated at the end of 2022. It was an astonishing climbdown for a man hailed as the most powerful leader since Mao. And it raised an ineluctable question about the durability of the CCP. The government did not crumble, but one thing was clear: there would be future protests. Citizens had learned that if their voices were unheard, they could take to the streets; that was what it took to bring about a change in policy. Economic growth had slowed under the zero-Covid policy. Debts mounted. With vaccination rates low and the Chinese vaccines not as effective as their Western counterparts, Covid tore through the country. When dynasties began their long falls in China's past, Chinese would talk of the mandate of heaven passing. The passage of that mandate in the past had come with certain warning signs: foreigners ranging themselves more firmly against China, greater and greater investment in policing recalcitrant territories, a populace losing faith in the ruling emperor and deciding to show it, panicked decision-making seeking to assuage protesters but instead only emboldening them. Signs came, too, from the natural world. Plagues would break out; the weather would become literally unlivable; dragons would flash across the sky.[21] Watching Xi's China struggle today, one could not help wondering if this was the beginning of the end for the CCP. The end might not come soon—decades elapsed between the Qing Empire's defeat in the Opium War and its final collapse—but some wounds are too deep to heal.

Regardless of the CCP's long-term prospects, the array of domestic troubles could have meant several different things for China's Taiwan policy. Xi might well have chosen to distract from the turbulence on the mainland with another set of military exercises directed against the island. Part of Mao's motivation during the second Taiwan Strait crisis in 1958, after all, had been to unite China behind the Great Leap Forward. Instead, the protests seemed to cause Xi to rein in his more adventurous impulses. There was uncertainty at home. China's refusal to break with Russia when Vladimir Putin decided to invade Ukraine had cost Xi European support. He was going to travel to the United States in November 2023 for the Asia-Pacific Economic Cooperation forum; achieving results there would require tact. This was no time to go looking for more trouble. This might explain the note of calm Xi struck on Taiwan in his New Year's address. There was no harping on China's right to use force this time. "The people on both sides of the Taiwan Strait are members of one and the same family," he declared. "I sincerely hope that our compatriots on both sides of the Strait will work together with a unity of purpose to jointly foster lasting prosperity of the Chinese nation."[22] Family over fury—it was a welcome change in tone.

Yet that old, hurt nationalism was still there. Xi's conciliatory note was missing from Foreign Minister Wang Yi's remarks at the Munich Security Conference. "'Taiwan independence' separatist activities and peace and stability across the Taiwan Strait," Wang declared, "are as irreconcilable as fire and water." If the international community could invoke territorial integrity and sovereignty in denouncing Russia's invasion of Ukraine, Wang argued, then following the "one China" principle was an obligation; otherwise, there would be "double standards on major issues." It was a tone-deaf argument given Beijing's support for Moscow, and Taipei exploited that. China's reluctance to break with Russia, Taiwan's Mainland Affairs Council stated, showed how little it could be trusted. Taiwan was a sovereign country, whatever China had to say about the matter.[23] Nationalistic passion is not something that can be turned on and off easily. It acquires a life of its own. Wang had yet to realize that heated indignation would only entrench Taiwan further in its position. As Tsai's last term as president came to completion, China still had not figured out what tone to take on its Taiwan problem.

To make matters worse, Beijing lost control of its equipment. Balloons started floating across the skies. On January 28, 2023, a wayward Chinese balloon wandered across North America. The United States was not going to tolerate such invasions: Biden ordered that the balloon be taken down. On February 4, the balloon was shot over the Atlantic and landed harmlessly in the water. This drew some wrath from Beijing. It had maintained that the balloon was an errant meteorological device; the Americans claimed it was engaged in surveillance. "The United States," declared Vice Foreign Minister Xie Feng, "turned a deaf ear and insisted on indiscriminate use of force against the civilian airship that was about to leave the United States airspace, obviously overreacted and seriously violated the spirit of international law and international practice." Overreaction or not, the move did inspire Taiwan to comment. It had been living with Chinese balloons itself, it claimed. Though one had yet to breach its defenses, any spy balloon coming from China over Taiwan would be shot down. Another Chinese balloon was spotted over Latin America. Meanwhile, North America kept up with the takedowns. A second "high-altitude object" was downed over Alaska on February 10. A third object was shot down over Canada the very next day. On February 12, yet another high-altitude object was shot down over Lake Huron. What the objects were or where they came from was left vague. This did not stop Senate majority leader Chuck Schumer from denouncing Beijing for a "crew of balloons. . . . They've probably been all over the world." The main casualty was a planned visit by Secretary of State Antony Blinken to China.[24] It was supposed to have been a chance for Beijing and Washington to talk over their differences. It was an opportunity that should have been seized. Face-to-face meetings, even if charged with hostility, at least open the possibility of staving off further damage. US-China relations have worked best when the two sides have maintained a commitment to keep talking to one another. But with the appearance of the balloons, the meeting would have to shelved. Like a balloon, hope is easily deflated.

Tsai Ing-wen's task was to keep Taiwan sovereign. To do so, she had to navigate an extremely treacherous set of currents. Keeping American support seemed easy; keeping that support without objections from her electorate or provoking China into war was far harder. Taiwan's voters knew, for the most part, that they wanted to stay separate from China. What they did not agree on was how best to achieve such separation. In a democracy, this type of disagreement is aired raucously, and it makes a leader's task infinitely harder.

The Russian invasion of Ukraine had shown that sovereignty was something not to be taken for granted. This was still a world where great powers invaded and the rest of the world watched. For Taiwanese, the questions were simple. Would China follow Russia's example? If it did, would Taiwanese be able to persevere in resistance as the Ukrainians had? On paper, Taiwan had a sizeable military: 190,000 active duty troops and some two million reservists. But the numbers masked the facts that military training lasted a grand total of four months and that the would-be fighters emerged woefully unprepared for combat. It was not just that Taiwan was not ready to fight the PRC; it was that it did not seem serious about getting ready. That had to change. A handful of Taiwanese took the initiative to seek out training for how to respond in the event of an attack. Organizations like Kuma Academy sprung up to show eager Taiwanese how to evade an enemy, read a map, and sniff out surveillance. If much of the population was far too busy to participate, the existence of Kuma Academy did, at least, show an inkling that the world could be cruel and some preparation was better than none. Meanwhile, Tsai took the chance to usher through long overdue military reforms. Explaining the necessity for reform to her citizens on December 27, 2022, she quoted Winston Churchill: "You were given the choice between war and dishonour. You chose dishonour, and you will have war." Hitherto, defending Taiwan had mainly been a job for reservists. Now there would be an active duty volunteer force, a garrison force, a civil defense force, and reservists. Conscription had been a four-month stint before; Tsai's plan would up it to a year. Military salaries would go up. Training had been outmoded—bayonet practice was still the norm—so Taiwan's soldiers would now practice the way American soldiers practiced, with things like Stinger missiles and drones. The small number of women who had military experience would be summoned to the reserves.[25] The reforms seemed pitifully inadequate set against the forces of the behemoth next door, but for Taiwan, they constituted massive change.

The move was far from universally popular. There was, as Tsai well knew, a deep-rooted suspicion of the military in a country that still associated soldiers with the tyranny of martial law. When the DPP had emphasized the need to strengthen civil-military relations back in 2014, it was precisely this suspicion it had sought to counter. Some criticized the reform for not being enough; others objected to the longer conscription. Lee Hsi-ming, former chief of general staff, had wanted Taiwan to adopt an asymmetric defense; the plan would have been to wage guerrilla war against an invader.[26] But Tsai's reform was not just about improving military efficacy. It was about showing the world—principally the United States—that Taiwan was prepared to fight for its democracy. Ukraine had won aid because it had shown itself willing to resist the Russian forces. It was all very well to talk about the virtues of democracy, but if Taiwan proved loath to stir in its own defense, it had no business expecting the Americans to help. If they wanted their island to survive sovereign, Taiwanese would have to show a willingness to do battle. The reforms, however imperfect, testified to that willingness.

Tsai would find some difficulty in tacking toward the United States because, much as her electorate was in favor of American protection, it was opposed to the strings that protection came with. The Americans came preaching the gospel of democracy, but they also wanted Taiwan to buy more of their goods. One of those goods was American pork, and herein lay a problem: Americans added ractopamine to their pig feed. To an American farmer, ractopamine was a harmless additive that accelerated the speed at which a pig put on muscle and made the meat leaner. To the European Union and to Taiwan (not to mention to China and to Russia), ractopamine was banned as a potentially dangerous chemical that could lead to an increased heart rate and anxiety. Opening the gates to American pork was opening the gates to ractopamine. Tsai, in her quest to keep the Americans satisfied, decided to drop her objections to ractopamine-laced pork. She found, too, that she could not compel the Americans to label their pork as bearing ractopamine. (There was more than a touch of irony here. It was Tsai, many years ago, who had lauded the protests against Ma Ying-jeou's decision to import American beef, which also came with a hefty dose of ractopamine.) Thousands marched against the decision. Among their number were the pig farmers who would now have to compete with cheaper pork. At the Legislative Yuan, the KMT flung pig intestines at the Taiwanese premier as a mark of protest; it was, admonished the DPP, wasting food. A referendum was held calling for a reversal of the decision on December 18, 2021. The referendum failed, so American pork was allowed in. But if Tsai was unable to ensure that the Americans labeled their pork as containing ractopamine, she could ensure that the pork was labeled by its country of origin—a ractopamine label without being a ractopamine label. The US trade representative was unhappy about the implication that American pork was unsafe, but on this, Taiwan did not budge.[27]

The whole saga showcased what the relationship with the United States was really like. The Americans would offer protection, though how that would pan out in an actual conflict was uncertain. But they would not do so for free. They would compel imports if they could, and the health and safety standards of the country they wished to protect were immaterial. It was an imperfect world, and Taiwan would just have to live with this. But it helped explain why, beneath the cordial bonhomie that would greet Lindsey Graham and Nancy Pelosi, there was an undercurrent of resentment directed toward the United States. Dependence is hard to stomach, especially when the dependent party is forced to accept things it does not wish to.

Though the referendum had failed, there was a mood that the KMT could capitalize on. Taiwan's swift lockdown and its excellent contact-tracing system allowed it to have a relatively good pandemic, but the cost was voters feeling that the economy was not doing as well as it should. Tsai had framed the local elections of 2022 as being another referendum on China. But life was not all about China; it was about putting food on the table, the cost of gasoline, subsidies, the ease with which one could navigate daily life. The KMT won most of the seats being contested, and an embarrassed Tsai resigned as DPP chairperson.[28]

Life on Taiwan was not all about China, but it could not be lived without thinking about China either. If the KMT was going to compete in the presidential elections of 2024, it would need to adjust its China policy. It had come to be identified as the party that favored some form of association with China. Its trouble was how to sell such an association to voters when China was behaving like an insufferable bully. In crafting that policy, the KMT sought a middle ground. Only the foolhardiest politician would try a pro-unification message now. There was a reason the KMT had been so vocal in dismissing "one country, two systems" when Xi threatened force in 2022. But there was a case to be made that placating China was a better path to continued safety and separation than antagonizing it. This was a hard case to make because China had changed. The rough muscularity it was demonstrating made it difficult to argue that greater amiability would help. Xi Jinping was no Jiang Zemin or Hu Jintao; it was unclear that anything other than complete surrender would placate him. But it was a stance the KMT deemed worth taking. "Vote for the DPP, youth go to the battlefield. Vote for the Kuomintang, there will be no battlefield on both sides of the strait," declared Ma Ying-jeou. In Ma's portrayal, Tsai was responsible for the building tension in the strait. War was best avoided by engagement with the mainland. Resuming the links between the offshore islands and China, which had been suspended due to the pandemic, would be a start.[29]

Ferries did start going directly between Kinmen and China again for the Lunar New Year on January 7, 2023. Tsai had made clear that even though she would prepare for war, she knew it was a far from ideal solution.[30] But what was the ideal solution? What was the line between working with the Americans and becoming subservient to them? How did Taiwan resist China without provoking it into a broader war, particularly when just being Taiwan was a provocation? There were no easy answers here, and the debate about them was crystallized by the dueling visits that Ma and Tsai undertook.

Ma Ying-jeou headed for China in March 2023. He celebrated the common descent of people on both sides of the strait. He honored his deceased ancestors at the family tomb in Xiangtan. He visited Sun Yat-sen's mausoleum in Nanjing. He toured historical sites and spoke of his hopes for peace. But there was no meeting with Xi Jinping this time.[31] It was a tough position; one could only marvel that Ma had sought it out. A failure to meet with Xi would be seen as a loss of face: the Chinese leader was too important to spare time for Ma. A meeting with Xi, by contrast, would be interpreted as courting

Chinese interference in Taiwan's elections yet again. Perhaps Ma had overreached. Criticizing Tsai's warmongering ways without the troublesome optics of a trip to China would have served the KMT better.

Tsai made her way to the Americas. Taiwan had lost yet another diplomatic partner, as Honduras decided the PRC had more to offer financially. Tsai needed to visit Guatemala and Belize, two of the dwindling number of countries that still recognized Taiwan. Important as this was, the stopovers in the United States on her way to and from Central America were what truly mattered. She received an award from the Hudson Institute in New York. On her way back, she met with Pelosi's successor as Speaker of the House, Kevin McCarthy, on April 5, 2023.

This was a meeting Beijing had warned against in the strictest of terms. It was therefore a meeting that both sides found necessary to have. China had to be shown that it could not dictate whom either Taiwan or the United States met with. On this, both Taipei and Washington were agreed. There had been some talk of McCarthy visiting Taipei, but it was decided—presumably to avoid a repeat of the Chinese military buildup that the Pelosi visit had wrought—that the meeting would take place at the Ronald Reagan Presidential Library in California instead. As meetings went, it was innocuous enough. Tsai paid graceful tribute to Reagan—she expressed her agreement with his precept "that to preserve peace, we must be strong"—and thanked Congress for all it had done to strengthen the US-Taiwan partnership. McCarthy vowed to continue arms sales and maintained that the bipartisan meeting had been held without intent of increasing tensions with China. Congresspeople like Mike Gallagher and Ashley Hinson got to show how unafraid they were. Pelosi congratulated the meeting for its bipartisanship. And the PRC delivered on its promised forceful response by engaging in military drills and sending warships and planes scudding around Taiwan. The median line and Taiwan's air defense identification zone were breached. One PLA aircraft carrier, the *Shandong*, entered the waters just south of Japan.[32] Violations of the "one China" principle, Beijing had to make clear, were not going to be taken quietly. And in seeking to make that clear, it deepened the risk of war.

Commentators dismissed Beijing's response to the Tsai-McCarthy meeting as less intense than the one that had attended the Pelosi visit. But the dismissal itself highlighted the gravity of the problem. A certain level of military activity had become normalized. It was as though the world now took for granted the presence of missiles and aircraft carriers, the shows of force that demanded a response in kind. The United States and the Philippines announced their own joint military exercises. It was a way of showing the PRC that there were other militaries that could operate in the region. New normal meant more ships and planes operating in close proximity to one another, mutual recrimination, and mutual suspicion. The risk of an accident had climbed, and Beijing and Washington had become desensitized to the level of risk. Comparisons between World War I and contemporary US-China relations are trite and often inaccurate. But in the militarization of foreign policy and in the failure to grasp the full significance of that militarization, a historian could not help but hear echoes of 1914. Mathematicians speak of the "edge of chaos": the final point separating order from chaos. A system operating at the edge of chaos has no room for error. A slight misstep means a plunge into doom.[33] This was where the accumulated weight of the past had brought the United States, China, and Taiwan. They had walked right up to the edge of a war that could go nuclear several times in the past: in 1954–1955, in 1958, and then again in 1996. Now, they seemed to be living on that edge permanently.

China had pursued a course that had alienated Taiwan completely. It had bullied, threatened, and displayed force, both at home and abroad. In doing so, it had made the thought of unification unacceptable to much of the Taiwanese electorate. It had sought to influence the democratic process there through meetings with KMT chieftains. In so doing, China had damaged the KMT's electoral prospects, perhaps irreparably. And in trying to isolate Taiwan diplomatically, the PRC had enjoyed only mixed success. True, it had managed to buy off many of Taiwan's erstwhile allies. But China's conduct over Covid and its support for Russia despite the invasion of Ukraine cost it friends too—and those former friends turned to the island across the strait. A seemingly endless parade of visitors came to Taiwan, and not all of them were American. A Japanese parliamentary delegation arrived. It spoke glowingly of Tsai's defense plans and made a point of emphasizing Japan's own determination to keep the status quo in the region from being "changed by force or unilaterally." The European Parliament sent a delegation to Taiwan. Raphaël Glucksmann, the head of the delegation, explained his purpose in terms that would have provoked howls in Beijing: "We in Europe are also confronted with interference from authoritarian regimes and we came here to learn from you." Germany sent its education minister to Taiwan, despite Beijing denouncing the visits as "vile." Liz Truss, onetime UK prime minister and a member of Parliament, showed up. The Czech president-elect, Petr Pavel, talked to Tsai on the phone, disregarding Beijing's threats.

Parliamentarians from Lithuania and Ukraine stood by Tsai's side in Taipei. Lithuania, as Tsai acknowledged, had established representative offices in Taiwan despite Beijing's anger. For Ukraine, it was a gesture of solidarity with a country that, unlike China, had been sharp in its criticism of Moscow.[34]

Beijing had only itself to blame. The wolf warrior nationalism had cost it European support. Its reluctance to break with Moscow had angered Europe further. For a country that had been hemorrhaging diplomatic partners, Taiwan was a wildly popular destination among politicians. It was unclear what kind of support these visits actually portended, but Beijing had managed to strengthen Taiwan's diplomatic position. Were these visits to translate into condemnation of China at the UN, the PRC could veto a Security Council resolution. In this case, like Russia, China would find itself a pariah state—and unlike Russia, China cares about how it is seen by the world. Its own corrosive nationalism had eaten into the body politic too. It had not torn itself apart in a bout of political bloodletting yet, but it had certainly let loose the kind of jingoism that would allow that to happen. What it would decide to do in a crisis was uncertain. Beijing itself did not know.

The United States, meanwhile, seemed intent on reviving a defense treaty that it had once spent over a decade trying to break. Taiwan had become a means of showing China just how tough America could get. The ultimate objective of this toughness was undefined. America was still not clear on how getting tough was going to alter the Chinese conduct it found objectionable. "Deterrence" was the concept invoked most often. A show of force would deter China from aggression by demonstrating that the United States meant business. But what if deterrence failed? Being deterred, after all, was a choice; China could choose not to be. What if the show of force backed China into a corner from which it felt it had no option but to lash out? To this, Washington had few answers beyond preparing for war. American pundits waxed lyrical about how they would fight a war with China. Taiwan, they opined, would be turned into a porcupine and the seas would turn into a no-go zone, with missiles and drones flying across them. One former defense official suggested the use of "low-yield tactical nuclear weapons" in the event of a conflict with China. Low-yield nuclear weapons were what the United States used against Hiroshima and Nagasaki. The possibility of Vladimir Putin using such weapons had sent shock waves of horror and disgust through the world. Yet the idea became quite normal in some circles. A war with China was coming, and nuclear weapons would have to be employed judiciously.[35] There was no guarantee that, once the nuclear taboo was breached, the weapons would stay "low yield." But the question of what would happen if the two nuclear powers escalated to higher yield arms and plunged the world into nuclear holocaust was left unresolved.

Douglas MacArthur had wanted to wage war against China in 1950. Dwight Eisenhower had considered using nuclear weapons against the PRC in 1955 and 1958. It was as though the United States was being haunted by all the ghosts of its long past with China and Taiwan, forcing it to relive questions it had once thought resolved. America abided by the "one China" principle, but it wanted Taiwan to enjoy "self-determination." It avowed commitment to the idea that it did not dispute the formulation that Taiwan was a part of China, but it would help Taiwan resist Chinese coercion. It wished to promote Taiwan's presence in international organizations, but it remained unwilling to recognize Taiwan itself. It had shifted from pure ambiguity to ambiguity with a tilt in favor of Taiwan—and it had done so because it had decided China was an enemy. Like China, it was mired in jingoism and confusion. Like China, it had no idea what it would do if things went wrong.

Every now and then, there was a flicker of hope that the two great powers would find a modus vivendi once more. Biden spoke optimistically in May 2023 of a coming "thaw" in the relationship. National Security Advisor Jake Sullivan met with politburo member Wang Yi in Vienna; the idea was just to get talking again. Trade talks resumed at APEC. Blinken finally made the China trip the balloons had blown off course. He met with Xi, who encouraged him to make "positive contributions to stabilizing China-US relations." Blinken made sure to emphasize that there was no change to America's "one China" policy. The US secretary of the Treasury, Janet Yellen, followed up with her own visit, espousing the "clear value in frank and in-depth discussions." It was a reminder that, for all the fury that had come to mark the bilateral relationship, there were still strong economic ties between the United States and China.[36] Maybe, just maybe, communication channels could be restored. If they could do that, the chances of all-out war would diminish.

But the forces pushing for conflict remained strong. American restrictions on the export of microchips used for artificial intelligence (among other strategically sensitive technology) to China remained intact. China had countered by tightening the exports of two rare earths—gallium and germanium—that were used for the manufacture of semiconductors and electric cars. With the US presidential election heating up, the one thing every candidate, Democrat or Republican, would have to do was show how tough they could get on China. That meant standing up for Taiwan. Republicans vying for the nomination got in on the act early. Ron DeSantis noted that Xi only understood strength. Nikki Haley asked that China be held responsible for Covid. Trump announced that French leader Emmanuel Macron was "kissing Xi's ass."[37] The competition for toughest candidate on China was well underway.

Taiwan was beginning to prepare for elections of its own, scheduled for January 13, 2024. The DPP's candidate, William Lai—whose more assertive stance on independence had once made him a challenger to Tsai for the presidential nomination—was now vowing not to alter the status quo, though he accused Beijing of doing so. Taiwan, he argued, was already sovereign. There was no need to change what worked. Becoming a candidate for the presidency seemed to have brought out a certain caution. But that caution soon vanished. American officials had been planning on Lai stopping somewhere in the United States on a transit visit (such as Tsai and others before her had enjoyed). Lai, however, while campaigning, defined success for Taiwan as his being able to visit the White House. This was a gauntlet thrown down. Taiwanese officials were blocked from visiting Washington, DC. Lai was daring America to turn him away. The Biden administration immediately demanded an explanation. This was not, American officials made clear, how the relationship was going to work.[38] Where Tsai had been prudent, Lai was willing to push his luck.

The DPP would need ingenuity and luck in the election, because the KMT had gone back to an old lesson: the party did well when it fielded a candidate who cared about Taiwan. After long internecine squabbling, the KMT nominated Hou You-yi as its candidate for president. Hou was mayor of New Taipei City, where he had proven popular. As a youth, he had captured pigs by jumping on them and tying them up; as a cop, he had done the same with criminals. He knew how to interact with people. He preferred glad-handing his constituents to shining on a stage. And Hou was clear that he was in this for Taiwan. If he did show something of the politician's propensity for nonanswer answers, his professed love for Taiwan was still sufficient to establish his patriotic bona fides. The country he wished to govern was the Republic of China, according to him, by which he meant he would protect Taiwan and the offshore islands. He would reject both "one country, two systems" and a formal move for independence, he said. But if Taiwan was attacked, he would face the challenge. Taiwan, he said, needed to be ready to do battle, though he would reverse the DPP's extension of military training.[39] On the crucial question of how to deal with China, there was little difference between the policies Lai and Hou espoused.

Far more dangerous than Hou for the DPP's prospects was the emergence of a third candidate. Ko Wen-je of the Taiwan People's Party had been mayor of Taipei. Though politically independent, he had been supportive of both Chen Shui-bian and Tsai. His campaign made clear, however, that he saw his hopes for the presidency as depending on votes from traditional KMT supporters: those who would have favored a closer relationship with China. Ko promised to revisit the Cross-Strait Service Trade Agreement while asking China to clarify what it meant by the '92 consensus. If placing this much trust in China seemed naive given all that had passed, Ko's answer was that China would change. As a plan for ensuring Taiwan's survival, that answer left much to be desired. As a ploy for winning votes that might otherwise have gone to Hou, it was sound policy. Ko rose steadily in the polls, not least because he had mastered the art of leaving things undefined. He was against politics as usual. He would find the middle ground between the KMT's appeasement of the PRC and the DPP's provocation of it. He would make

Taiwan a bridge for Sino-American communication rather than a front in a Sino-American war. He never explained how he proposed to do this, but somehow this did not stop Taiwanese of both green (pro-independence) and blue (KMT supporters) persuasion deciding that they would vote for him. And a fourth candidate, Terry Gou, eventually joined the race as an independent too. Gou was a tech mogul and billionaire, with a direct channel to higher powers. He had angled for the KMT nomination for presidency in 2020, when Mazu, goddess of the sea, had told him to. When the KMT and Mazu disagreed, he considered running as an independent, but eventually withdrew. His poll numbers for the 2024 race were not encouraging. But any new candidate had the potential, at least, to siphon off votes from the two main parties.[40]

A brown smog hung over Taipei in the run-up to election day. China sent balloons and a satellite Taiwan's way, along with stern admonitions about the dangers of electing William Lai. Terry Gou had dropped out of the race, but Ko Wen-je had hung in. There had been talk, at one point, of his joining forces with the KMT's Hou You-yi, but it had come to nothing. Ko's tenacity had left the election too close to call; with a third candidate hoovering up votes, neither the DPP nor the KMT could be assured of the presidency. Pundits wrote furiously about what it all meant. Meanwhile, people grumbled about the things that weigh heavy on the mind at election time: the conundrum of China, gay marriage, the price of eggs.

By January 13, 2024, the smog had lifted. It was a glorious day for a stroll. At the Chiang Kai-shek memorial hall, the hourly changing of the guards at the generalissimo's statue took place with a martial pomp and style that would have pleased him. Crowds raised cellphones to film the ceremony. Couples sauntered the verdant grounds of the 228 memorial park, holding hands and laughing. A man snored gently on the grass, while a sullen pond heron surveyed the scene. A shabby encampment bore posters demanding aboriginal land rights—a reminder that there was still a deeper past unaddressed, still peoples for whom the drama of democracy versus authoritarianism was just drama. A boombox started blaring *Hotel California*: "Some dance to remember, some dance to forget."

That evening, Lai won the presidency. It was not the ringing triumph Tsai had won four years earlier. Lai scraped through with a mere 40 percent of the vote, his victory made easier by the fact that Hou and Ko had failed to join forces. As he prepared to take office in May, he was facing a deeply divided, volatile populace and a legislature in which the DPP was bereft of a majority.

This was a point China had been quick to underline. The DPP, it huffed, was not representative of "majority public opinion." What was lost on Beijing was that both the other candidates had made clear that unification was not something they were willing to countenance either. Hou indeed had made a point of not inviting Ma Ying-jeou to his rallies; to associate himself with former president's embrace of China would have doomed his candidacy. Beijing still did not understand Taiwan. The United States continued to disavow support for Taiwanese independence while making plans for further delegations to the island. With the American presidential election going into fifth gear, the risk of miscalculation would only rise.[41]

At the edge of chaos, a single choice can make the difference between order and catastrophe. Eighty years on from Cairo, we can see that there were myriad moments when different decisions could have yielded different outcomes, for better or for worse. If FDR had insisted on self-determination for Taiwan after the war, if the ROC police had been gentler on February 27, if the Korean War had not happened, if Beijing had made "one country, two systems" work the way it was meant to, if Taiwan had developed a nuclear weapon, if Nancy Pelosi's plane had indeed been shot at—if someone had made a different decision at any of those moments, the world would be a radically different place. When deterrence, toughness, and pride drive policy, the room for error diminishes to virtually nil. The three countries are at a point where the choices they make could spell the difference between peace and nuclear holocaust. Those choices are best made with the historical record—and all its unrealized possibilities—firmly in mind.

Epilogue

I n following the paths the United States, China, and Taiwan took, it becomes clear that there was nothing foreordained about their arrival at the edge of chaos. Commentators like to portray the contemporary US-China relationship as an ineluctable function of great power politics. Revisionist and status quo powers, we are told, invariably clash; just look at Germany and Britain during World War I or Athens and Sparta in the Peloponnesian War. Telling the story in this manner obscures the role of choice in bringing us to our current juncture. (For that matter, it obscures the role of choice in past great power rivalries too.)[1] Decision-makers in Washington, Beijing, and Taipei were not the helpless victims of circumstance. The decisions they made yielded the outcomes we live with today. If those same decisions had gone another way, the world would be in a very different place. Tempting as it is to frame those decisions in terms of virtue—good versus evil, freedom versus authoritarianism—the historical record does not bear that out. For the most part, the choices made were the result of confusion, panic, stubbornness, and a stunning inability to think through long-term consequences. Gaps opened up between intention and outcome. Leaders did often find their choices constrained by forces that had spiraled out of their control, such as nationalism and credibility. But those forces themselves were the product of decisions made by human beings. And if they narrowed the range of options available to decision-makers, they did not eliminate all roads but one. Other presents were possible.

The United States, like the European empires it purported to deplore, had drawn lines and assigned territory in parts of the world it barely understood. Instead of pursuing trusteeship for Taiwan, it had consigned the island to Chiang Kai-shek. Taiwan's response was a struggle similar to so many of the struggles that broke out when great powers carved the world up. It was a natural reaction to people not being consulted on their own political future. The United States had then intervened in the Korean War in a fit of panic and, in doing so, plunged itself into a Chinese Civil War it had desperately tried to stay out of. For decades, it refused to recognize the government running China and propped up a dictator on Taiwan in the name of freedom. Having finally managed to terminate the US-ROC defense treaty, it lacked the clarity of vision to go all the way and perfect the rapprochement with China. And it finally decided that China was a mortal foe. Taiwan became a matter of face, a means of standing up to the PRC. A series of American decisions, made in fits of confusion, led to the current imbroglio.

The PRC had its share of choices too. It had, before it was established, maintained that the full extent of the country's territories was negotiable. There was a certain easy pragmatism to its thinking about territorial possessions, which would remain evident in its dealing with territorial disputes.[2] For the most part, it would insist on territory that was geostrategically vital; the rest could be bartered off in the name of goodwill won from neighbors. The bitterness of the civil war, however, clouded Mao's judgment. He could have granted Taiwan independence at the outset, much as he ceded territory to North Korea and Pakistan. The PRC was still trying to figure out what it was at the time. This was the moment to leave Chinese citizens convinced that Taiwan, while tied to China ethnically, was a politically distinct unit. Doing so by no means entailed recognizing Chiang Kai-shek's government. Mao could have dismissed it as that of a defeated tyrant and urged the world to get rid of the generalissimo. Instead, Mao stuck to the line that Taiwan was a part of China. He then proceeded to govern by mass campaign, and in that governance, the idea that Taiwan had always been a part of China became impossible to shake. A poisonous nationalism was deliberately fomented in the country, which would make compromise almost impossible.

If this was China's original sin in its approach to Taiwan, worse was to come. The Deng Xiaoping years had promised a future in which belonging to China would not have seemed altogether the worst deal in the world. "One country, two systems" could, had China really stuck with it, have been a model that Taiwan might have followed. The economic pull China exerted was being felt in Taiwan, and, in the days when it promised to be a responsible stakeholder, the PRC seemed to be winning American support for its position too. Persisting in that course, without resorting to threats, was probably China's best chance of achieving peaceful unification. There was clear evidence—notably in the 1996 elections—that bullying, intimidation, and interference backfired when it came to dealing with Taiwan. But Xi Jinping decided to dismantle "one country, two systems" completely. Hong Kong and China proper were now both places that no sensible Taiwanese would want to be part of.

The brutish nationalism that came after Covid only deepened the estrangement. Faith in a future with China, once lost, was not coming back. To generations of Taiwanese, unification with China has become unacceptable. Xi and China have only themselves to blame for this.

Of all three countries, it was Taiwan whose choices varied most dramatically. Chiang Kai-shek and Chiang Ching-kuo chose to preside over an authoritarian police state. But they also chose to keep that state separate from the mainland, which Chiang Kai-shek, at least, had dreamed of conquering. This was by no means a given. It required cunning and manipulation to keep the United States committed to the ROC's defense. And it required determination to persevere in the ROC's course after the normalization of US-China relations. Chiang Ching-kuo could have been tempted to throw in his lot with Deng's China, especially if the ROC had been allowed to keep its own forces. Theirs, as Tsai Ing-wen's remarks on the younger Chiang reflected, was a disquietingly mixed legacy. They had perpetrated enormous violence upon their population. They had also kept that population outside the PRC's reach.

Had Taiwan returned to China at any point before the nineties, it would have been difficult for an outsider to feel much sympathy. The Republic of China had been a cruel, dictatorial state; its absorption by another cruel, dictatorial state would have excited interest but not sorrow. But Taiwan did democratize. Lee Teng-hui chose to take the political risk of pushing his fellow politicians into retirement. He chose to open his own office up for election. Succeeding presidents chose to abide by a democratic system. For a onetime police state, this was remarkable—all the more so given how many fledgling democracies fail. Defying all the burdens the past has placed on it, Taiwan has carried out free and fair elections, transferred power peacefully after those elections (American politicians have much to learn here), and waged an intense political debate about how its power should best be wielded. The state it has created is one that deserves a shot at survival. But it is a state still struggling with the costs of asserting its newfound identity. If it has acquired an independence that it dare not give voice to yet, it remains dependent on China economically and on America for defense. At some point, living with that tension between liberty and dependence might become untenable.

This emphasis on choice does more than help apportion blame. By restoring choice—constrained, imperfect, but still there—to the historical picture, one understands how malleable the past was. And that understanding suggests that the future might be malleable too. Nuclear holocaust is only one among the several possible futures we might bring into being. Historians are usually wary of speculating on the future; they are far too apt to get it wrong. But speculation can be helpful, if only to show us what we should try to avoid and what we might aim for.

In an ideal world, Xi Jinping would simply opt to grant Taiwan independence. He could declare it magnanimously, a gift from the emperor to an errant people. States usually find it hard to consent to such dismemberment, though the example of Czechoslovakia's peaceful split into the Czech Republic and Slovakia shows it is far from impossible. Empires—including the Qing—could and did adjust territorial claims in this manner. China, as inheritor of the territories that made up the Qing Empire, might be able to hearken back to Mao's line on self-determination and issue an amicable divorce to Taiwan.

From a geostrategic perspective, this makes sense. Rather than incur the expense of policing another recalcitrant outpost, Beijing could let Taiwan continue balancing between the great powers. Taipei would be far more willing to cooperate with Beijing under such circumstances than if under occupation. Those old ties of language and ethnicity, coupled with economic interest, would be a far greater guarantee of unity. And this would go a long way toward removing some of the world's fears of the PRC. The biggest obstacle, of course, is that, having whipped its citizens into a patriotic fervor about Taiwan for so long, China would find it immensely hard to portray such a move as anything other than an unacceptable loss of face. But it might just be doable. Mao, after all, managed to make peace with the United States after decades spent castigating American imperialism. Deng oversaw a complete transformation of the economic system that had acquired the sacredness of religion. Communist China was capitalist in all but name by the time Deng was done, and most Chinese knew it. If Xi were to explain that Taiwan had been conquered by the reviled Qing Empire and that Mao Zedong had espoused a tradition of self-determination, the message might be easier to sell domestically. A populace scarred by the trials of the last few years might well find that it cares less about Taiwan than Beijing feared. There has already been some criticism of China's initiatives abroad when people at home are suffering. Whether or not such China-first sentiments extend to Taiwan is uncertain. But it would be possible to find out.

If the CCP finds it cannot go this far, there is a halfway step. It could declare its willingness to hold off on the use of force for a specified period of time—a century, say, or fifty years. Naturally, there is no holding any country to such a commitment. But the declaration, if followed through on, might go some way toward dialing down tension with Taiwan. Eliminating flights over the median line and keeping warships distant from the island can only help. It would behoove Taiwan not to crow about the virtues of standing firm here, but rather to accept it calmly and move on. A temporary moratorium on the use of force would not require Beijing to renounce its claims. It would simply be a chance to let economic and cultural ties do their work without the countervailing influence the threat of force has. It is unlikely that Taiwan will decide to trust China in the near future; it will take a while for the impressions of the last few years to fade. But people do move on. A few decades down the line, the world could look different. A commonwealth model—Nixon once floated this idea—might look attractive. Tact is a far better bet for Beijing than trying to threaten Taiwan into submission.

If these two options and the status quo prove intolerable to the PRC, it has, broadly speaking, two options for taking Taiwan. The first is a coup. China would locate enough politicians and military officials who would, for a handsome sum, be willing to turn the island over. This was how the CCP took Beijing (among other places) in the civil war, and over the years the PRC has not been shy of courting Taiwan's leaders. At least initially, this might be a less violent option than all-out war. But it is much harder to accomplish than it might seem. Taiwan's leaders are aware of the risk and are taking steps to counter it. The Anti-infiltration Act of 2019 was aimed at curbing precisely the kind of influence that could lead to a loss of sovereignty in this manner. How effective such defenses prove will only be clear in the event. But even if the PRC were to successfully take Taiwan with a silent coup, its problems would have just begun. Taiwanese citizens would almost certainly rally against the takeover, much like Ukrainians did at the Maidan in Kyiv. The PRC might be able to put such protests down, but the cost would be immense. There is no telling how long such an operation would drag out or what the ultimate toll for the PRC would be.

The same holds true for the second option the PRC has for taking Taiwan: all-out war. This carries the risk of a broader Sino-American war. It is not clear what the United States would do if Taiwan were attacked—and Beijing would have no way of knowing until war had begun. But even if the United States were to stay out, Taiwan could make it a longer, bloodier conflict than expected. Nothing is certain in a war. Ukraine was not supposed to prove this hard for Russia to handle. How PLA soldiers would feel about butchering people they have looked upon as their own, how they would fare in combat, how much guerrilla resistance Taiwan could muster, what damage Taiwanese missiles could do to Chinese cities—all this is difficult to predict. China might well prevail, but at a cost that would make all but the most foolishly jingoistic Chinese wonder if it was worth it.

Both coup and military assault would leave the PRC hobbled with two problems. The first would be the task of governing a conquered Taiwan. The population that would be incorporated into the PRC would be a raucous one, used to public debate and criticism of public servants. These habits do not die easily. Once upon a time, the PRC was worried about ideas of democracy infecting both party and people. Taking Taiwan into the fold would risk exactly that infection. The surveillance and policing methods honed in Xinjiang might prove sufficient to quell the threat. But this has been difficult even in Hong Kong. In the long term, true, all dissidents might flee or be imprisoned, but it would take substantial amounts of time, money, and energy to get to that point. The costs would mount up. China might be unable to stand them.

The second problem would be the international fallout a takeover of Taiwan would cause. Most people will not be duped by assertions of Taiwan's willingness to be unified. It is conceivable, of course, that much of the world will shrug and move on, much as it did after Tiananmen. But, given the goodwill Taiwan has won through its handling of the pandemic, this is far from certain. A resolution of condemnation could circle through the UN General Assembly. China's possession of veto power in the Security Council would rob such a resolution of practical consequences, but the blow to legitimacy—particularly for a country so heavily invested in the success of multilateral organizations—would be severe. Far and away the most severe consequence would be geopolitical. For countries in the Asia-Pacific, a Chinese takeover of Taiwan would be an unignorable wake-up call. Australia, Japan, the Philippines, and Vietnam are already leery of China. If Taiwan were to be taken, they would up their military budgets and strengthen their efforts to counter Chinese power. A nuclear arms race, with Japan in the lead, might ensue. The net result would be a far less secure geostrategic environment for the PRC to operate in, never mind that it would undo many of the economic gains China has made since Deng Xiaoping set the course for reform and opening.

The PRC's response, both to domestic unrest in Taiwan and to geostrategic challenges, would be to throw money at the problem. There would be investment in police work and camera installation; a rise in rivals' military budgets would be met with concomitant rises in the PRC's. But this is exactly how great powers go into "imperial overstretch": their commitments outstrip their resources, and their economy is cannibalized by military spending. Deng, who was wary of letting military spending damage the economy, was well aware of this. The greatest guarantee of his security, he held, was the goodwill of his neighbors.[3] This is a precept China has ignored of late. Continuing to ignore it will come with a cost. If swallowing Taiwan leads to the fall and perhaps eventual collapse of China, the PRC's would be a Pyrrhic victory indeed.

If brandishing arms promises little but ill for the PRC, the same holds true for the United States. The idea of using light, tactical nuclear weapons that has gained some currency in Washington is misguided and dangerous in the extreme. A Sino-American war could end in a nuclear holocaust. It is grotesquely easy to see how such a war would come about. One possibility involves an accident. A collision between American and Chinese warships or an errant PLA pilot coming too close to the plane of a visiting American dignitary would lead to a loss of life. Demands for a response in both countries would cause violence to escalate. Absent regular communication, the response would broaden to war. Once nuclear weapons are used, there is no telling where the carnage will stop. The other possibility is that Beijing would decide, for whatever reason, that the moment to invade Taiwan had come. A panicked United States would behave exactly as it behaved during the Korean War and rush to intervene, even if it had not committed itself to the defense of Taiwan. Once that great power war begins, the risk of nuclear weapons being used goes up dramatically. It is terrifying that the United States does not have a "no first use" policy, a vow not to be the first to use nuclear weapons in a conflict. Such a vow is unenforceable, but it does help a country set the norms by which it governs its own conduct. There will be no winners in such a war. Taiwan would be a pile of ash and rock. Saying China started it would provide little comfort.

The United States needs clarity. Taiwan policy cannot be a product of how tough Washington wants to be with Beijing. It needs to be based on an assessment of how much Washington values Taipei, what it is willing to do about it, and which options are actually in the realm of practical policy. One option is to arm Taiwan with a nuclear deterrent of its own. This might prevent a Chinese invasion. But it would spell an end to the nonproliferation regime and probably spark an arms race across East Asia. And while great powers have generally shown themselves unwilling to attack smaller countries armed with nuclear weapons, there is no guarantee that that rule would hold forever. Beijing might well miscalculate, with Armageddon as the result.

The first essential step is to reestablish communication lines and make sure that the United States and China survive the tiffs they seem especially prone to just now. Regular talks on climate change, cybersecurity, or perhaps even arms reduction—issues on which there is either substantial agreement or the hope of finding some—would help remind each side what a dialogue feels like. Ensuring regular communication between the defense establishments of the two countries would be the next step (ideally without key policymakers on the Chinese side disappearing inexplicably; trust takes time to build). The idea is not to reach agreement on Taiwan. The idea is to produce enough interactions—tiresome as they may be—to impede the rush to war. There was a reason a simple cup of tea at Warsaw eased communication. It reminded the two diplomats that, for all that divided them, they were still human beings.

Where does this leave Taiwan? If the United States could keep its legislators under control, it might have offered to swap a moratorium on the use of force by the PRC for a commitment to terminate official visits to Taiwan. The suggestion might sound bizarre, but as a way of ratcheting down tension, it might help. In the American political system, this is not doable. Legislators chart their own course, as the Pelosi visit showed, and most of those courses are Taipei bound. It is also true, unfortunately, that commitments to refrain from the use of force can be reneged upon with ease.[4] Trade concessions might be worth exploring. The least worst course perhaps would be to make clear to China, privately, without the loss of face an open confrontation involves, that any attempt to alter the status quo would be met by unparalleled sanctions.[5] The threat would be to turn China into a giant version of North Korea. The many assets Chinese officials have parked in North America would be seized immediately. Visas for children and relatives of Chinese officials would not just be more difficult to get; they would be gone, the relics of a different era. Soybean exports would come to an end. This would require enormous determination and commitment in rallying allies and partners to make sure the sanctions held. It would require making sure, through bribery, threat, or some mix of both, that smaller powers—Brazil, South Africa, South Korea—not play spoiler. They would have to know that trading with China was beyond the range of acceptable conduct.

Following through on such a threat—and no threat is worth making unless it is followed through on—would cause harm and suffering in the United States too. The costs of such sanctions would be staggeringly high. But Taiwan cannot be defended on the cheap. If America is serious about confronting China over Taiwan, then there will be pain. Whether or not the American public is ready for that level of pain is unclear. An overhaul of the US tax code could help—progressive taxation could counter the economic pain an embargo on China would create—though it would create political difficulties that would need to be addressed.[6] But in a democracy, these are matters that are up for debate. Laying the costs of great power confrontation before the public and asking how it would feel about entering such a conflict is something responsible politicians should do. If the difficulties of actually confronting China are too great, the decent thing to do would be to let Taiwan know now.

Taiwan, for its part, does not take American assistance for granted. It has dealt with the United States long enough to know that it might well have to face China on its own. It is possible that at some point in the future it will seek its own nuclear deterrent. If it chooses not to breach that taboo, it might opt to deter China by having missiles aimed at major dams and crucial infrastructure across the strait. The threat to China would be simple: nuclear weapons will not be used, but the damage will be enormous—enough to turn the Chinese people against the CCP.

Before then, Taiwan would need to make sure that its support went beyond just the United States. Winning over UN members who would at the very least condemn the PRC would weaken Beijing's diplomatic hand. Security assistance from Japan might be forthcoming, particularly given Taiwan's proximity to the Senkaku Islands. The greatest challenge, perhaps, remains the economic bond with China. Continuing to assert independence while remaining that reliant on the PRC is hard. The best that can be done is to continue to diversify economic partnerships, so that if sanctions come, the island is braced for them.

And what if the worst were to come and China successfully took over the island? That Taiwan could make the occupation painful and expensive if it so chose is clear. Guerrilla resistance and general protests would make life hard for China. But it would be infinitely harder for Taiwanese. And yet, the island's own past would be a source of hope. Taiwan has had experience with a Chinese occupying force before. It managed, somehow, to keep alive an idea of an independent Taiwan, despite the suffering meted out to it. Dissidents met behind closed doors. Some agitated in Japan, others at home. Some printed magazines, and others detonated bombs. Their eventual success was unlikely, but it came. How long the CCP could survive in the world it would have created by occupying Taiwan is unclear. But if and when the CCP falls, one suspects that the idea of an independent Taiwan will still be there, ready to take root and flourish once more.

Wars are not predictable things. They can be staved off when they seem inevitable. They can emerge suddenly when least expected. But the normalization of force as an answer to complex problems does increase the possibility of error—error that could be catastrophic. As 2023 came to a close, the staggeringly high number of PRC incursions into Taiwan's air defense identification zone—more than 1,600—was in keeping with the new normal 2022 had set. The Pelosi visit had spurred China to new levels of aggression. The American defense secretary, Lloyd Austin, warned that conflict over Taiwan would be "devastating." But his answer to the problem embodied the philosophy that had brought all three sides to the precipice. "Deterrence is strong today," he said at the Shangri-La security dialogue in Singapore in June 2023, "and it's our job to keep it that way."[7] Missing here was the realization that luck, as much as deterrence, had kept America and China from tumbling into cataclysm. Valuable as a military deterrent can be, the "job" extends well beyond threatening to meet force with force. It requires trying to figure out what the United States wants from China and what Washington's long-term goal for Taiwan is. It requires asking if those objectives involve futures that the PRC and Taiwan can live with. And it requires making sure that channels of communication between Washington and Beijing remain open, for it is communication, along with luck, that could mark the boundary between deterrence and warfare.

It is in the myopic embrace of force, perhaps, rather than in the usual facile comparisons with the kaiser's Germany, that the real parallels to 1914 can be found. But if those parallels disturb us—and they should—they can also offer comfort. Cataclysm was not inevitable then. And it is not inevitable now.

SUGGESTIONS FOR FURTHER READING

The reader perusing the notes to this manuscript will have noticed how heavily I rely on some of the truly excellent work that has been done on the United States, China, and Taiwan. I do hope that this book has stimulated curiosity; to that end, I am discussing some of the English-language books that others might wish to turn to. This is far from an exhaustive catalogue (as the notes show), but it should provide hours of happy reading. With interest in Taiwan peaking, further excellent volumes are no doubt forthcoming.

For two volumes that take in the broad sweep of Chinese history, including the relationship with Taiwan, see Jonathan Spence, *The Search for Modern China*, and Odd Arne Westad, *Restless Empire*. A good introductory survey to the triangular relationship is Kerry Brown and Kalley Wu Tzu Hui, *The Trouble with Taiwan*. For the establishment of Chiang Kai-shek's rule over the island in the twentieth century, Hsiao-ting Lin's *Accidental State* is the indispensable volume. Chiang himself has been the subject of two informative biographies: Jay Taylor, *The Generalissimo*, and Alexander Pantsov, *Victorious in Defeat*. For China's involvement in World War II, Rana Mitter's *Forgotten Ally* is excellent. I still find Barbara Tuchman's

Stilwell and the American Experience in China a thoroughly reward-ing read. Odd Arne Westad's *Decisive Encounters* is the classic on the Chinese Civil War.

American policy toward Taiwan is best covered by the superb Nancy Bernkopf Tucker, *Strait Talk*. The best account of the Mao era is still Chen Jian, *Mao's China and the Cold War*, which gives the shrewdest analysis of Mao's calculus on Taiwan that we have. The Deng era is well served by Ezra Vogel, *Deng Xiaoping and the Trans-formation of China*.

Contemporary Taiwan has inspired some superb scholarship. Syaru Shirley Lin's *Taiwan's China Dilemma* is a fascinating explo-ration of Taiwanese identity, political economy, and geopolitics. Shelley Rigger has written several excellent works on politics and economy; see in particular her study of the DPP, *From Opposition to Power*, and *The Tiger Leading the Dragon*, which is an eye-opening account of how important Taiwan was to China's economic boom. J. Bruce Jacobs was that rare scholar who was both caught up in the events he describes and fair-minded; *The Kaohsiung Incident in Tai-wan and Memoirs of a Foreign Big Beard* is a truly worthwhile read. On the Sunflower Movement, see Ming-sho Ho, *Challenging Bei-jing's Mandate of Heaven*.

ACKNOWLEDGMENTS

Two former colleagues at the Fletcher School provided the initial impetus for this book. Gerard Sheehan asked me to organize a panel on Taiwan for the students of the Fletcher School. The panelists (more on Lin Hsiao-ting, Shirley Lin, Michael Glennon, and Chia-Chun Chung below) were the best one could possibly have on the subject, and I learned an immense amount from them that evening. Then, Bob Loynd, now at Lincoln Laboratory, asked me to come give a talk on the triangular relationship. I found myself wishing I had reading to assign—and then realized that there might be a book to write here. At that point, my excellent literary agent, Andrew Gordon, offered his usual sound judgment on the proposal; he then allowed me to disappear to the tropics just as we were trying to figure out where this book would go. Thanks to Andrew, the book found the two perfect editors. Brandon Proia at Basic Books was a thoughtful interlocutor who "got" the book from our earliest discussions (which is all any writer can hope for). His enthusiasm for the project kept my own from flagging. Brandon was kind when I got curmudgeonly about titles and when I asked for "just one more day"; it is to him, too, that I owe the Spock reference. Simon Winder, at Allen Lane, reminded me of the need to spell out things I took for granted and to set the book in the broader global context (here, I fear, I only half succeeded). Simon's passion for maps matched my own; I was delighted when he asked for more. It was a pleasure to work with the deeply knowledgeable Kelly Sandefer, of Beehive Mapping, on cartography. Liz Dana did a superb job on copyediting. My thanks, too, to Kelly Lenkevich, Alex Cullina, and Eva Hodgkin.

The Wilson Center once again agreed to fund my work. Thanks to Chuck Kraus, Pieter Biersteker, and Raedina Thompson for their help (and to Chuck for providing primary sources yet again). Particular thanks to my dear friend Christian Ostermann, who does so much to make work like this possible and whose hospitality at Tulip Hill Farm has been a boon.

Several people have educated me on matters related to Taiwan over the years. Lin Hsiao-ting, who sets an impossibly high standard for scholarship on this topic, continues to chart my course through archives and has remained an indispensable source of wisdom for over a decade. Wang Wenlung shared his fund of knowledge on all matters archival and his equally vast fund of knowledge on where to get the best *niurou mian*. I first heard Shirley Lin talk about her own work in Tokyo, and it was a revelation. I had not known then how deep a study in political economy could cut. Shirley generously offered feedback on a version of this manuscript at a time when I had no business even asking her to look at it. Chia-Chun Chung, with her idealism, integrity, and meticulousness, has contributed a ton to my learning. She is the essential port of call on all matters Taiwan related. I never came away from a conversation with Chen Yun-Ru without being struck anew by her razor-sharp insight and originality of mind. Yun-Ru being Yun-Ru, the learning went hand in hand with helpless laughter, for which I am deeply grateful.

At several points, I had to consult those better informed than I. Chen Jian, Sergey Radchenko, and Mary Sarotte continued to provide invaluable information on sources. Jim Stavridis provided insight on UNCLOS and "no first use" policy. Ryan Irwin, Victor McFarland, Charlie Laderman, and Cookie Monster continue to field questions on historiography.

Once again, Lupita Ervin had my back—and if Lupita has your back, you can face any army. I have been beyond lucky to have her in my corner.

Josephine Wolff checked the manuscript for mathematical accuracy and offered gourmet meals. On drives to train stations and walks across Cambridge, her company has been a delight (notwithstanding her utterly wrongheaded opinions on Mantel's Cromwell trilogy). With her usual extraordinary levels of energy, Elisabeth Leake braved a draft of the entire manuscript and sent it back thoroughly (and helpfully) marked up. Her sarcastic wit and her steadfast friendship have been welcome additions to my little corner of the world. Michael Glennon shared his own knowledge of the Taiwan Relations Act and kept a watchful eye out to make sure that I did not get into too much trouble. The name Daniel Drezner brings an affectionate smile to the faces of those who know that character's boisterous good humor. I smile affectionately too, and thank him for his reminders to keep my temper. Toni Chayes twinkled encouragement and mischief. For their help, collegiality, and goodwill, my thanks to Alexandra Ryan, Katie Mulroy, Kristen Zecchi, Mieke Wansem, Jillian DeStone, Jessica Daniels, Michael Klein, Eileen Babbitt, Dyan

Mazurana, Leila Fawaz, Alex de Waal, Melissa McCracken, and Abi Linnington.

Cyndi Rubino and Anulfo Baez stressed out about this book on my behalf. Ellen McDonald—when not off on a tangent about ChatGPT—performed her usual quiet miracles of finding sources that were impossible to find and answering questions that mere mortals cannot. For reasons best known to her, Ellen continues to care about me. My wandering ways would not be possible without her provision of a homestead. I owe her a ton.

John Gaddis shared his *FRUS* volumes and typically laconic, but helpful, advice. Paul Kennedy gently encouraged me to get the book done. Not a day went by working on this book when I did not find myself wishing I could talk to Charlie Hill about it. I miss him dearly. Thank you to Toni Dorfman, Cynthia Farrar, Norma Thompson, Allie Sacharuk, Susie Jakes, Jeff Prescott, Amalia Prescott, Phoebe Prescott, Zhang Taisu, Zhao Xiaoxue, Zaka Shafiq, Tamara Momand, Rushdia Yusuf, Paul O'Connell, Judy Yao, Christopher Walker, and Tracy and Lee Jackson for being there.

Kelly and Kingsley Goddard of Barberry Hill Farm provided the perfect space in which to write. Kelly also made sure I was properly fed and encouraged me in some dubious animal husbandry experiments. Luna Kressin and Aaron McMullen cat sat when I ran away to do research and offered excellent company when I was home. So did Mio Yamada, who returned from Japan just as this book was being plotted; taking a break from the proposal to go off in quest of coyotes and barred owls with her was just what the doctor ordered. Mia Lazarewicz quite literally saved my back and taught me the term "brain lazy." I learned more from her than she knows. Ranger Dan Barvir continues to let me accompany him on his adventures.

This is not the book I promised Regina Asmutis-Silvia and Laura Howes when they let me into their worlds. That book will come, but this one would not have been possible without the healing they and their teams made possible. It was a lucky day when my path crossed Regina's. She has been an inspiration, teacher, comrade in arms, and trusted friend. The voyage she and Dave Silvia took us on was an incomparable gift. Laura is the best boss I will ever have. Monica Pepe was patient when this book got in the way of what I owed her. Colin Greeley kept me dreaming, let me stow away, and shared his inexhaustible supply of bad puns. Bruna Silva provided the finest coffee I have ever tasted and, at just the right moment, summoned me back for a truly glorious day on the water. The wonderful Deb Ridings quizzed me on this book and raised my eyes from computer screen to distant spouts. Jon Brink, fellow shearwater enthusiast and dreamer, invited me for a six-hour ride among minkes, phalaropes, and gray seals.

My mother reminded me that I was stuck on a hillock and asked what was taking so long with this book. I hope she finds it better than average. My father sent me photos of Khayyam and Jehan, so that I could keep an eye on my nephew and niece from afar. Maryam and Bilal performed the vital task of making sure that all was well in Lahore.

Koshka the cat was my inseparable writing companion. She bumped noses just when I wanted to type, placed her paw on the books I wanted, and purred her way into the writing.

To Anna Beth Keim, I owe thanks on two levels. For one thing, she shared her own tremendous expertise on Taiwan—including her remarkable manuscript and knowledge of sources—shaping this book indelibly. But she also gave me the pure joy of morning walks to the mulch or the sound, on which she would tell stories of Taiwan then and now, plot journeys for days and months and years ahead, point out wildly colorful mushrooms, or just hold my hand. Whether busting out of old bunkers on a Taiwan beach or surviving a stampede at a political rally, gleefully mulling yet another source or braving the general annoyances of life, she defines resilience and courage and determination. And love.

Odd Arne Westad urged me to do this book (for which miscalculation he had to suffer yet another draft from me). Much more importantly, he gave the gift of understanding. In Arne's company, quixotic fantasies become things to plan and do; you remember that dreams are meant to be lived, and that life is meant to be fun. Ingunn Bjornson would tell me not to be "away with the fairies." But she herself combines sound common sense with a fairy's expansive sense of possibility. Ingunn is one of the most gallantly adventurous souls I know, whether scrambling across a wood pile or inviting two wanderers into her home while a pandemic rages in the world beyond. For epic meals that ended by a warm fire and *Wild Earth*, for strolls across salt marsh amid harriers and herons, and for a love that was both easy and profound, this book is dedicated to them.

NOTES

INTRODUCTION

1. Michael Martina and David Brunnstrom, "Exclusive: Biden Sends Former Top Defense Officials to Taiwan in Show of Support," Reuters, February 28, 2022, www.reuters.com/world/china/exclusive-biden-sends-former-top-defense-officials-taiwan-show-support-2022-02-28; "Peace in Taiwan Strait a Global Concern, Says Mullen," AP, March 2, 2022; https://apnews.com/article/russia-ukraine-china-taiwan-europe-joint-chiefs-of-staff-1d133ce85b3a79fae056c38248fa08d2; Kayleigh Madjar et al., "Pompeo Urges US to Recognize ROC," *Taipei Times*, March 5, 2022, www.taipeitimes.com/News/front/archives/2022/03/05/2003774214.

2. Tom Mitchell and Demetri Sevastopulo, "Chinese Anger Over Taiwan Visit Grows After Nancy Pelosi Departs on Asia Tour," *Financial Times*, July 31, 2022, www.ft.com/content/9abd2646-5562-4a32-9bb8-19645ed8601f; Vincent Ni, "Nancy Pelosi's Taiwan Trip 'Not a Good Idea Right Now,' Says Biden," *Guardian*, July 21, 2022, www.theguardian.com/us-news/2022/jul/21/nancy-pelosi-taiwan-trip-not-good-idea-right-now-joe-biden; Chen Yi-chieh, "Peiluoxi lai le!," *Taibei baodo*, August 2, 2022, www.setn.com/News.aspx?NewsID=1155373; Chris Horton and Amy Chang Chien, "Ahead of Pelosi's Trip, Quiet Defiance in Taiwan," *New York Times*, August 2, 2022, https://cn.nytimes.com/asia-pacific/20220802/pelosi-trip-taiwan/dual/.

3. Anders Hagstrom, "US Lawmakers Visit Taiwan in Unannounced Trip on the Heels of the Nancy Pelosi Uproar," Fox News, August 14, 2022, www.foxnews.com/politics/lawmakers-visit-taiwan-unannounced-visit-heels-nancy-pelosi-uproar; Office of the President Republic of China (Taiwan), "President Tsai Meets Indiana Governor Eric Holcomb," news release, August 22, 2022, https://english.president.gov.tw/NEWS/6304#:~:text=Governor%20Holcomb%20is%20leading%20a,deepening%20of%20Taiwan%2DUS%20relations; Lawrence Chung, "Pompeo in Taiwan Calls for End to US 'Blind Engagement' with Beijing," *South China Morning Post*, September 27, 2022, www.scmp.com/news/china/diplomacy/article/3193997/pompeo-taiwan-calls-end-us-blind-engagement-beijing; Helen Davidson, "China Used Drills to Prepare for Invasion, Taiwan Foreign Minister Says," *Guardian*, August 9, 2022, https://www.theguardian.com/world/2022/aug/09/china-used-drills-to-prepare-for-invasion-taiwan-foreign-minister-says.

4. "Chinese Warship Comes Within 150 Yards of U.S. Missile Destroyer in Taiwan Strait," CBS News, June 3, 2023, www.cbsnews.com/news/chinese-warship-u-s-missile-destroyer-tai wan-strait-close-call uss-chung-hoon/; Patrick Smith and Courtney Kube, "US Releases Video Showing Close Call with Chinese Warship in Taiwan Strait," NBC, June 5, 2023, www.nbcnews .com/news/world/us-releases-video-encounter-chinese-warship-taiwan-strait-rcna87669.

5. Antony J. Blinken, "The Administration's Approach to the People's Republic of China" (speech, George Washington University, Washington, DC, May 26, 2022), www.state.gov/the-administrations-approach-to-the-peoples-republic-of-china/; David Brunnstrom and Trevor Hunnicutt, "Biden Says U.S. Forces Would Defend Taiwan in the Event of a Chinese Invasion," Reuters, September 19, 2022, www.reuters.com/world /biden-says-us-forces-would-defend-taiwanevent-chinese-invasion-2022-09-18/; "Xi Jinping kan wang canjia zhenxie huiyi de minjian gongshang lianjie weiyuan shi qiang diao," Gov.cn, March 6, 2023, https://archive.ph/MFIi0; Yew Lun Tian and Ben Blanchard, "China Will Never Renounce Right to Use Force Over Taiwan, Xi Says," Reuters, October 16, 2022, www.reuters.com/world/china/xi-china-will-never-renounce-right-use-force -over-taiwan-2022-10-16/; Zubaidah Abdul Jalil, "China Sends 30 Warplanes into Taiwan Air Defence Zone," BBC, May 31, 2022, www.bbc.com/news/world-asia-61642217.

6. Department of Defense, National Defense Strategy of the United States, 2022 https://media.defense.gov/2022/Oct/27/2003103845/-1/-1/1/2022-NATIONAL-DEFENSE -STRATEGY-NPR-MDR.PDF; Lai Ching-te, "My Plan to Preserve Peace in the Taiwan Strait," *Wall Street Journal*, July 4, 2023.

7. A quick glance at the notes will show the reader how indebted I am to the work of Hsiao-ting Lin, Shirley Lin, Nancy Tucker, and Shelley Rigger, among others. Most of the existing literature concentrates on, at most, two of the three parties involved. The best overall survey is still the classic by Nancy Tucker, *Strait Talk: United States-Taiwan Relations and the Crisis with China* (Cambridge, MA: Harvard University Press, 2011), which concentrates on US-Taiwan relations. Tucker does not give much space to the crucial pre-1950 period, and many of the more recent developments had not taken place when her book was published. The formation of the Republic of China is best covered by the outstanding Hsiao-ting Lin, *Accidental State: Chiang Kai-shek, the United States, and the Making of Taiwan* (Cambridge, MA: Harvard University Press, 2016). No reader looking at Taiwanese democratization and cross-strait relations can afford to ignore the work of Shelley Rigger. Syaru Shirley Lin, *Tai-wan's China Dilemma: Contested Identities and Multiple Interests in Taiwan's Cross-Strait Economic Policy* (Stanford, CA: Stanford University Press, 2016), offers the deepest, most illuminating examination of political economy and identity that I have come across—not just on Taiwan, but on any country. See also the useful Kerry Brown and Kalley Wu Tzu Hui, *The Trouble with Taiwan: History, the United States and a Rising China* (London: Zed Books, 2019). For a helpful compendium on US policy toward Taiwan, see Ryan Hass, Bonnie Glaser, and Richard Bush, *US-Taiwan Relations: Will China's Challenge Lead to a Crisis?* (Washington, DC: Brookings, 2023). Chinese archives no longer offer the primary sources historians once took for granted. Nevertheless, several scholars (including myself) collected documents from there in happier times; these were then deposited at the Wilson Center in DC. Archival collections in Taiwan and the United States remain easy to access.

CHAPTER 1: THE MAKING OF THE TAIWAN PROBLEM

1. Winston Churchill, *The Second World War*, vol. 5, *Closing the Ring* (London: Cassell and Co., 1952). Video at "The Cairo Conference (1943)," British Pathé, posted April 13, 2014, YouTube, www.youtube.com/watch?v=TTl6RC43h7g.

2. "The Cairo Declaration," November 26, 1943, Wilson Center Digital Archive, in *FRUS: Diplomatic Papers, The Conferences at Cairo and Tehran, 1943*, eds. William M. Franklin and William Gerber (Washington, DC: US Government Printing Office, 1961), 448–449, https://digitalarchive.wilsoncenter.org/document/122101.

3. Chen Di quoted in Laurence G. Thompson, "The Earliest Chinese Eyewitness Accounts of the Formosan Aborigines," *Monumenta Serica* 23, no. 1 (1964): 163–204. On the Qing Empire in general, the best introduction is William Rowe, *China's Last Empire: The Great Qing* (Cambridge, MA: Harvard University Press, 2012). For the origins of Qing and the conquest of Central Asia, Peter C. Perdue, *China Marches West: The Qing Conquest of Central Eurasia* (Cambridge, MA: Harvard University Press, 2010), is indispensable.

4. For an extremely useful review of the literature on pre-Qing Taiwan, see J. Bruce Jacobs, "The History of Taiwan," *China Journal* (January 2011). Early Chinese indifference to Taiwan is chronicled in Emma Jinhua Teng, *Taiwan's Imagined Geography: Chinese Colonial Travel Writing and Pictures, 1683–1895* (Cambridge, MA: Harvard University Press, 2006). The best accounts of Taiwan's encounters with the Dutch and the Qing have come from the remarkable Tonio Andrade; see Andrade, *Lost Colony: The Untold Story of China's First Great Victory Over the West* (Princeton, NJ: Princeton University Press, 2011) and Andrade, *How Taiwan Became Chinese: Dutch, Spanish, and Han Colonization in the Seventeenth Century* (New York: Columbia University Press, 2008).

5. See Rowe, *China's Last Empire* for a summary.

6. For a rich discussion of Qing administration of Taiwan, see John Robert Shepherd, *Statecraft and Political Economy on the Taiwan Frontier, 1600–1800* (Stanford, CA: Stanford University Press, 1993). See also Wan-yao Chou, *A New Illustrated History of Taiwan*, trans. Carol Plackitt and Tim Casey (Taipei: SMC Publishing, 2015).

7. These developments are well covered by the literature. See Jonathan Spence, *The Search for Modern China* (New York: W. W. Norton, 2020), for a starting point. On imperial overstretch, see Paul Kennedy, *The Rise and Fall of the Great Powers* (New York: Vintage, 2010).

8 On the Qing war with Japan, see Stewart Lone, *Japan's First Modern War: Army and Society in the Conflict with China, 1894–5* (London: Macmillan, 1994).

9. See Spence, *Search for Modern China*, for a starting point.

10. For an overview of the fall of the Qing and Yuan Shikai, see Spence, *Search for Modern China*. On the warlord era, see Hans van de Ven, *War and Nationalism in China: 1925–1945* (London: Routledge, 2003), and Arthur Waldron, *From War to Nationalism: China's Turning Point, 1924–1925* (Cambridge: Cambridge University Press, 1995).

11. On Chiang, see Jay Taylor, *The Generalissimo: Chiang Kai-shek and the Struggle for Modern China* (Cambridge, MA: Belknap, 2011), and Alexander Pantsov, *Victorious*

in Defeat: The Life and Times of Chiang Kai-shek, China, 1887–1975 (New Haven, CT: Yale University Press, 2023). The nature of the state he established—with its reliance on a loose-knit coalition of warlords—is crying out for further study.

12. These developments are well served by the literature; see Spence, *Search for Modern China*, for a starting point. For a look at Soviet decision-making, see Paul Gregory, Hsiao-ting Lin, and Lisa Nguyen, "Chiang Chooses His Enemies," *Hoover Digest*, April 21, 2010, www.hoover.org/research/chiang-chooses-his-enemies. For Chiang's own thoughts on how to govern, see Chiang Kai-shek, *China's Destiny* (New York: Roy Publishers, 1947).

13. Sulmaan Wasif Khan, *Haunted by Chaos: China's Grand Strategy from Mao Zedong to Xi Jinping* (Cambridge, MA: Harvard University Press, 2022). For the fate of the CCP in the far west, the best source is Xiaoyuan Liu, *Frontier Passages: Ethnopolitics and the Rise of Chinese Communism, 1921–1945* (Stanford, CA: Stanford University Press, 2004).

14. On Japanese policy in East Asia, see the excellent S. C. M. Paine, *The Japanese Empire: Grand Strategy from the Meiji Restoration to the Pacific War* (Cambridge: Cambridge University Press, 2017).

15. For a detailed account, see Pantsov, *Victorious in Defeat*.

16. The best recent account of the war—and of Wang Jingwei in particular—is Rana Mitter, *Forgotten Ally: China's World War II, 1937–1945* (New York: Houghton Mifflin Harcourt, 2013).

17. Information on Sino-American relations in the preceding paragraphs drawn from Odd Arne Westad, *Restless Empire: China and the World Since 1750* (New York: Basic, 2012), Joanna Waley-Cohen, *Sextants of Beijing: Global Currents in Chinese History* (New York: W. W. Norton, 2000), and George C. Herring, *From Colony to Superpower: US Foreign Relations Since 1776* (Oxford: Oxford University Press, 2008). A glorious analysis of the Open Door policy is provided by George Kennan, *American Diplomacy* (Chicago: University of Chicago Press, 2012).

18. On US-Japan relations during this period, see Eri Hotta, *Japan 1941: Countdown to Infamy* (New York: Vintage, 2014). Mitter, *Forgotten Ally* provides an excellent account of the war in China. On Stimson, see Herring, *From Colony to Superpower*. The best account of Stilwell is still the superb Barbara Tuchman, *Stilwell and the American Experience in China: 1911–1945* (New York: Random House, 2017).

19. "Memorandum by the Second Secretary of Embassy in China (Davies) to the Ambassador in China (Gauss)," March 9, 1943, in *FRUS: Diplomatic Papers, 1943, China*, eds. G. Bernard Noble and E. R. Perkins (Washington, DC: US Government Printing Office, 1957), https://history.state.gov/historicaldocuments/frus1943China/d17; "Memorandum by Mr. O. Edmund Clubb of the Division of Chinese Affairs," May 10, 1944, in *FRUS: Diplomatic Papers, 1944, China*, vol. 6, eds. E. Ralph Perkins et al. (Washington, DC: US Government Printing Office, 1967), https://history.state.gov/historical-documents/frus1944v06/d341. Several truly excellent recent works—including Mitter, *Forgotten Ally*, on which I rely heavily—have been kinder to Chiang than Davies was in his memorandum. Scholarship has focused on the generalissimo's patriotism and on how galling American condescension could be. This is correct, but to my less forgiving

temperament, Chiang's patriotism was marred by self-worship; he (like Mao) saw his survival as crucial to that of China. His willingness to explore a deal with Japan even as he received American aid was understandable, but it does suggest that the survival of his own regime was paramount. Stilwell was intemperate in his criticism of the generalissimo, but he was far from being unprovoked.

20. See here Herring, *From Colony to Superpower*, and Pantsov, *Victorious in Defeat*. Tuchman, *Stilwell* is still invaluable.

21. The best source here is the outstanding Xiaoyuan Liu, *A Partnership for Disorder: China, the United States, and Their Policies for the Postwar Disposition of the Japanese Empire, 1941–1945* (Cambridge: Cambridge University Press, 2002). Information on thinking on bases from "Minutes of the Presidents Meeting With the Joint Chiefs of Staff, November 19, 1943, 2 P.M., Admiral's Cabin, U. S. S. 'Iowa'," Moscow, November 19, 1943, in *The Conferences at Cairo and Tehran*, https://history.state.gov/historicaldocuments/frus 1943CairoTehran/d238.

22. "Minutes of the Presidents Meeting With the Joint Chiefs of Staff, November 19, 1943, 2 P.M., Admiral's Cabin, U. S. S. 'Iowa'," Moscow, November 19, 1943; "Agreement Regarding Entry of the Soviet Union into the War Against Japan," February 11, 1945, in *FRUS: Diplomatic Papers, Conferences at Malta and Yalta, 1945*, ed. Bryton Barron (Washington, DC: US Government Printing Office, 1955), https://history.state.gov/historical documents/frus1945Malta/d503; "Memorandum by the Ambassador in the Soviet Union (Harriman)," July 18, 1945, in *FRUS: Diplomatic Papers, 1945, The Far East, China*, vol. 7, eds. Ralph R. Goodwin et al. (Washington, DC: US Government Printing Office, 1969), https://his tory.state.gov/historicaldocuments/frus1945v07/d665; "Bohlen Minutes," November 30, 1943, in *The Conferences at Cairo and Tehran*, https://history.state.gov/historicaldocuments /frus1943CairoTehran/d371; "Bohlen Minutes," November 28, 1943, in *The Conferences at Cairo and Tehran*, https://history.state.gov/historicaldocuments/frus1943CairoTehran /d358; "Bohlen Minutes, November 29, 1943, in *The Conferences at Cairo and Tehran*, https://history.state.gov/historicaldocuments/frus1943CairoTehran/d365; Liu, *A Partnership for Disorder*; Keith Allan Clark, "Imagined Territory: The Republic of China's 1955 Veto of Mongolian Membership in the United Nations,'" *Journal of American-East Asian Relations* 25, no. 3 (2018): 263–295, www.jstor.org/stable/26549248.

23. See Bob Bergin, "The Dixie Mission 1944: The First US Intelligence Encounter with the Chinese Communists," *Studies in Intelligence* 63, no. 3 (September 2019). See also Tuchman, *Stilwell*, and Khan, *Haunted by Chaos*.

24. On Japanese casualties, see Lone, *Japan's First Modern War*. For a starting point on Taiwan's history under Japanese rule, see Ping-hui Liao and David Der-wei Wang, eds., *Taiwan Under Japanese Colonial Rule, 1895–1945: History, Culture, Memory* (New York: Columbia University Press, 2006). Some of the Taiwanese groups seeking to overthrow Japan did reach out to the KMT to see what a future with Taiwan as part of China might look like. Interestingly enough, these groups sought guarantees of liberal governance that might allow them a status greater than mere territory of the KMT. The KMT seemed unwilling to grant this. See Liu, *A Partnership for Disorder*. The subject is crying out for further research.

25. Shi Ming, *Shi Ming Huiyi lu* (Taipei: Qianjie shi, 2016), 143, 148, 225–226, 284–289. Shi Ming was Su Beng's pen name.

26. Peng Ming-min, *A Taste of Freedom: Memoirs of a Formosan Independence Leader* (New York: Holt McDougal, 1972), 11–12.

27. X. Qin et al., eds., *Guang fu Taiwan zhi chou hua yu shou xiang jie shou*, (Taipei: Zhongguo guo min dang zhong yang wei yuan hui dang shi wei yuan hui, 1990), 59–64.

28. The best guide to these events is Tsuyoshi Hasegawa, *Racing the Enemy: Stalin, Truman, and the Surrender of Japan* (Cambridge, MA: Harvard University Press, 2005).

29. Odd Arne Westad, *The Cold War: A World History* (New York: Basic, 2017); Xixiao Guo, "Paradise or Hell Hole? US Marines in Post World War II China," *Journal of American-East Asian Relations* (1998). Information on how many Japanese were scattered across the erstwhile empire gathered from Pantsov, *Victorious in Defeat*, and Barak Kushner and Andrew Levidis, eds., *In the Ruins of the Japanese Empire: Imperial Violence, State Destruction, and the Reordering of Modern East Asia* (Hong Kong: Hong Kong University Press, 2020). Note that a small handful of Japanese would remain on the island and serve as military advisors to Chiang; see here Lin Hsiao-ting, "U.S.-Taiwan Military Diplomacy Revisited: Chiang Kai-Shek, Baituan, and the 1954 Mutual Defense Pact," *Diplomatic History* 37, no. 5 (2013): 971–994. The story of the Japanese passage back to Japan—many of those making the journey had been born in Taiwan and knew no other home—deserves further scholarly research.

30. Population estimates vary. I have drawn upon Dominic Meng-Hsuan Yang, *The Great Exodus from China: Trauma, Memory, and Identity in Modern Taiwan* (Cambridge: Cambridge University Press, 2021); Pantsov, *Victorious in Defeat*; Odd Arne Westad, *Decisive Encounters: The Chinese Civil War, 1946–1950* (Stanford, CA: Stanford University Press, 2003), and the official Taiwanese government estimate, available at "History," Taiwan.gov.tw, accessed on September 24, 2023, www.taiwan.gov.tw/content_3.php.

31. Qin et al., *Guang fu Taiwan*, 204–205. On Taiwanese perceptions, see Peng, *Taste of Freedom*; and George Kerr, *Formosa Betrayed: The Definitive First-Hand Account of Modern Taiwan's Founding Tragedy* (Manchester: Camphor Press, 2018). Information on Chen's employment of mainlanders from UK National Archives, Kew, FO 371/63425, "Situation in Taiwan," 1947.

32. Westad, *Cold War*.

33. My thoughts on the Marshall mission have been influenced by Daniel Kurtz-Phelan, *The China Mission: George Marshall's Unfinished War, 1945–1947* (New York: W. W. Norton, 2019). Kurtz-Phelan does not share my characterization of the mission as a success, but his careful narrative made it difficult for me to see it in any other light. See also Chen Jian, *Mao's China and the Cold War* (Chapel Hill: University of North Carolina Press, 2001). On the possibility of Mao living with a temporary division, see Khan, *Haunted by Chaos*.

34. In addition to Kurtz-Phelan, *China Mission*, see Ernest R. May, "1947–48: When Marshall Kept the US Out of War in China," *Journal of Military History* 66, no. 4 (2002): 1001–1010.

35. By far the best account—and unlikely to be superseded—is still Westad, *Decisive Encounters*.

36. Accounts abound. For a memoir recounting the events, see George Kerr, *Formosa Betrayed* (Manchester: Camphor, 2018). The standard, if somewhat problematic, account is Z. Lai and R. H. Myers, *A Tragic Beginning: The Taiwan Uprising of February 28, 1947* (Stanford, CA: Stanford, 1991). The meticulous Lin, *Accidental State*, covers this time period superbly. Scholars differ on the exact starting point of the White Terror: some argue for 1947, with the crackdown following the 228 incident, whereas others date it to the reimposition of martial law in 1949. There is a strong case to be made for either. I have inclined to 1947 because this was when fear of the state began to take hold of the populace. Nineteen forty-nine augmented the fear, but it did not originate it.

37. Peng, *A Taste of Freedom*; Shi Ming, *Shi Ming Huiyi lu*, 419–420.

38. Kerr's own memoir is telling. The best historical account is Lin, *Accidental State*.

39. "General Wedemeyer to the Secretary of State," July 29, 1947, in *FRUS, 1947, The Far East: China*, vol. 7, eds. Ralph E. Goodwin et al. (Washington, DC: US Government Printing Office, 1972), https://history.state.gov/historicaldocuments/frus1947v07/d562; "General Wedemeyer to the Secretary of State," August 17, 1947, in *1947, The Far East: China*, vol. 7, https://history.state.gov/historicaldocuments/frus1947v07/d582.

40. See Kerr, *Formosa Betrayed*, here. Wedemeyer's report would eventually be released as part of the State Department's white paper on China: see *The China White Paper: August 1949* (Stanford, CA: Stanford University Press, 1967), https://ia800 203.us.archive.org/32/items/VanSlykeLymanTheChinaWhitePaper1949/Van%20 Slyke%2C%20Lyman%20-%20The%20China%20White%20Paper%201949.pdf.

41. "Memorandum by the Director of the Policy Planning Staff (Kennan)," PPS 53, in *FRUS, 1949, The Far East: China*, vol. 9, eds. Francis C. Prescott, Herbert A. Fine, and Velma Hastings Cassidy (Washington, DC: US Government Printing Office, 1974), https://history.state.gov/historicaldocuments/frus1949v09/d402.

42. "Memorandum by the Director." See also John Lewis Gaddis, *George F. Kennan: An American Life* (New York: Penguin, 2011).

43. On the possibility of a declaration of autonomy, see Lin, *Accidental State*, 72–73.

44. Gaddis, *George F. Kennan*. On the cancellation and possible involvement of John Paton Davies, see Gaddis, *George F. Kennan*. See also Paul J. Heer. *Mr. X and the Pacific: George F. Kennan and American Policy in East Asia* (Ithaca, NY: Cornell University Press, 2018); Kennan, *American Diplomacy*; "Memorandum by the Director of the Policy Planning Staff (Kennan)," PPS 53. It is safe to say that, prescient as he was, Kennan did not foresee the reimagining of dinosaurs as swift, warm-blooded beasts that Michael Crichton would popularize.

45. Lin, *Accidental State*; see also Pantsov, *Victorious in Defeat*. On Fu Zuoyi, see Khan, *Haunted by Chaos*.

46. See here Lin, *Accidental State*.

47. Lin, *Accidental State*.

48. I owe this point to Timothy Snyder, who made it while lecturing on Eastern Europe. On Chiang Ching-kuo, see Jay Taylor, *The Generalissimo's Son: Chiang Ching-kuo*

and the Revolutions in China and Taiwan (Cambridge, MA: Harvard University Press, 2009).

49. Estimates of the arrested and dead vary, not least because archival access is still incomplete. The best source—which charts the difficulties of arriving at a proper estimate—is Chou Wan-yao, *Zhuanxing zhengyi zhi lu* (China: Yushan she, 2022). See also Taylor, *Generalissimo's Son*. I benefited greatly here from Anna Beth Keim's draft manuscript, *Heaven Does Not Block All Roads* (forthcoming).

50. "Introduction," Constitution of the Republic of China (Taiwan), Office of the President Republic of China (Taiwan), accessed September 24, 2023, https://english.president .gov.tw/page/93. On Li, see Lin, *Accidental State*, and Pantsov, *Victorious in Defeat*. On judiciary's role, see J. Bruce Jacobs, *The Kaohsiung Incident in Taiwan and Memoirs of a Foreign Big Beard* (Leiden: Brill, 2016).

51. "The Chargé in China (Strong) to the Secretary of State," June 2, 1950, in *FRUS, 1950, East Asia and the Pacific*, vol. 11, eds. Neal H. Petersen et al. (Washington, DC: US Government Printing Office, 1976), https://history.state.gov/historicaldocuments/frus1950v06/d186.

52. Liu, *Frontier Passages*; Edgar Snow, "Interviews With Mao Tse-tung," July 16, 1936, Marxists Internet Archive, 2014, www.marxists.org/reference/archive/mao/works/1936/11/ x01.htm.

53. Sergey Radchenko, "Lost Chance for Peace: The 1945 CCP-Kuomintang Peace Talks Revisited," *Journal of Cold War Studies* 19, no. 2 (2017): 84–114, https://doi.org /10.1162/JCWS_a_00742; Khan, *Haunted by Chaos*.

54. See Taylor, *The Generalissimo*, and Khan, *Haunted by Chaos*.

55. See Khan, *Haunted by Chaos*. The Mao-Stalin discussions are available at "Record of Conversation Between I.V. Stalin and Chairman of the Central People's Government of the People's Republic of China Mao Zedong on 16 December 1949," December 16, 1949, trans. Danny Rozas, Wilson Center Digital Archive, Archive of the President, Russian Federation (APRF), fond (f.) 45, opis (op.) 1, delo (d.) 329, listy (ll.) 9-17, https://digitalarchive .wilsoncenter.org/document/record-conversation-between-iv-stalin-and-chairman-central -peoples-government-peoples.

56. "The Charge in the Soviet Union (Kennan) to the Secretary of State," February 22, 1946, National Security Archive, George Washington University, https://nsarchive2.gwu. edu/coldwar/documents/episode-1/kennan.htm; Mao Zedong, "On the People's Democratic Dictatorship: In Commemoration of the Twenty-Eighth Anniversary of the Communist Party of China," June 30, 1949, Wilson Center Digital Archive, in *Selected Works of Mao Tse-tung*, vol. 4 (Peking: Foreign Languages Press, 1961), 411–423, https://digitalarchive .wilsoncenter.org/document/119300; "Ambassador in China (Stuart) to Secretary of State," May 13, 1949, in *FRUS, 1949, The Far East: China*, vol. 8, eds. Francis C. Prescott et al. (Washington, DC: US Government Printing Office, 1978), https://history.state.gov/ historicaldocuments/frus1949v08/d889. On Cold War developments, see John Lewis Gaddis, *The Cold War: A New History* (New York: Penguin, 2006). On Mao's attempts at balance of power politics, see Khan, *Haunted by Chaos*. For a different perspective that emphasizes the role of ideology more than I do, see the superb Chen, *Mao's China*.

57. "The United States Representative at the United Nations (Austin) to the Secretary of State," August 17, 1949, in *1949, The Far East: China*, vol. 9, https://history.state.gov/historicaldocuments/frus1949v09/d1451; *China White Paper*. For a full account of just how deep the confusion went, see Lin, *Accidental State*, which in addition to the details mentioned here, provides an account of various fruitless plans to unseat Chiang. On anti-Communism in America, see John Earl Haynes and Harvey Klehr, *Early Cold War Spies: The Espionage Trials that Shaped American Politics* (Cambridge: Cambridge University Press, 2012). By far the most insightful account of the "loss of China" debate and its impact on American foreign policy (an impact, remarkably, that persists to this day) is still David Halberstam, *The Best and the Brightest* (New York: Ballantine Books, 1993).

58. "Memorandum of Conversation, by the Secretary of State," January 5, 1950, in *FRUS, 1950, East Asia and the Pacific*, vol. 11, eds. Neal H. Petersen et al. (Washington, DC: US Government Printing Office, 1976), https://history.state.gov/historicaldocuments/frus1950v06/d127.

59. "Editorial note," in *1950, East Asia and the Pacific*, vol. 11, https://history.state.gov/historicaldocuments/frus1950v06/d128; "Extract from a Draft Memorandum by the Assistant Secretary of State for Far Eastern Affairs (Rusk) to the Secretary of State," May 30, 1950, in *1950, East Asia and the Pacific*, vol. 11, https://history.state.gov/historicaldocuments/frus1950v06/d183; "Memorandum by the Deputy Special Assistant for Intelligence (Howe) to Mr. W. Park Armstrong, Special Assistant to the Secretary of State for Intelligence and Research," May 31, 1950, in *1950, East Asia and the Pacific*, vol. 11, https://history.state.gov/historicaldocuments/frus1950v06/d182.

60. John Lewis Gaddis, *Strategies of Containment: A Critical Appraisal of American National Security Policy during the Cold War* (New York: Oxford University Press, 2005).

61. "Remarks by Dean Acheson Before the National Press Club," January 12, 1950, Harry S. Truman Library and Museum (underlining in original text), www.trumanlibrary.gov/library/research-files/remarks-dean-acheson-national-press-club?documentid=NA&pagenumber=2. On motivations for Acheson's speech, see James I. Matray, "Dean Acheson's Press Club Speech Reexamined," *Journal of Conflict Studies* 22, no. 1 (2002): 28–55.

62. See Westad, *Cold War*.

63. Harry S. Truman, *Memoirs*, vol. 1, *Year of Decisions* (New York: Doubleday, 1955); Gaddis, *Cold War*.

64. For the PRC perspective on its exclusion from the United Nations at the time, see "Struggle to Restore China's Lawful Seat in the United Nations," Ministry of Foreign Affairs of the People's Republic of China, www.fmprc.gov.cn/eng/ziliao_665539/3602_665543/3604_665547/200011/t20001117_697805.html. The Soviet boycott of the Security Council is well covered in the literature; see Gaddis, *Cold War*.

65. Harry S. Truman, *Memoirs*, vol. 2, *Years of Trial and Hope* (New York: Doubleday, 1956), 337. Truman gives a good account of the considerations motivating him at the time. "The Secretary of State to All Diplomatic and Certain Consular Offices," July 1, 1950, in

1950, East Asia and the Pacific, vol. 11, https://history.state.gov/historicaldocuments/frus 1950v06/d196.

66. Pantsov, *Victorious in Defeat*, 443.

67. "Memorandum of Conversation, by the Ambassador at Large (Jessup)," June 25, 1950, in *FRUS, 1950, Korea*, vol. 7, ed. John P. Glennon (Washington, DC: US Government Printing Office, 1976), https://history.state.gov/historicaldocuments/frus1950v07/d86.

68. "Extracts of a Memorandum of Conversations, by Mr. W. Averell Harriman, Special Assistant to the President, with General MacArthur in Tokyo on August 6 and 8, 1950," in *1950, East Asia and the Pacific*, vol. 11, https://history.state.gov/historicaldocuments /frus1950v06/d253.

69. Harry S. Truman, "Message to General MacArthur Regarding the Withdrawal of the General's Message to the Veterans of Foreign Wars," August 29, 1950, American Presidency Project, www.presidency.ucsb.edu/node/230181. On MacArthur's talks with Chiang, see Lin, *Accidental State*.

70. "Memorandum of Conversation, by the Ambassador at Large (Jessup)."

71. See Khan, *Haunted by Chaos*.

72. The best account of the sequence of events is Chen, *Mao's China*.

73. For a starting point, see Westad, *Cold War*. MacArthur's speech is available at "Gen. Douglas MacArthur's 'Old Soldiers Never Die' Address to Congress," April 19, 1951, Library of Congress, www.loc.gov/resource/mcc.034/?st=gallery.

74. See Chen, *Mao's China*; Khan, *Haunted by Chaos*.

75. On the Korean War, see Chen, *Mao's China*. On San Francisco, see Kimie Hara, "50 Years from San Francisco: Re-Examining the Peace Treaty and Japan's Territorial Problems," *Pacific Affairs* 74, no. 3 (2001): 361–382, https://doi.org/10.2307/3557753. The Soviet Union was not party to the Treaty of San Francisco either.

CHAPTER 2: CHOOSING BETWEEN TWO TYRANNIES

1. "No. 115: Memorandum of Discussion at the 237th Meeting of the National Security Council, Washington, February 17, 1955," in *FRUS, 1955–1957, China*, vol. 2, ed. Harriet D. Schwar (Washington, DC: US Government Printing Office, 1986), https://history .state.gov/historicaldocuments/frus1955-57v02/d115. On Eisenhower as a strategist and the processes of policymaking, see William Hitchcock, *The Age of Eisenhower: America and the World in the 1950s* (New York: Simon & Schuster, 2019). See also Gaddis, *Cold War*, and *The Long Peace: Inquiries into the History of the Cold War* (Oxford: Oxford University Press, 1989).

2. "No. 139: Memorandum of Conversation," July 9, 1971, in *FRUS, 1969–1976*, vol. 17, *China, 1969–1972*, ed. Steven E. Phillips (Washington, DC: US Government Printing Office, 2006), https://history.state.gov/historicaldocuments/frus1969-76v17/d139. On Mao Zedong's general strategy, see Khan, *Haunted by Chaos*.

3. "No. 75: Message from the President to the Congress," February 2, 1953, in *FRUS, 1952–1954, China and Japan*, vol. 14, part 1, eds. David W. Mabon and Harriet D. Schwar (Washington, DC: US Government Printing Office, 1985), https://history.state.gov/histor

icaldocuments/frus1952-54v14p1/d75. On McCarthy, Marshall, and Eisenhower, see Halberstam, *The Best and the Brightest*. McCarthy's denunciation of Marshall is available
at Joseph McCarthy, "The History of George Catlett Marshall, 1951" (speech delivered
before the Senate, June 14, 1951), Internet Modern History Sourcebook, Fordham University, https://sourcebooks.fordham.edu/mod/1951mccarthy-marshall.asp.

4. "No. 80: The Ambassador in India (Bowles) to the Department of State," February
10, 1953, in *1952–1954, China and Japan*, vol. 14, part 1, https://history.state.gov/histori-
caldocuments/frus1952-54v14p1/d80; "No. 73: Memorandum by the Assistant Secretary
of State for Far Eastern Affairs (Allison) to the President," February 2, 1953, in *1952–1954,
China and Japan*, vol. 14, part 1, https://history.state.gov/historicaldocuments/frus1952-
54v14p1/d73; "No. 76: *The Chargé in the United Kingdom (Holmes) to the Department of
State,*" February 4, 1953, in *1952–1954, China and Japan*, vol. 14, part 1, https://history.state
.gov/historicaldocuments/frus1952-54v14p1/d76.

5. "No. 68: Memorandum of Conversation, by the Assistant Secretary of State for
Far Eastern Affairs (Allison)," January 28, 1953, in *1952–1954, China and Japan*, vol. 14,
part 1, https://history.state.gov/historicaldocuments/frus1952-54v14p1/d68; "No. 78: The
Chief of the Military Assistance Advisory Group, Formosa (Chase) to the Chief of General Staff, Republic of China Taipei," February 5, 1953, in *1952–1954, China and Japan*,
vol. 14, part 1, https://history.state.gov/historicaldocuments/frus1952-54v14p1/d78.

6. "No. 74: Memorandum of Conversation, by the Assistant Secretary of State for
Far Eastern Affairs (Allison)," February 2, 1953, in *1952–1954, China and Japan*, vol.
14, part 1, https://history.state.gov/historicaldocuments/frus1952-54v14p1/d74; "No. 83:
*Memorandum of Conversation, by the Assistant Secretary of State for Far Eastern Affairs
(Allison),*" March 19, 1953, in *1952–1954, China and Japan*, vol. 14, part 1, https://history
.state.gov/historicaldocuments/frus1952-54v14p1/d83; "No. 86: *Memorandum of the Substance of Discussion at a Department of State–Joint Chiefs of Staff Meeting, Held at the Pentagon, March 27, 1953, 11:30 a.m.,*" in *1952–1954, China and Japan*, vol. 14, part 1, https://history
.state.gov/historicaldocuments/frus1952-54v14p1/d86.

7. "No. 93: Memorandum of Discussion at the 139th Meeting of the National Security
Council, Washington, April 8, 1953," in *1952–1954, China and Japan*, vol. 14, part 1, https
://history.state.gov/historicaldocuments/frus1952-54v14p1/d93.

8. "No. 93: Memorandum"; "No. 98: The Ambassador in the Republic of China
(Rankin) to the Department of State," April 16, 1953, in *1952–1954, China and Japan*, vol.
14, part 1, https://history.state.gov/historicaldocuments/frus1952-54v14p1/d98; "No. 95:
*Memorandum of the Substance of Discussion at a Department of State–Joint Chiefs of Staff
Meeting, Held at the Pentagon, April 10, 1953, 11 a.m.,*" in *1952–1954, China and Japan*,
vol. 14, part 1, https://history.state.gov/historicaldocuments/frus1952-54v14p1/d95; "No.
101: The Chargé in the Republic of China (Jones) to the Department of State," April 23,
1953, in *1952–1954, China and Japan*, vol. 14, part 1, https://history.state.gov/historical-
documents/frus1952-54v14p1/d101; "No. 94: *The Ambassador in the Republic of China
(Rankin) to the Director of the Office of Chinese Affairs (McConaughy),*" April 10, 1953, in
1952–1954, China and Japan, vol. 14, part 1, https://history.state.gov/historicaldocuments
/frus1952-54v14p1/d94.

9. "No. 216: Memorandum of Telephone Conversation, Prepared in the White House," June 16, 1954, in *1952–1954, China and Japan*, vol. 14, part 1, https://history.state .gov/historicaldocuments/frus1952-54v14p1/d216.

10. "No. 224: The Ambassador in the Republic of China (Rankin) to the Department of State," June 24, 1954, in *1952–1954, China and Japan*, vol. 14, part 1, https://history. state.gov/historicaldocuments/frus1952-54v14p1/d224; "No. 229: The Secretary of State to the Embassy in the Republic of China Washington," July 9, 1954, in *1952–1954, China and Japan*, vol. 14, part 1, https://history.state.gov/historicaldocuments/frus1952-54v14p1 /d229; "No. 230: The Chargé in the Republic of China (Cochran) to the Department of State," July 13, 1954, in *1952–1954, China and Japan*, vol. 14, part 1, https://history.state.gov /historicaldocuments/frus1952-54v14p1/d230.

11. "No. 155: The Ambassador in the Republic of China (Rankin) to the Department of State," November 30, 1953, in *1952–1954, China and Japan*, vol. 14, part 1, https://history .state.gov/historicaldocuments/frus1952-54v14p1/d155.

12. "No. 88: Memorandum by the Deputy Under Secretary of State (Matthews) to the Secretary of State," March 31, 1953," in *1952–1954, China and Japan*, vol. 14, part 1, https://history.state.gov/historicaldocuments/frus1952-54v14p1/d88; "No. 97: The President of the Republic of China (Chiang Kai-shek) to President Eisenhower," April 15, 1953, in *1952–1954, China and Japan*, vol. 14, part 1, https://history.state.gov/histor-icaldocuments/frus1952-54v14p1/d97; "No. 108: The President of the Republic of China (Chiang Kai-shek) to President Eisenhower," June 7, 1953, in *1952–1954, China and Japan*, vol. 14, part 1, https://history.state.gov/historicaldocuments/frus1952-54v14p1/d108. On the negotiations about the prisoners of war, see the excellent David Cheng Chang, *The Hijacked War: The Story of Chinese POWs in the Korean War* (Stanford, CA: Stanford University Press, 2020).

13. "No. 193: Memorandum of Conversation, by the Director of the Office of Chinese Affairs (McConaughy)," May 19, 1954, in *1952–1954, China and Japan*, vol. 14, part 1, https://history.state.gov/historicaldocuments/frus1952-54v14p1/d193.

14. "No. 262: Memorandum by the Assistant Secretary of State for Far Eastern Affairs (Robertson) to the Secretary of State," August 25, 1954, in *1952–1954, China and Japan*, vol. 14, part 1, https://history.state.gov/historicaldocuments/frus1952-54v14p1 /d262. SEATO is well-covered in the literature; for a basic sketch, see "Southeast Asia Treaty Organization (SEATO), 1954," Milestones: 1953–1960, Office of the Historian, US Department of State, https://history.state.gov/milestones/1953-1960/seato.

15. "No. 269: Memorandum by the Acting Secretary of State to the Assistant Secretary of State for Far Eastern Affairs (Robertson)," September 1, 1954, in *1952–1954, China and Japan*, vol. 14, part 1, https://history.state.gov/historicaldocuments/frus1952-54v14p1/d269.

16. Pang Xianzhi and Zhong gong zhong yang wen xian yan jiu shi, eds., *Mao Zedong nian pu: yi jiu si jiu - yi jiu qi liu* (Beijing: Zhong yang wen xian chu ban she, 2013), 2:263. The best account of the crises in the strait during the Mao era is still Chen, *Mao's China*. See also Tucker, *Strait Talk*, and Khan, *Haunted by Chaos*.

17. See Chen, *Mao's China*.

18. "No. 289: Memorandum of Discussion at the 213th Meeting of the National Security Council, Washington, September 9, 1954," in *1952–1954, China and Japan*, vol. 14, part 1, https://history.state.gov/historicaldocuments/frus1952-54v14p1/d289; "No. 293: *Memorandum of Discussion at the 214th Meeting of the National Security Council, Denver, September 12, 1954*," in *1952–1954, China and Japan*, vol. 14, part 1, https://history.state .gov/historicaldocuments/frus1952-54v14p1/d293; No. 291, *Memorandum by the Chairman of the Joint Chiefs of Staff (Radford) to the Secretary of Defense (Wilson)* Washington, 11 September 1954" in *1952–1954, China and Japan*, vol. 14, part 1.

19. "No. 293: Memorandum of Discussion"; "No. 364: Memorandum of Discussion at the 220th Meeting of the National Security Council, Washington, October 28, 1954," in *1952–1954, China and Japan*, vol. 14, part 1, https://history.state.gov/historicaldocuments /frus1952-54v14p1/d364.

20. "No. 364: Memorandum of Discussion."

21. "No. 362: Memorandum of Conversation, by the Director of the Office of Chinese Affairs (McConaughy)," October 27, 1954, in *1952–1954, China and Japan*, vol. 14, part 1, https://history.state.gov/historicaldocuments/frus1952-54v14p1/d362; "Mutual Defense Treaty Between the United States and the Republic of China; December 2, 1954," Avalon Project, in *American Foreign Policy 1950–1955: Basic Documents*, vols. 1 and 2 (Washington, DC: US Government Printing Office, 1957), https://avalon.law.yale.edu/20th _century/chin001.asp; "No. 375: Memorandum of Discussion at the 221st Meeting of the National Security Council, Washington, November 2, 1954," in *1952–1954, China and Japan*, vol. 14, part 1, https://history.state.gov/historicaldocuments/frus1952-54v14p1/d375.

22. "No. 8: Memorandum of a Conversation, Department of State, Washington, January 12, 1955," in *1955–1957, China*, vol. 2, https://history.state.gov/historicaldocuments/ frus1955-57v02/d8; "No. 23: Memorandum of Discussion at the 232nd Meeting of the National Security Council, Washington, January 20, 1955," in *1955–1957, China*, vol. 2, https://history.state.gov/historicaldocuments/frus1955-57v02/d23.

23. "No. 23: Memorandum of Discussion"; "No. 8: Memorandum of a Conversation." On Mao's contemplation of military action, see Khan, *Haunted by Chaos*.

24. "No. 56: Joint Resolution by the Congress," January 29, 1955, in *1955–1957, China*, vol. 2, https://history.state.gov/historicaldocuments/frus1955-57v02/d56; "No. 60: Telegram from the Ambassador in the Republic of China (Rankin) to the Department of State Taipei," January 30, 1955, in *1955–1957, China*, vol. 2, https://history.state.gov/historical-documents/frus1955-57v02/d60. Congress appears to have been thinking of what modern students of geopolitics call the "first island chain," not the second, which is farther west and encompasses Micronesia.

25. "No. 94: Telegram from the Ambassador in the Republic of China (Rankin) to the Department of State," February 7, 1955, in *1955–1957, China*, vol. 2, https://history.state.gov /historicaldocuments/frus1955-57v02/d94; "No. 115: Memorandum of Discussion."

26. "No. 141: Memorandum of a Conversation Between the President and the Secretary of State, Washington, March 6, 1955, 5:15 p.m.," in *1955–1957, China*, vol. 2, https://history .state.gov/historicaldocuments/frus1955-57v02/d141; "No. 146: Memorandum of Discussion

at the 240th Meeting of the National Security Council, Washington, March 10, 1955," in *1955–1957, China*, vol. 2, https://history.state.gov/historicaldocuments/frus1955-57v02 /d146; "No. 185. Memorandum from the Under Secretary of State (Hoover) to the Secretary of State," April 1, 1955, in *1955–1957, China*, vol. 2, https://history.state.gov /historicaldocuments/frus1955-57v02/d185.

27. See Chen, *Mao's China*, and Khan, *Haunted by Chaos*.

28. "No. 219: Message from the Assistant Secretary of State for Far Eastern Affairs (Robertson) to the Secretary of State," April 25, 1955, in *1955–1957, China*, vol. 2, https://history .state.gov/historicaldocuments/frus1955-57v02/d219.

29. Quoted in Chen, *Mao's China*, 180.

30. Information here and in preceding paragraph drawn from Chen, *Mao's China*, and Khan, *Haunted by Chaos*.

31. Khan, *Haunted by Chaos*.

32. "No. 28: Memorandum of Meeting," August 8, 1958, in *FRUS, 1958–1960, China*, vol. 19, ed. Harriet Dashiell Schwar (Washington, DC: US Government Printing Office, 1996), https://history.state.gov/historicaldocuments/frus1958-60v19/d28; "No. 43: Memorandum of Meeting," August 25, 1958, in *1958–1960, China*, vol. 19, https://history.state .gov/historicaldocuments/frus1958-60v19/d43; "No. 67: Memorandum Prepared by Secretary of State Dulles," September 4, 1958, in *1958–1960, China*, vol. 19, https://history. state.gov/historicaldocuments/frus1958-60v19/d67.

33. "No. 185: Draft Talking Paper Prepared by Secretary of State Dulles," October 13, 1958, in *1958–1960, China*, vol. 19, https://history.state.gov/historicaldocuments/frus 1958-60v19/d185; "No. 59. Telegram from the Embassy in the Republic of China to the Department of State," September 1, 1958, in *1958–1960, China*, vol. 19, https://history. state.gov/historicaldocuments/frus1958-60v19/d59; "No. 203: Memorandum of Conversation," October 22, 1958, in *1958–1960, China*, vol. 19, https://history.state.gov/historicaldocuments/frus1958-60v19/d203; "No. 204: Memorandum of Conversation," October 22, 1958, in *1958–1960, China*, vol. 19, https://history.state.gov/historicaldocuments /frus1958-60v19/d204; "No. 210: Telegram from Secretary of State Dulles to the Department of State," October 23, 1958, in *1958–1960, China*, vol. 19, https://history.state.gov /historicaldocuments/frus1958-60v19/d210.

34. Chen, *Mao's China*; "The Taiwan Straits Crises: 1954–55 and 1958," Milestones: 1953–1960, Office of the Historian, US Department of State, https://history.state.gov /milestones/1953-1960/taiwan-strait-crises.

35 "No. 256: Memorandum of Discussion at the 211th Meeting of the National Security Council, Washington, August 18, 1954," in *1952–1954, China and Japan*, vol. 14, part 1, https://history.state.gov/historicaldocuments/frus1952-54v14p1/d256; "No. 146: Memorandum by the Director of the Office of Chinese Affairs (McConaughy) to the Assistant Secretary of State for Far Eastern Affairs (Robertson)," November 4, 1953, in *1952–1954, China and Japan*, vol. 14, part 1, https://history.state.gov/historicaldocuments/frus1952-54v14p1/d146.

36. "No. 144: Memorandum by the Regional Planning Adviser for Far Eastern Affairs (Ogburn) to the Director of the Office of Chinese Affairs (McConaughy)," October 30, 1953, in *1952–1954, China and Japan*, vol. 14, part 1, https://history.state.gov/historical-documents/frus1952-54v14p1/d144; "No. 185: Memorandum of Discussion at the 193rd Meeting of the National Security Council, Washington, April 13, 1954," in *1952–1954, China and Japan*, vol. 14, part 1, https://history.state.gov/historicaldocuments/frus1952 -54v14p1/d185; "No. 419: Memorandum of Discussion at the 226th Meeting of the National Security Council, Washington, December 1, 1954," in *1952–1954, China and Japan*, vol. 14, part 1, https://history.state.gov/historicaldocuments/frus1952-54v14p1 /d419; "No. 375: Memorandum of Discussion at the 221st Meeting of the National Security Council, Washington, November 2, 1954," in *1952–1954, China and Japan*, vol. 14, part 1, https://history.state.gov/historicaldocuments/frus1952-54v14p1/d375. On the Eisenhower-Dulles scheme for trying to split the Soviet Union and China through pressure, see Gaddis, *Long Peace*. The plan was not well conceived.

37. Tucker, *Strait Talk*, provides a good overview. On the Sino-Soviet split, see Sergey Radchenko, *Two Suns in the Heavens: The Sino-Soviet Struggle for Supremacy, 1962–1967* (Stanford, CA: Stanford University Press, 2009), and Lorenz M. Lüthi, *The Sino-Soviet Split: Cold War in the Communist World* (Princeton, NJ: Princeton University Press, 2008). On American appraisals of the Sino-Soviet relationship, see Gaddis, *Strategies of Containment*, and, for a harsher view, Halberstam, *Best and the Brightest*.

38. See Khan, *Haunted by Chaos*.

39. Li Jian, *Liang an mou he zuji zhuizong* (Beijing: Huawen, 1996), 73–74. See also Gong Li, "Tension Across the Taiwan Strait in the 1950s Chinese Strategy and Tactics," in *Re-examining the Cold War: US-China Diplomacy, 1954–1973*, eds. Robert S. Ross and Changbin Jiang (Leiden, Netherlands: Brill, 2020). The United States was aware that Chiang might be communicating with the CCP as Tucker, *Strait Talk*, points out. On Tibet, see Liu Xiaoyuan, *To the End of Revolution: The Chinese Communist Party and Tibet, 1949–1959* (New York: Columbia University Press, 2019), and Sulmaan Wasif Khan, *Muslim, Trader, Nomad, Spy* (Chapel Hill: University of North Carolina Press, 2015).

40. Li, *Liang an*, 140–162.

41. Li, *Liang an*, 166–171.

42. CCP Central Committee, "Central Committee Issues the Central Propaganda Department's 'Report on the Basic Conditions of and Suggestions for Improvement of Propaganda Work Towards Taiwan,'" February 26, 1956, trans. Simon Schuchat, Wilson Center Digital Archive, Fujian Provincial Archives, 101-5-814, 18-24, https://digitalarchive .wilsoncenter.org/document/cable-ccp-central-committee-central-committee-issues -central-propaganda-departments-report.

43. "No. 260: Memorandum of a Conversation, Taipei, May 27, 1957," in *FRUS, 1955–1957, China*, vol. 3, eds. Harriet D. Schwar and Louis J. Smith (Washington, DC: US Government Printing Office, 1986), https://history.state.gov/historicaldocuments

/frus1955-57v03/d260; "No. 259: Telegram from the Ambassador in the Republic of China (Rankin) to the Department of State," May 26, 1957, in *1955–1957, China*, vol. 3, https://history.state.gov/historicaldocuments/frus1955-57v03/d259; "No. 261: Memorandum of Discussion at the 325th Meeting of the National Security Council, Washington, May 27, 1957," in *1955–1957, China*, vol. 3, https://history.state.gov/historicaldocuments /frus1955-57v03/d261. See also Han Cheung, "Taiwan in Time: A 'Great National Shame,'" *Taipei Times*, May 20, 2018, https://www.taipeitimes.com/News/feat/archives/2018/05/20 /2003693380.

44. "No. 53: Telegram from the Embassy in Poland to the Department of State," August 16, 1961, in *FRUS, 1961–1963*, vol. 22, *Northeast Asia*, eds. Edward C. Keefer, David W. Mabon, and Harriet Dashiell Schwar (Washington, DC: US Government Printing Office, 1996), https://history.state.gov/historicaldocuments/frus1961-63v22/d53. The best account of the Warsaw Talks is Yafeng Xia, *Negotiating with the Enemy: U.S.-China Talks During the Cold War, 1949–1972* (Bloomington: Indiana University Press, 2006).

45. "No. 119: Memorandum from the Director of the Bureau of Intelligence and Research (Hilsman) to Secretary of State Rusk," June 18, 1962, in *1961–1963*, vol. 22, *Northeast Asia*, https://history.state.gov/historicaldocuments/frus1961-63v22/d119; "No. 131: Telegram from the Embassy in Poland to the Department of State," June 23, 1962, in *1961–1963*, vol. 22, *Northeast Asia*, https://history.state.gov/historicaldocuments/frus1961-63v22 /d131. On Chiang's grand plans for conquest, see Khan, *Muslim, Trader*.

46. "No. 156: Telegram from the Consulate General at Singapore to the Department of State," November 13, 1962, in *1961–1963*, vol. 22, *Northeast Asia*, https://history.state. gov/historicaldocuments/frus1961-63v22/d156; "No. 145: Telegram from the Department of State to the Embassy in the Republic of China," July 28, 1962, in *1961–1963*, vol. 22, *Northeast Asia*, https://history.state.gov/historicaldocuments/frus1961-63v22/d145.

47. The literature on Kissinger abounds. See John Lewis Gaddis, "Rescuing Choice from Circumstance: The Statecraft of Henry Kissinger," in *The Diplomats, 1939–1979*, eds. Gordon A. Craig and Francis L. Loewenheim (Princeton, NJ: Princeton University Press, 1994), for a starting point. Kissinger's work on Bismarck is still worth reading: Henry Kissinger, "The White Revolutionary: Reflections on Bismarck," *Daedalus* 97, no. 3 (Summer 1968): 888–924.

48. "No. 163: Memorandum of Discussion at the 177th Meeting of the National Security Council, Washington, December 23, 1953," in *1952–1954, China and Japan*, vol. 14, part 1, https://history.state.gov/historicaldocuments/frus1952-54v14p1/d163; US Assistant to the President for National Security Affairs, "Meeting Between the President, Ambassador Chow, and Henry A. Kissinger (U.S. Relations with China and Taiwan; Includes Action Memorandum Entitled 'Chinese Representation at the United Nations')," April 12, 1971, Digital National Security Archive, ProQuest, accessed April 26, 2023. See also Elis Eastmund (@eliseastmund1030), "There's an Old Vulcan Proverb . . . 'Only Nixon Could Go to China'," YouTube, September 5, 2016, www.youtube.com/watch?v=X_gwnFSFzv0.

49. White House, "Meeting Between Henry Kissinger and Zhou Enlai," July 9, 1971, Digital National Security Archive, ProQuest, accessed April 26, 2023; "Communiqué

[Meeting of Henry Kissinger and Zhou Enlai]," October 25, 1971, Digital National Security Archive.

50. "Kissinger Transcripts, Memorandum of Conversation," November 12, 1973, Digital National Security Archive; "No. 203: Joint Statement Following Discussions with Leaders of the People's Republic of China," February 27, 1972, in *FRUS, 1969–1976*, vol. 17, *China, 1969–1972*, ed. Steven E. Phillips (Washington, DC: US Government Printing Office, 2006), https://history.state.gov/historicaldocuments/frus1969-76v17/d203.

51. Tucker, *Strait Talk*, is rightly critical of Kissinger here.

52. Lin, *Accidental State*, makes an excellent case on economic reform; see also Chen Cheng and Zhilin He, *Chen Cheng xian sheng hui yi lu: liu shi zi shu* (Taipei: Guoshiguan, 2012), 885. Chiang's governance principles are well-documented by the man himself; see Chiang, *China's Destiny*. For a deplorable perspective on "Free China" today, see Danielle Pletka and Marc Thiessen, "Like It or Not, Taiwan Is Free China," American Enterprise Institute, April 20, 2020, www.aei.org/foreign-and-defense-policy/like-it-or-not-taiwan-is-free-china/. "No. 141: Memorandum for the Files, by the Director of the Office of Chinese Affairs (McConaughy)," November 13, 1953, in *1952–1954, China and Japan*, vol. 14, part 1, https://history.state.gov/historicaldocuments/frus1952-54v14p1/d141.

53. Taiwan National Archives, A383130000C/0059/215/008/1/003; Taiwan National Archives, A303000000B/0047/006.3/008/1/041; Shi Ming, *Shi Ming Huiyi lu*, 467–468.

54. *Mao Zedong Nianpu*, 2:263. On mass mobilization, see Chen, *Mao's China*.

55. Peng, *Taste of Freedom*, 101–199; Memoranda for the President Beginning February 20, 1972, National Archives, Nixon Presidential Materials Project, White House Special Files, President's Office Files, box 87, https://nsarchive2.gwu.edu/NSAEBB/NSAEBB106/NZ-3.pdf.

56. Memoranda for the President Beginning February 20, 1972.

57. Jill Lepore, *These Truths: A History of the United States* (New York: W. W. Norton, 2018); John W. Finney, "Nixon Wins Broad Approval of Congress on China Talks but Some Criticism Arises," *New York Times*, February 29, 1972; "Richard Nixon and Ronald W. Reagan on 26 October 1971," transcript, eds. Ken Hughes et al., Presidential Recordings Digital Edition, University of Virginia, https://prde.upress.virginia.edu/conversations/4002192.

CHAPTER 3: TOWARD ANOTHER CRISIS

1. "No. 20: Conversation Between President Nixon and His Assistant for National Security Affairs (Kissinger)," March 12, 1973, in *FRUS, 1969–1976*, vol. 18, *China, 1973–1976*, ed. David P. Nickles (Washington, DC: US Government Printing Office, 2007), https://history.state.gov/historicaldocuments/frus1969-76v18/d20.

2. For a look at China after Mao and Deng's impact, see Ezra Vogel, *Deng Xiaoping and the Transformation of China* (Cambridge, MA: Harvard University Press, 2011). Deng did not succeed Mao as paramount leader immediately; Hua Guofeng was the chairman's immediate successor.

3. "No. 5: Conversation Between President Nixon and His Assistant for National Security Affairs (Kissinger)," February 1, 1973, in vol. 18, *China, 1973–1976*, https://history.state.gov/historicaldocuments/frus1969-76v18/d5; "No. 43: Memorandum of Conversation," July 19, 1973, in vol. 18, *China, 1973–1976*, https://history.state.gov/historicaldocuments/frus1969-76v18/d43. On Japan's understanding of the "one China" principle, see Adam Liff, "Japan, Taiwan and the 'One China' Framework after 50 Years," *China Quarterly* 252 (2022): 1066–1093, https://doi.org/10.1017/S0305741022001357.

4. "No. 9: Memorandum of Conversation," February 16, 1973, in vol. 18, *China, 1973–1976*, https://history.state.gov/historicaldocuments/frus1969-76v18/d9; "No. 10: Memorandum of Conversation," February 17, 1973, in vol. 18, *China, 1973–1976*, https://history.state.gov/historicaldocuments/frus1969-76v18/d10. On troop levels, see "Does America Have Troops in Taiwan?," *Economist*, October 8, 2021, www.economist.com/the-economist-explains/2021/10/08/does-america-have-troops-in-taiwan; "US Military Bases in Taiwan," GlobalSecurity.org, www.globalsecurity.org/military/facility/taiwan.htm; and CIA, "Mr. Nixon and Taiwan," Freedom of Information Act Reading Room, December 9, 2016, www.cia.gov/readingroom/document/cia-rdp80-01601r000800180001-7.

5. "No. 43: Memorandum of Conversation."

6. "No. 41: Memorandum of Conversation," July 6, 1973, in vol. 18, *China, 1973–1976*, https://history.state.gov/historicaldocuments/frus1969-76v18/d41. The most authoritative source on Zhou's travails at this time is Chen Jian, *Zhou Enlai: A Life* (Cambridge, MA: Harvard University Press, 2024). See also Khan, *Haunted by Chaos*, and Tucker, *Strait Talk*.

7. "No. 56: Memorandum of Conversation," Beijing, November 11, 1973 in vol. 18, *China, 1973–1976*, https://history.state.gov/historicaldocuments/frus1969-76v18/d56; "No: 59: Memorandum of Conversation," November 13, 1973, in vol. 18, *China, 1973–1976*, https://history.state.gov/historicaldocuments/frus1969-76v18/d59; "No. 62: Memorandum from the President's Assistant for National Security Affairs (Kissinger) to President Nixon," November 19, 1973, in vol. 18, *China, 1973–1976*, https://history.state.gov/historicaldocuments/frus1969-76v18/d62.

8. "No. 78: Memorandum of Conversation," April 14, 1974, in vol. 18, *China, 1973–1976*, https://history.state.gov/historicaldocuments/frus1969-76v18/d78.

9. "No. 94: Memorandum of Conversation," November 26, 1974, in vol. 18, *China, 1973–1976*, https://history.state.gov/historicaldocuments/frus1969-76v18/d94; "No. 95: Memorandum of Conversation," November 27, 1974, in vol. 18, *China, 1973–1976*, https://history.state.gov/historicaldocuments/frus1969-76v18/d95.

10. "No. 112: Memorandum from the Assistant Secretary of State for East Asian and Pacific Affairs (Habib), the Deputy Assistant Secretary of State for East Asian and Pacific Affairs (Gleysteen), the Director of the Policy Planning Staff (Lord), and Richard H. Solomon of the National Security Council Staff to Secretary of State Kissinger," July 3, 1975, in vol. 18, *China, 1973–1976*, https://history.state.gov/historicaldocuments/frus1969-76v18/d112; "No. 120: Memorandum of Conversation," October 17, 1975, in vol. 18, *China, 1973–1976*, https://history.state.gov/historicaldocuments/frus1969-76v18/d120; "No. 129: Mem-

orandum of Conversation," October 25, 1975, in vol. 18, *China, 1973–1976*, https://history .state.gov/historicaldocuments/frus1969-76v18/d129; "No. 125: Memorandum of Conversation," October 22, 1975, in vol. 18, *China, 1973–1976*, https://history.state.gov /historicaldocuments/frus1969-76v18/d125; "No. 137: Memorandum of Conversation," December 4, 1975, in vol. 18, *China, 1973–1976*, https://history.state.gov/historicaldocuments/frus1969-76v18/d137; "No. 133: Editorial Note," in vol. 18, *China, 1973–1976*, https://history.state.gov/historicaldocuments/frus1969-76v18/d133.

11. "Chiang Kai-shek Is Dead in Taipei at 87; Last of Allied Big Four of World War II," *New York Times*, April 6, 1975, www.nytimes.com/1975/04/06/archives/chiang-kaishek -is-dead-in-taipei-at-87-last-of-allied-big-four-of.html. On Goldwater's role, see Tucker, *Strait Talk*.

12. Fox Butterfield, "Free Congressional Trips to Taiwan Are Linked to the Nationalist Government," *New York Times*, October 18, 1975; "No. 40: Memorandum from the President's Assistant for National Security Affairs (Brzezinski) to President Carter," July 29, 1977, in *FRUS, 1977–1980*, vol. 13, *China*, ed. David P. Nickles (Washington, DC: US Government Printing Office, 2013), https://history.state.gov/historicaldocuments /frus1977-80v13/d40; "Republican Party Platform of 1976," August 18, 1976, American Presidency Project, www.presidency.ucsb.edu/documents/republican-party-platform-1976; "No. 153: Memorandum for the Record," August 25, 1976, in vol. 18, *China, 1973–1976*, https:// history.state.gov/historicaldocuments/frus1969-76v18/d153; "Presidential Campaign Debate Between Gerald R. Ford and Jimmy Carter," October 6, 1976, Gerald R. Ford Presidential Library and Museum, www.fordlibrarymuseum.gov/library/speeches/760854.asp; "No. 203: Joint Statement Following Discussions with Leaders of the People's Republic of China," February 27, 1972, in vol. 18, *China, 1973–1976*, https://history.state.gov/his toricaldocuments/frus1969-76v17/d203; "No. 157. Memorandum of Conversation," October 8, 1976, in vol. 18, *China, 1973–1976*, https://history.state.gov/historicaldocuments /frus1969-76v18/d157. On Goldwater, see Tucker, *Strait Talk*.

13. "No. 137: Memorandum of Conversation," December 4, 1975, in vol. 18, *China, 1973–1976*, https://history.state.gov/historicaldocuments/frus1969-76v18/d137; "No. 2: Memorandum of Conversation," January 8, 1977, in *1977–1980*, vol. 13, *China*, https://history.state .gov/historicaldocuments/frus1977-80v13/d2; "No. 28: Memorandum from the President's Assistant for National Security Affairs (Brzezinski) to President Carter," May 24, 1977, in *1977–1980*, vol. 13, *China*, https://history.state.gov/historicaldocuments/frus1977-80v13/d28.

14. "No. 41: Memorandum of Conversation," July 30, 1977, in *1977–1980*, vol. 13, *China*, https://history.state.gov/historicaldocuments/frus1977-80v13/d41.

15. "No. 50: Memorandum of Conversation," August 24, 1977, in *1977–1980*, vol. 13, *China*, https://history.state.gov/historicaldocuments/frus1977-80v13/d50.

16. "No. 110: Memorandum of Conversation," May 21, 1978, in *1977–1980*, vol. 13, *China*, https://history.state.gov/historicaldocuments/frus1977-80v13/d110.

17. "No. 154: Memorandum from the Joint Chiefs of Staff to Secretary of Defense Brown," November 20, 1978, in *1977–1980*, vol. 13, *China*, https://history.state.gov/historical documents/frus1977-80v13/d154; "No. 170: Backchannel Message from the Chief of

the Liaison Office in China (Woodcock) to Secretary of State Vance and the President's Assistant for National Security Affairs (Brzezinski)," December 15, 1978, in *1977–1980*, vol. 13, *China*, https://history.state.gov/historicaldocuments/frus1977-80v13/d170. "No. 168: Backchannel Message from the Chief of the Liaison Office in China (Woodcock) to Secretary of State Vance and the President's Assistant for National Security Affairs (Brzezinski)," December 14, 1978, in *1977–1980*, vol. 13, *China*, https://history.state.gov /historicaldocuments/frus1977-80v13/d168.

18. Tucker, *Strait Talk*; "No. 230: Telegram from the Embassy in China to the Department of State," March 16, 1979, in *1977–1980*, vol. 13, *China*, https://history.state.gov/ historicaldocuments/frus1977-80v13/d230.

19. Goldwater v. Carter, 444 U.S. 996 (1979), decided December 13, 1979, by vote of six to three; Taiwan Relations Act, H. R. 2479, 96th Cong. (1979), www.congress.gov/ bill/96th-congress/house-bill/2479; "No. 264: Memorandum of Conversation," August 27, 1979, in *1977–1980*, vol. 13, *China*, https://history.state.gov/historicaldocuments/ frus1977-80v13/d264.

20. See Tucker, *Strait Talk*.

21. On Reagan's adventures in China policy, see Tucker, *Strait Talk*, and Vogel, *Deng Xiaoping*. The afterlife of the six assurances is best covered by Susan V. Lawrence, "President Reagan's Six Assurances to Taiwan," Congressional Research Service, last modified June 13, 2023, https://sgp.fas.org/crs/row/IF11665.pdf.

22. "Meeting with China's Ambassador Zhu Qizhen," memorandum of conversation, June 25, 1991, George H. W. Bush Presidential Library and Museum, https://bush41library.tamu.edu/files/memcons-telcons/1991-06-25--Qizhen.pdf.

23. "No. 7: Telegram from the Department of State to the Embassy in the Republic of China," February 10, 1977, in *1977–1980*, vol. 13, *China*, https://history.state.gov/historicaldocuments/frus1977-80v13/d7. On outreach to the Soviets, see Hsiao-ting Lin, *Taiwan, the United States, and the Hidden History of the Cold War in Asia* (New York: Routledge, 2022). On Soviet initiatives in Asia at this time, see also Sergey Radchenko, *Unwanted Visionaries: The Soviet Failure in Asia at the End of the Cold War* (Oxford: Oxford University Press, 2014). Deng's lack of concern about the possibility of a Taiwan-Soviet rapprochement was evident in his conversation with Brzezinski: "No. 110: Memorandum of Conversation," May 21, 1978, in *1977–1980*, vol. 13, *China*, https://history.state.gov/ historicaldocuments/frus1977-80v13/d110.

24. On nuclear weapons, see David Albright and Andrea Stricker, *Taiwan's Former Nuclear Weapons Program: Nuclear Weapons On-Demand* (Washington, DC: Institute for Science and International Security, 2018), https://isis-online.org/uploads/isis-reports /documents/TaiwansFormerNuclearWeaponsProgram_POD_color_withCover.pdf.

25. On Chinese remarks about US Taiwan policy at the time, see Khan, *Haunted by Chaos*.

26. The best recent study on cross-strait economic connections is the thought-provoking Shelley Rigger, *The Tiger Leading the Dragon: How Taiwan Propelled China's Economic Rise* (Lanham, MD: Rowman & Littlefield, 2021). Deng's policies as a whole are best covered by Vogel, *Deng Xiaoping*.

27. Rigger, *Tiger Leading the Dragon*. Statistics drawn from the invaluable Weng Cheng Shou, "Taishang touzi dalu de huigu yu zhangwang," *Jingji xue dongtai* (July 1995).

28. On Tibet, see the magisterial Xiaoyuan Liu, *To the End of Revolution: The Chinese Communist Party and Tibet, 1949–1959* (New York: Columbia University Press, 2020). Information on "one country, two systems" from Khan, *Muslim, Trader* and *Haunted by Chaos*.

29. See Khan, *Haunted by Chaos*.

30. Ye Jianying's promise from Li, *Liang An*, 262.

31. On Chiang Ching-kuo, see Taylor, *Generalissimo's Son*. J. Bruce Jacobs, *The Kaohsiung Incident in Taiwan and Memoirs of a Foreign Big Beard* (Leiden, Netherlands: Brill, 2016), is a first-rate account of the events in Kaohsiung and their aftermath.

32. Zhen Lei and Zheng Fu, *Lei Zhen yu Zi you Zhongguo: Lei Zhen wen xuan* (Taipei: Gui guan tu shu gu fen you xian gong si: Fa xing Jiu bo tu shu gu fen you xian gong si, 1989).

33. The best source here is Jacobs, *Kaohsiung Incident*, on which I have relied in telling the story of the 1978 elections and the crackdown. On elections, see John F. Copper, "Taiwan's Recent Elections: Fulfilling the Democratic Promise," Maryland Series in Contemporary Asian Studies 1990, no. 6 (1990): 1.

34. Jacobs, *Kaohsiung Incident*.

35. Weimin Liao, *Wo de dang wai qing chun: dang wai za zhi de gu shi* (Taipei: Yun chen wen hua shi ye gu fen you xian gong si, 2015), 57; Jacobs, *Kaohsiung Incident*.

36. Taylor, *Generalissimo's Son*.

37. Yung Wei, "Recognition of Divided States: Implication and Application of Concepts of Multi-System Nations, Political Entities, and Intra-National Commonwealth," *International Lawyer* 34, no. 3 (2000): 997–1011.

38. Li, *Liang An*, 326–377; "KMT Gives Boot to Hu for Talking to Reds," *Taiwan Today*, September 26, 1988.

39. Khan, *Haunted by Chaos*; Mark Arax, "Rooted in Taiwan Connection: The Plot to Kill Henry Liu—Slayers Confess Details," *Los Angeles Times*, March 3, 1985; Taylor, *Generalissimo's Son*; Bryan Curtis, *Taiwan Releases Prisoners*, January 1, 1991, UPI, https://www.upi.com/Archives/1991/01/01/Taiwan-releases-prisoners/3580662706000/; Ming-sho Ho, "Changing Memory of the Tiananmen Incident in Taiwan: From Patriotism to Universal Values (1989–2019)," *China Information* 36, no. 1 (November 24, 2020): 90–111, https://doi.org/10.1177/0920203X20971454; Eric Pace, "Chiang Ching-kuo Dies at 77, Ending a Dynasty on Taiwan," *New York Times*, January 14, 1988, www.nytimes.com/1988/01/14/obituaries/chiang-ching-kuo-dies-at-77-ending-a-dynasty-on-taiwan.html.

40. Pace, "Chiang Ching-kuo Dies"; Taylor, *Generalissimo's Son*; Tucker, *Strait Talk*.

41. Taylor, *Generalissimo's Son*; Pace, "Chiang Ching-kuo Dies."

42. Lee Teng-hui, *Jian zheng Taiwan: Jiang Jingguo zong tong yu wo* (Taipei: Taibei Xian Xindian Shi: Yun chen wen hua shi ye gu fen you xian gong si; Guo shi guan, 2004); Lee

Teng-hui, *The Road to Democracy: Taiwan's Pursuit of Identity* (Tokyo: PHP Institute, 1999); Taylor, *Generalissimo's Son*. Lee himself is still crying out for the biography he deserves.

43. Lee, *Jian zheng Taiwan*, 258. See also Taylor, *The Generalissimo's Son*.

44. Information here and in preceding paragraph from Lee, *Road to Democracy*; "Lee Teng-hui (7th–9th Terms)," Presidents Since 1947, Office of the President Republic of China (Taiwan), https://english.president.gov.tw/Page/86. For the ins and outs of Lee's political maneuvering, see J. Bruce Jacobs, "Democratisation in Taiwan Revisited," *Asian Studies Review* 21, no. 2–3 (1997): 149–157, https://doi.org/10.1080/03147539708713169. On the National Affairs Conference, in addition to Jacobs, see *Hearing Before the Subcommittee on Asian and Pacific Affairs of the Committee on Foreign Affairs House of Representatives: One Hundred First Congress, Second Session, October 11, 1990* (Washington, DC: US Government Printing Office, 1991), https://digitalcommons.law.umaryland.edu/cgi/viewcontent.cgi?article=1025&context=cong_test. On the Wild Lily movement, Han Cheung, "Taiwan in Time: The 'Communist Rebellion' Finally Ends," *Taipei Times*, April 25, 2021, www.taipeitimes.com/News/feat/archives/2021/04/25/2003756299. On Hau, see the obituary at Aaron Tu and Jake Chung, "Former Premier Hau Pei-tsun Passes Away at Age 100," *Taipei Times*, March 31, 2020, www.taipeitimes.com/News/taiwan/archives/2020/03/31/2003733717.

45. Additional Articles of the Constitution of the Republic of China, Office of the President, June 10, 2005, https://law.moj.gov.tw/ENG/LawClass/LawAll.aspx?pcode=A0000002; Lee Teng-hui, "Building a Democracy for Unification," *World Affairs* 155, no. 3 (1993): 130–131, https://heinonline.org/HOL/LandingPage?handle=hein.journals/wrldaf155&div=28&id=&page=.

46. Lee, "Building a Democracy"; Lin, *Taiwan's China Dilemma*; Lee, *Road to Democracy*.

47. Lee, *Road to Democracy*. See also Tucker, *Strait Talk*; and Jyh-Jia Chen, "Reforming Textbooks, Reshaping School Knowledge: Taiwan's Textbook Deregulation in the 1990s," *Pedagogy, Culture & Society* 10, no. 1 (2002), 39–72, doi.org/10.1080/14681360200200129.

48. Li, *Liang An*.

49. The best account is Tucker, *Strait Talk*. My interpretation of Lee's skill and congressional motivations differs slightly from hers but follows her basic narrative. The idea that there comes a time when a great power cannot be pushed around anymore was one I got from Paul Kennedy, who got it from A. J. P. Taylor.

50. "Pres. Lee Teng-Hui, Cornell University Commencement Address, June 9, 1995," USC US-China Institute, https://china.usc.edu/pres-lee-teng-hui-cornell-university-commencement-address-june-9-1995. On China and democracy, see Merle Goldman, *Sowing the Seeds of Democracy in China: Political Reform in the Deng Xiaoping Era* (Cambridge, MA: Harvard University Press, 1995).

51. Robert Ross, "The 1995–96 Taiwan Strait Confrontation: Coercion, Credibility, and the Use of Force," *International Security* 25, no. 2 (2000): 87–123.

52. National Security Council and NSC Records Management System, "Declassified Documents Regarding President Jiang Zemin of China," *Clinton Digital Library*,

accessed November 25, 2023, https://clinton.presidentiallibraries.us/items/show/118735; Ross, "The 1995–96 Taiwan Strait Confrontation." See also Khan, *Haunted by Chaos*. The account of the 1995–1996 crisis here draws on these sources.

53. Accounts abound. See Tun-jen Cheng, "Taiwan in 1996: From Euphoria to Melodrama," *Asian Survey* 37, no. 1 (1997): 43–51; Patrick Tyler, "Taiwan's Leader Wins Its Election and a Mandate," *New York Times*, March 24, 1996.

54. Ross, "1995–96 Taiwan Strait Confrontation"; Khan, *Haunted by Chaos*.

55. Lee, *Road to Democracy*, 131; Barton Gellman, "US and China Nearly Came to Blows in '96," *Washington Post*, June 21, 1998.

CHAPTER 4: THE HARDENING LINE

1. The phrase was coined by Robert Zoellick in a speech, "Whither China? From Membership to Responsibility," to the National Committee on US-China Relations in 2005, https://www.ncuscr.org/wp-content/uploads/2020/04/migration_Zoellick_remarks _notes06_winter_spring.pdf.

2. "Memorandum of Conversation—Vice President Al Gore and President Jiang Zemin of China," November 16, 1998, Clinton Digital Library, https://clinton.presidential libraries.us/items/show/101542; John Pomfret, "Taiwanese Negotiator, Jiang Meet in Beijing," *Washington Post*, October 19, 1998, www.washingtonpost.com/wp-srv/inatl /longterm/china/stories/meeting101998.htm. On Clinton's exchanges with Jiang, see Khan, *Hauntedby Chaos*.

3. Lee, *Road to Democracy*, 120–133; Lijun Sheng, "Lee Teng-hui and the 'Two-States' Theory," in *China and Taiwan: Cross-Strait Relations Under Chen Shui-bian* (Singapore: ISEAS-Yusof Ishak Institute, 2002), 11–39.

4. "Lee Teng-hui (7th–9th Terms)"; Han Cheung, "Taiwan in Time: 228, After the Apology," *Taipei Times*, February 24, 2019, www.taipeitimes.com/News/feat/archives /2019/02/24/2003710307.

5. "Chen Shui-bian (10th–11th Terms)," Presidents Since 1947, Office of the President Republic of China (Taiwan), https://english.president.gov.tw/Page/87; John F. Copper, *Taiwan's 2000 Presidential and Vice Presidential Election: Consolidating Democracy and Creating a New Era of Politics* (Baltimore: University of Maryland School of Law, 2000), https://digitalcommons.law.umaryland.edu/cgi/viewcontent.cgi?article=1156&context =mscas. On the DPP's development, see Shelley Rigger, *From Opposition to Power* (Boulder, CO: Lynne Rienner, 2001).

6. Zhu Rongji press conference, March 15, 2000, www.gov.cn/gongbao/content /2000/content_60076.htm.

7. See Copper, *Taiwan's 2000 Presidential and Vice Presidential Election*.

8. Chen Shui-bian, "Taiwan Stands Up: Presidential Inauguration Address," May 20, 2000, USC US-China Institute, https://china.usc.edu/chen-shui-bian-"taiwan-stands -presidential-inauguration-address"-may-20-2000.

9. On factions within the DPP, Rigger, *From Opposition to Power*, is excellent. On the Taiwan Solidarity Union, see Lin Chieh-yu and Crystal Hsu, "Party with Ties to Lee

Picks Name," *Taipei Times*, July 25, 2001, https://www.taipeitimes.com/News/front/archi ves/2001/07/25/0000095588.

10. Tucker, *Strait Talk*.

11. Bush cited in Tucker, *Strait Talk*, and Shirley A. Kan, "China/Taiwan: Evolution of the 'One China' Policy—Key Statements from Washington, Beijing, and Taipei," Congressional Research Service, June 1, 2004, www.everycrsreport.com/files/20040601 _RL30341_cc47b6416bec38f7e036fd8ad823c752ed9f5957.pdf; AP, "Taiwan Welcomes Powell Clarification," NBC News, October 28, 2004, www.nbcnews.com/id/wbna6353727.

12. Han Cheung, "Taiwan in Time: The Dawn of the Referendum Era," *Taipei Times*, December 2, 2018, www.taipeitimes.com/News/feat/archives/2018/12/02/2003705330.

13. These developments were well covered by the press at the time. For an overview, see John F. Copper, "Taiwan's 2004 Legislative Election: Putting it in Perspective," *Maryland Series in Contemporary Asian Studies* 2004, no. 4; John F. Copper, "Taiwan's 2004 Presidential and Vice Presidential Election: Democracy's Consolidation or Devolution?," *Maryland Series in Contemporary Asian Studies* 2004, no. 1, https://digitalcommons.law. umaryland.edu/cgi/viewcontent.cgi?article=1175&context=mscas.

14. CGTN, "Xi Jinping Meets with Former KMT Chairman Lien Chan," YouTube, July 13, 2018, www.youtube.com/watch?v=ESqzVqMxESA; Khan, *Haunted by Chaos*.

15. Lee, *Road to Democracy*.

16. Jane Rickards, "Protesters Call on Taiwan's Leader to Quit, Chen Urged to Take Responsibility for Alleged Wrongdoing by Relatives, Aides," *Washington Post*, September 9, 2006; Tania Branigan, "Taiwan Court Jails Former President for Corruption," *Guardian*, September 11, 2009.

17. Ma Yingjeou and Xiao Xucen, *Ba nian zhi zheng hui yi lu* (Taibei Shi: Yuan jian tian xia wen hua chu ban gu fen you xian gong si, 2018), 170, 431.

18. Ma and Xiao, *Ba nian zhi zheng hui yi lu*, 117–128. On the ECFA, the best source is Lin, *Taiwan's China Dilemma*.

19. Ma and Xiao, *Ba nian zhi zheng hui yi lu*, 126.

20. Ma and Xiao, *Ba nian zhi zheng hui yi lu*, 171–175.

21. My thoughts here were provoked in part by Bill Emmott.

22. AP, "Costa Rica Breaks Relations with Taiwan," NBC News, June 7, 2007, www .nbcnews.com/id/wbna19080068; author's conversations with Costa Ricans and Taiwanese fishermen; Randall Arauz, "Sharks and Fisheries: Costa Rica," WFN, https://whitleyaward.org/winners/sharks-fisheries-costa-rica/.

23. Lin, *Taiwan's China Dilemma*. This is the indispensable work on contemporary China-Taiwan relations. No one interested in international affairs can afford to be without it.

24. "Lee Teng-hui Endorses Tsai Ing-wen in Open Letter," January 11, 2012, Kuomintang Official Website, www1.kmt.org.tw/english/page.aspx?type=article&mnum=112&anum=10738; Chris Wang and Shih Hsiu-chuan, "2012 Elections: DPP Grateful for Lee

Teng-hui Endorsement," *Taipei Times*, January 12, 2012, www.taipeitimes.com/News/front/archives/2012/01/12/2003523020.

25. The best guides here are Syaru Shirley Lin, "Sunflowers and Umbrellas: Government Responses to Student-led Protests in Taiwan and Hong Kong," Asan Forum, December 10, 2015, https://theasanforum.org/sunflowers-and-umbrellas-government-responses-to-student-led-protests-in-taiwan-and-hong-kong/; and Ming-sho Ho, *Challenging Beijing's Mandate of Heaven: Taiwan's Sunflower Movement and Hong Kong's Umbrella Movement* (Philadelphia, PA: Temple University Press, 2019).

26. Lin, "Sunflowers and Umbrellas"; Xiao Ye et al., *Cong women de yanjing kan jian daoyu tianguang* (Taipei: Youlu wen hua shiye you xian gong si, 2014), 293.

27. Lin, "Sunflowers and Umbrellas"; Xiao et al., *Cong women de yanjing*, 293; Ming-sho Ho, "Occupy Congress in Taiwan: Political Opportunity, Threat, and the Sunflower Movement," *Journal of East Asian Studies* 15, no. 1 (2015): 69–97.

28. Ma and Xiao, *Ba nian zhi zheng hui yi lu*, 304–333.

29. On the difference between Xi and his predecessors, see Khan, *Haunted by Chaos*. On Hong Kong, see Louisa Lim, *Indelible City: Dispossession and Defiance in Hong Kong* (New York: Riverhead Books, 2022), and Ho, *Challenging Beijing's Mandate of Heaven*.

30. Anna Beth Keim, "Those Taiwanese Blues," *ChinaFile*, January 13, 2016, www.chinafile.com/reporting-opinion/features/those-taiwanese-blues.

31. Ma and Xiao, *Ba nian zhi zheng hui yi lu*, 360–389.

32. "President Tsai," President & Vice President, Office of the President Republic of China (Taiwan), https://english.president.gov.tw/Page/40; Anna Fifield, Robin Kwong, and Kathrin Hille, "US Concerned About Taiwan Candidate," *Financial Times*, September 15, 2011, www.ft.com/content/f926fd14-df93-11e0-845a-00144feabdc0#axzz3eeXlcwfN.

33. For an insider's account, see Kurt Campbell, *The Pivot: The Future of American Statecraft in Asia* (London: Hachette UK, 2016).

34. Tom Phillips, Nicola Smith, and Nicky Woolf, "Trump's Phone Call with Taiwan President Risks China's Wrath," *Guardian*, December 3, 2016, www.theguardian.com/us-news/2016/dec/03/trump-angers-beijing-with-provocative-phone-call-to-taiwan-president; Chinese Foreign Minister, "FM: Trump-Tsai Phone Call Will Not Change One-China Situation," news release, December 3, 2016, www.china.org.cn/world/2016-12/03/content_39842086.htm; Caren Bohan and David Brunnstrom, "Trump Says U.S. Not Necessarily Bound by 'One China' Policy," Reuters, December 11, 2016, www.reuters.com/article/us-usa-trump-china/trump-says-u-s-not-necessarily-bound-by-one-china-policy-idUSKBN1400TY.

35. "Timeline: Trump Questions Then Honors 'One China' Policy," Reuters, February 10, 2017, www.reuters.com/article/us-usa-trump-china-xi-timeline/timeline-trump-questions-then-honors-one-china-policy-idUSKBN15P0OQ.

36. Khan, *Haunted by Chaos*; Reuters, "Trump Says He Could Intervene in the Case Against Huawei CFO if It Helps US-China Deal," CNBC, December 11, 2018, www.cnbc.com/2018/12/12/huawei-cfo-arrest-trump-could-intervene-if-it-helps-us-china-deal.html.

37. John Hendel, "Republicans Soften ZTE Ban in Concession to Trump," *Politico*, July 20, 2018, www.politico.com/story/2018/07/20/congress-zte-ban-trump-734955.

38. White House, "National Security Strategy of the United States," December 2017, https://trumpwhitehouse.archives.gov/wp-content/uploads/2017/12/NSS-FInal-12-18-2017-0905.pdf.

39. Richard Haas and David Sacks, "American Support for Taiwan Must Be Unambiguous," *Foreign Affairs*, September 2, 2020.

40. Nahal Toosi and Laura Seligman, "Trump Seizes a New Cudgel to Bash China: Taiwan," *Politico*, May 21, 2020, www.politico.com/news/2020/05/21/trump-cudgel-china-taiwan-274160; Edward Wong, "U.S. Tries to Bolster Taiwan's Status, Short of Recognizing Sovereignty," *New York Times*, August 17, 2020, www.nytimes.com/2020/08/17/us/politics/trump-china-taiwan-hong-kong.html; White House, "U.S. Strategic Framework for the Indo-Pacific," declassified January 5, 2021, https://trumpwhitehouse.archives.gov/wp-content/uploads/2021/01/IPS-Final-Declass.pdf; US Department of State, "A Free and Open Indo-Pacific: Advancing a Shared Vision," November 4, 2019, www.state.gov/wp-content/uploads/2019/11/Free-and-Open-Indo-Pacific-4Nov2019.pdf; Taiwan Allies International Protection and Enhancement Initiative (TAIPEI) Act of 2019, S.1678, 116th Cong. (2019), www.congress.gov/bill/116th-congress/senate-bill/1678/text.

41. Tseng-Chang Su, "DPP's Defense Agenda," Defense Policy Blue Paper no. 1, New Frontier Foundation, June 2023, www.ustaiwandefense.com/tdnswp/wp-content/uploads/2013/06/20130606_DPP_Defense_Blue_Paper_1.pdf; Defense Policy Advisory Committee, "China's Military Threats Against Taiwan in 2025," Defense Policy Blue Paper no. 5, New Frontier Foundation, March 2014, www.ustaiwandefense.com/tdnswp/wp-content/uploads/2014/03/20140303_DPP_Defense_Blue_Paper_5.pdf; Defense Policy Advisory Committee, "Preparing the Development of Indigenous Defense Industry," Defense Policy Blue Paper no. 12, New Frontier Foundation, May 2015, www.ustaiwandefense.com/tdnswp/wp-content/uploads/2014/12/20150526_DPP_Defense_Blue_Paper_12.pdf; David An, Matt Schrader, and Ned Collins-Chase, "Taiwan's Indigenous Defense Industry: Centralized Control of Abundant Suppliers," Global Taiwan Institute, May 2018, https://globaltaiwan.org/wp-content/uploads/2022/08/GTI-TW-Indig-Defense-Occasional-Report-May-2018-final.pdf; Johnson Lai and Huizhong Wu, "Taiwan Launches the Island's First Domestically Made Submarine for Testing," AP, September 28, 2023, https://apnews.com/articletaiwan-domestic-submarine-tests-cd69c0be2dfc0acac949ee797130558e; "Taiwan: Issues for Congress," *Congressional Research Service*, October 30, 2017, https://crsreports.congress.gov/product/pdf/R/R44996; "Taiwan: Defense and Military Issues," *Congressional Research Service*, September 19, 2023, https://crsreports.congress.gov/product/pdf/IF/IF12481#:~:text=share%20of%20gross%20domestic%20product,a%2010%25%20increase%20from%202022.

42. Lin, *Taiwan's China Dilemma*; Wei (Azim) Hung, "The New Southbound Policy: Where Do We Go from Here?," *New Bloom*, March 6, 2020, https://newbloommag.net/2020/03/06/nsp-directions-assessment/; author's conversations with Japanese business people.

43. Hunter Marston and Richard C. Bush, "Taiwan's Engagement with Southeast Asia Is Making Progress Under the New Southbound Policy," Brookings, July 30, 2018, www

.brookings.edu/opinions/taiwans-engagement-with-southeast-asia-is-making-progress-under-the-new-southbound-policy/; author's observations; "China Unhappy as Philippines Signs Investment Deal with Taiwan," Reuters, December 8, 2017, www.reuters .com/article/us-china-taiwan-philippines/china-unhappy-as-philippines-signs-investment -deal-with-taiwan-idUSKBN1E217F; Evelyn Cheng, "Taiwan's Trade with China Is Far Bigger Than Its Trade with the U.S.," CNBC, August 4, 2022, www.cnbc.com/2022/08/05 /taiwans-trade-with-china-is-far-bigger-than-its-trade-with-the-us.html.

44. Liu Lirong, "Tsai Ing-wen Zongtong jiu zhiyan shuo Zhong ying wen quan wen," CNA, May 20, 2016, www.cna.com.tw/news/firstnews/201605205012.aspx; Department of Information Services, Executive Yuan, "Progress Hailed in Historical and Transitional Justice for Indigenous Peoples," news release, August 1, 2018, https://english.ey.gov.tw/Page /61BF20C3E89B856/9fe754e7-1216-456f-b3b1-2958805c662c.

45. Courtney Donovan Smith, "President Tsai Embraces Nuanced View of Former Taiwan Dictator," *Taiwan News*, January 23, 2022, www.taiwannews.com.tw/en/news /4418935; Wen Guixiang, "Tsai Zongtong: Chiang Ching-kuo jianjue fan gong bao tai lichangshi renmin zui da gongshi," CNA, January 22, 2022, www.cna.com.tw/news /aipl/202201220050.aspx.

46. Brian Hioe, "William Lai Declares Challenge to Tsai for the DPP's 2020 Presidential Nomination," *New Bloom*, March 19, 2019, https://newbloommag.net/2019/03/19 /william-lai-challenge/; Sean Lin, "Tsai Asked Not to Run for Re-election," *Taipei Times*, January 4, 2019, www.taipeitimes.com/News/front/archives/2019/01/04/2003707304.

47. Anna Beth Keim, "As Taiwan's Election Nears, a Sense of Foreboding Grips Voters from Different Camps," *ChinaFile*, January 9, 2020, www.chinafile.com/reporting-opinion /postcard/taiwans-election-nears-sense-of-foreboding-grips-voters-different-camps.

48 "Key Dates in Hong Kong's Anti-government Protests," Reuters, June 2, 2020, www .reuters.com/article/us-hongkong-protests-anniversary-timelin/key-dates-in-hong-kongs -anti-government-protests-idUSKBN23A0QD; "Hong Kong's National Security Law: 10 Things You Need to Know," Amnesty International, July 17, 2020, www.amnesty.org/en /latest/news/2020/07/hong-kong-national-security-law-10-things-you-need-to-know/.

49. The best source on PRC disinformation is the Doublethink Lab in Taiwan. See Lilly Min-Chen Lee et al., *Deafening Whispers: China's Information Operation and Taiwan's 2020 Election* (Taipei City: Doublethink Lab, 2021), https://drive.google. com/file/d/1FW35t93GvMJ3W6rqbPhAm6lNZ4uy66jD/view; author's conversations; Lily Kuo, Taiwan election: "Tsai Ing-Wen Wins Landslide in Rebuke to China," *Guardian*, January 11, 2020, www.theguardian.com/world/2020/jan/11/taiwan-re-elects-tsai-ing -wen-as-president-in-clear-message-to-china.

50. The initial American position on UNCLOS, taken in the Reagan years, is explored in James Stavridis, "Marine Technology Transfer and the Law of the Sea," *Naval War College Review* 36, no. 4 (July–August 1983): 38–49. Additional objections to the treaty accumulated over time and are ripe for a full study.

CHAPTER 5: AFTER COVID

1. Lily Kuo, "Coronavirus: Wuhan Doctor Speaks Out Against Authorities," *Guardian*, March 11, 2020, www.theguardian.com/world/2020/mar/11/coronavirus-wuhan-doctor-ai-fen-speaks-out-against-authorities; James Griffiths, "Did Xi Jinping Know About the Coronavirus Outbreak Earlier Than First Suggested?," CNN, February 17, 2020, www.cnn.com/2020/02/17/asia/china-coronavirus-xi-jinping-intl-hnk/index.html; World Health Organization, "WHO, China Leaders Discuss Next Steps in Battle Against Coronavirus Outbreak," news release, January 28, 2020, www.who.int/news/item/28-01-2020-who-china-leaders-discuss-next-steps-in-battle-against-coronavirus-outbreak.

2. Kow-Tong Chen et al., "SARS in Taiwan: An Overview and Lessons Learned," *International Journal of Infectious Diseases* 9, no. 2 (2005): 77–85; Chien-Jen Chen, "Taiwan-US Cooperation in Public Health and Pandemic Containment," East-West Center, July 19, 2022, www.eastwestcenter.org/publications/taiwan-us-cooperation-in-public-health-and-pandemic-containment; Taiwan Centers for Disease Control, "The Facts Regarding Taiwan's Email to Alert WHO to Possible Danger of COVID-19," news release, April 11, 2020, www.cdc.gov.tw/En/Bulletin/Detail/PAD-lbwDHeN_bLa-viBOuw?typeid=158.

3. Stephen Buranyi, "The WHO v Coronavirus: Why It Can't Handle the Pandemic," *Guardian*, April 10, 2020, www.theguardian.com/news/2020/apr/10/world-health-organization-who-v-coronavirus-why-it-cant-handle-pandemic; World Health Organization, COVID-19 Virtual Press Conference, April 20, 2020, transcript, www.who.int/docs/default-source/coronaviruse/transcripts/who-audio-emergencies-coronavirus-press-conference-20apr2020.pdf; Ben Blanchard, "Taiwan Rebuffs Accusations It Racially Attacked WHO Chief," Reuters, April 9, 2020, www.reuters.com/article/us-health-coronavirus-taiwan-who/taiwan-rebuffs-accusations-it-racially-attacked-who-chief-idUSKCN21R04R.

4. Sulmaan Wasif Khan, "Wolf Warriors Killed China's Grand Strategy," *Foreign Policy*, May 28, 2021, https://foreignpolicy.com/2021/05/28/china-grand-strategy-wolf-warrior-nationalism/.

5. US Senate Committee on Finance, letter to Tedros Adhanom Ghebreyesus, April 9, 2020, www.finance.senate.gov/imo/media/doc/2020-04-09%20CEG%20letter%20to%20WHO.pdf.

6. Katie Rogers, Lara Jakes, and Ana Swanson, "Trump Defends Using 'Chinese Virus' Label, Ignoring Growing Criticism," *New York Times*, March 18, 2020, www.nytimes.com/2020/03/18/us/politics/china-virus.html; "President Trump Calls Coronavirus 'Kung Flu,'" BBC, June 24, 2020, www.bbc.com/news/av/world-us-canada-53173436; Doina Chiacu and David Brunnstrom, "Trump Says Doesn't Want to Talk to Xi, Could Even Cut China Ties," Reuters, May 14, 2020, www.reuters.com/article/us-health-coronavirus-usa-china/trump-says-doesnt-want-to-talk-to-xi-could-even-cut-china-ties-idUSKBN22Q2BD; Alex Ward, "Trump at the UN: America Is Good, China Is Bad," *Vox*, September 22, 2020, www.vox.com/world/2020/9/22/21450727/trump-unga-speech-2020-full-text-china; Lauly Li and Cheng Ting-Fang, "Taiwan's Tsai Faces Fierce China Isolation Campaign in New Term," Nikkei, May 19, 2020, https://asia.nikkei.com/Politics/Taiwan-s-Tsai-faces-fierce-China-isolation-campaign-in-new-term; Lin Chia-nan, "Taiwan Not Part of China, Pompeo Says," *Taipei Times*, November 14,

2020, www.taipeitimes.com/News/front/archives/2020/11/14/2003746883; Idrees Ali and David Brunnstrom, "Pompeo Lifts Restrictions on U.S.-Taiwan Relationship as Clock Runs out on Trump Administration," Reuters, January 9, 2021, www.reuters.com/article/us-usa-taiwan-diplomacy/pompeo-lifts-restrictions-on-u-s-taiwan-relationship-as-clock-runs-out-on-trump-administration-idUSKBN29E0Q6.

7. "New Relationship with Taiwan Approved," *CQ Almanac*, 1979, https://library.cqpress.com/cqalmanac/document.php?id=cqal79-1184415; Barack Obama, *A Promised Land* (New York: Crown, 2020).

8. White House, "Indo-Pacific Strategy of the United States," February 2022, www.whitehouse.gov/wp-content/uploads/2022/02/U.S.-Indo-Pacific-Strategy.pdf.

9. White House, "National Security Strategy," October 2022, www.whitehouse.gov/wp-content/uploads/2022/10/Biden-Harris-Administrations-National-Security-Strategy-10.2022.pdf; C. Todd Lopez, "U.S. Partnership with U.K., Australia Enhances Security," US Department of Defense, May 25, 2023, www.defense.gov/News/News-Stories/Article/Article/3407275/us-partnership-with-uk-australia-enhances-security/; White House, "Joint Statement from Quad Leaders," news release, September 24, 2021, www.whitehouse.gov/briefing-room/statements-releases/2021/09/24/joint-statement-from-quad-leaders/; Loveday Morris et al., "China and Russia Are Using Coronavirus Vaccines to Expand Their Influence. The U.S. Is on the Sidelines," *Washington Post*, November 24, 2020, www.washingtonpost.com/world/vaccine-russia-china-influence/2020/11/23/b93daaca-25e5-11eb-9c4a-0dc6242c4814_story.html.

10. "Full Transcript of ABC News' George Stephanopoulos' Interview with President Joe Biden," ABC News, August 19, 2021, https://abcnews.go.com/Politics/full-transcript-abc-news-george-stephanopoulos-interview-president/story?id=79535643.

11. John Ruwitch, "Biden, Again, Says U.S. Would Help Taiwan if China Attacks," NPR, September 19, 2022, www.npr.org/2022/09/19/1123759127/biden-again-says-us-would-help-taiwan-if-china-attacks.

12. Taiwan Policy Act of 2022, S.4428, 117th Cong. (2022), www.congress.gov/bill/117th-congress/senate-bill/4428/text; US Senate Foreign Relations Committee, "Chairman Menendez Announces Historic Inclusion of Taiwan Legislation in Annual Defense Bill," news release, December 7, 2022, www.foreign.senate.gov/press/dem/release/chairman-menendez-announces-historic-inclusion-of-taiwan-legislation-in-annual-defense-bill; Patricia Zengerle and Mike Stone, "U.S. Lawmakers Authorize $800 Million More for Ukraine in Defense Bill," Reuters, December 7, 2022, www.reuters.com/world/us-lawmakers-authorize-800-million-more-ukraine-defense-bill-2022-12-07/.

13. Melissa Zhu, "Nancy Pelosi's Long History of Opposing Beijing," BBC, August 2, 2022, www.bbc.com/news/world-asia-china-62343675; Phelim Kine, "How Biden Bungled the Pelosi Trip," *Politico*, August 3, 2022, www.politico.com/news/2022/08/03/biden-pelosi-taiwan-trip-beijing-00049625; "Chinese Nationalist Commentator Deletes Pelosi Tweet After Twitter Blocks Account," Reuters, July 30, 2022, www.reuters.com/world/china/chinese-nationalist-commentator-deletes-pelosi-tweet-after-twitter-blocks-2022-07-30/.

14. Liu Xuanzun, "PLA Sent Nearly 200 Aircraft Near Taiwan in Record Month," *Global Times*, November 1, 2021, www.globaltimes.cn/page/202111/1237849.shtml; AP, "US Military Makes Plans for Nancy Pelosi's Potential Taiwan Visit," *Guardian*, July 27, 2022, www.theguardian.com/us-news/2022/jul/27/nancy-pelosi-taiwan-us-military -security. For a summary of the Hainan spy plane incident, see Khan, *Haunted by Chaos*.

15. Khushboo Razdan, "Nancy Pelosi Criticised for Including Son in Taiwan Delega- tion," *South China Morning Post*, August 13, 2022, www.scmp.com/news/china/diplomacy /article/3188767/us-house-speaker-draws-criticism-including-son-taiwan; Wang Qi and Zhang Han, "DPP Authorities Urged to Explain Financial Relationship After Pelosi's Son Found to Be Among Her Delegation," *Global Times*, August 13, 2022, www.globaltimes.cn /page/202208/1272871.shtml.

16. Kelly Hooper, Lara Seligman, and Paul McLeary, "China Sends Warships to Surround Taiwan Amid Pelosi Visit," *Politico*, August 2, 2022, www.politico.com/news/2022/08/02/ pelosi-lands-in-taiwan-00049234; David Rising, "China's Response to Pelosi Visit a Sign of Future Intentions," AP, August 19, 2022, https://apnews.com/article/taiwan-china-beijing -congress-8857910a1e44cefa70bc4dfd184ef880; Jessie Yeung, "China Suspends Cooperation with US on Range of Issues, Sanctions Pelosi Over Taiwan Trip," CNN, August 5, 2022, www.cnn.com/2022/08/05/asia/nancy-pelosi-taiwan-china-tokyo-intl-hnk/index.html.

17. Ellen Mitchell, "General's Memo Spurs Debate: Could China Invade Taiwan by 2025?," *Hill*, February 2, 2023, https://thehill.com/policy/defense/3840337-generals -memo-spurs-debate-could-china-invade-taiwan-by-2025/; Helen Davidson, "China Could Invade Taiwan in Next Six Years, Top US Admiral Warns," *Guardian*, March 10, 2021, www.theguardian.com/world/2021/mar/10/china-could-invade-taiwan-in-next-six -years-top-us-admiral-warns; "US Commander Pushes Back Against Colleagues 'Guess- ing' Taiwan Invasion Date," *Financial Times*, April 18, 2023, www.ft.com/content/753bec2b -9c55-49a8-9d34-7c286af505f3.

18. Ben Westcott and Steven Jiang, "China Is Embracing a New Brand of Foreign Pol- icy. Here's What Wolf Warrior Diplomacy Means," CNN, May 29, 2020, www.cnn.com /2020/05/28/asia/china-wolf-warrior-diplomacy-intl-hnk/index.html; Khan, "Wolf War- riors"; Michelle Nichols and Steve Holland, "U.S.-China Tensions Take Center Stage at U.N. as Trump Accuses Beijing of Unleashing 'Plague,'" Reuters, September 22, 2022, www .reuters.com/article/uk-un-assembly-idUKKCN26D2FM; Jessica Chen Weiss, "China's Self-Defeating Nationalism," *Foreign Affairs*, July 16, 2020, www.foreignaffairs.com/articles /china/2020-07-16/chinas-self-defeating-nationalism.

19. "Xinhua Headlines: Xi Says 'China Must Be, Will Be Reunified' as Key Anniversary Marked," Xinhua, January 2, 2019, www.xinhuanet.com/english/2019-01/02/c_137714898 .htm; Teddy Ng, "Update: Xi Jinping Says Efforts Must Be Made to Close the China-Taiwan Political Divide," *South China Morning Post*, October 6, 2013, www.scmp.com/news /china/article/1325761/xi-jinping-says-political-solution-taiwan-cant-wait-forever; Yew Lun Tian and Tony Munroe, "China's Xi Clinches Third Term, Packs Leadership with Loyalists," Reuters, October 24, 2022, www.reuters.com/world/china/chinas-com munist-party-politburo-standing-committee-unveiled-2022-10-23/; Yew Lun Tian and Ben Blanchard, "China Will Never Renounce Right to Use Force Over Taiwan, Xi Says,"

Reuters, October 16, 2022, www.reuters.com/world/china/xi-china-will-never-renounce
-right-use-force-over-taiwan-2022-10-16/. On the response in Taiwan, see Chen Yu-fu
and Liu Tzu-hsuan, "Taipei Slams Xi's Speech on Taiwan," *Taipei Times*, October 17,
2022, https://www.taipeitimes.com/News/front/archives/2022/10/17/2003787171.

20. Helen Davidson and Verna Yu, "Anti-CCP Protest and Lockdown Fears Fuel China
Tensions Before Congress," *Guardian*, October 13, 2022; Kathy Huang and Mengyu Han,
"Chinese Domestic Protests Go International," Council on Foreign Relations, October 24, 2022,
www.cfr.org/blog/chinese-domestic-protests-go-international; Erin Hale and Andy Peñafuerte,
"China's COVID Rebellion," *Al Jazeera*, December 22, 2022, www.aljazeera.com/economy
/longform/2022/12/22/the-protests-that-exposed-cracks-in-chinas-middle-class-dream.

21. Julie Zhu, Yew Lun Tian, and Engen Tham, "Insight: How China's New No. 2
Hastened the End of Xi's Zero-COVID Policy," Reuters, March 3, 2023, www.reuters.com
/world/china/how-chinas-new-no2-hastened-end-xis-zero-covid-policy-2023-03-03/.
Explorations of the mandate of heaven and its loss abound. See Timothy Brook, *Great
State: China and the World* (New York: Harper, 2020), for a thought-provoking example.

22. Ministry of Foreign Affairs of the People's Republic of China, "Full Text: 2023 New
Year Address by President Xi Jinping," news release, December 31, 2022, www.fmprc.gov.cn
/eng/zxxx_662805/202212/t20221231_10999475.html.

23. Ministry of Foreign Affairs of the People's Republic of China, "Wang Yi: To
Safeguard Peace Across the Taiwan Strait, We Must Resolutely Oppose 'Taiwan Independence,'" news release, February 18, 2023, www.fmprc.gov.cn/mfa_eng/zxxx_662805/202302
t20230222_11029275.html; Keoni Everington, "MAC Blasts Wang Yi's Claim Taiwan Is
Part of China," *Taiwan News*, February 21, 2023, https://www.taiwannews.com.tw/en
/news/4817023#:~:text=%27Taiwan%20has%20never%20been%20part,be%20in%20the
%20future%27%3A%20MAC&text=TAIPEI%20(Taiwan%20News)%20—%20Taiwan
%27s,Taiwan%20is%20part%20of%20China.

24. AP, "China Decries U.S. Decision to Shoot Down Suspected Spy Balloon," PBS,
February 6, 2023, www.pbs.org/newshour/politics/china-decries-u-s-decision-to-shoot-down
-suspected-spy-balloon; AP, "Taiwan Threatens to Shoot Down Any Chinese Balloons,"
VOA, February 14, 2023, www.voanews.com/a/taiwan-threatens-to-shoot-down-any
-chinese-balloons/6962649.html; "Second Spy Balloon Spotted Over Latin America, Says
Pentagon, as Blinken Postpones China Trip," *Guardian*, February 4, 2023, www.theguardian
.com/us-news/2023/feb/04/second-spy-balloon-spotted-over-latin-america-says-pentagon
-as-blinken-postpones-china-trip; Thomas Mackintosh and Kathryn Armstrong, "Chuck
Schumer: Two More Flying Objects Shot Down Were Likely Balloons," BBC, February 12,
2023, www.bbc.com/news/world-us-canada-64614098; "Mystery Surrounds Objects Shot
Down by US Military," BBC, February 13, 2023, www.bbc.com/news/world-us-canada
-64620064; Julian Borger and Helen Davidson, "US Secretary of State Postpones China Visit
After Spy Balloon Flies Over Montana," *Guardian*, February 3, 2023, www.theguardian
.com/us-news/2023/feb/03/china-spy-balloon-secretary-of-state-trip-postponed.

25. For one trainee's description see Chin Hsueh, "Taiwanese Compulsory Military
Service Should Be Improved, Not Extended," *Financial Times*, June 23, 2022, www.ft
.com/content/7bdfadf0-f3fb-4bb5-9b93-3ddc845c5e72; Kelvin Chen, "Taiwan's Kuma

Academy Holds 1st Session Simulating War," *Taiwan News*, January 17, 2023, www.taiwan news.com.tw/en/news/4783652; Yang Zhiqiang and Kung Delian, "Tsai zhengfu tui zhong bang guofang gaige," *Baodao zhe*, December 26, 2022, www.twreporter.org/a/national -defense-reform-obligatory-military-service-extension; Wayne Chang, "Taiwan to Allow Women into Military Reserve Force Training as China Fears Grow," CNN, January 18, 2023, www.cnn.com/2023/01/18/asia/taiwan-women-military-reserve-intl-hnk-ml/index .html.

26. Defense Policy Advisory Committee, "New Generation of Soldiers," Defense Policy Blue Paper no. 6, New Frontier Foundation, August 2014,www.ustaiwandefense .com/tdnswp/wp-content/uploads/2014/03/20140822_DPP_Defense_Blue_Paper_6 .pdf; "Mixed Reaction Over Pay Raise with Military Service Extension," *Focus Taiwan*, December 28, 2022, https://focustaiwan.tw/society/202212280005; "Taiwan Counts on Military Conscription Reform to Deter China Invasion," *Financial Times*, January 1, 2023, www.ft.com/content/c8762364-da8f-4543-a440-1ea72ccfabbf.

27. "Pig Guts Fly as Taiwan Lawmakers Brawl Over US Pork Imports," BBC, November 27, 2020, www.bbc.com/news/world-asia-55097091; Shelley Shan, "Pork Import Ban Referendum Fails," *Taipei Times*, December 19, 2021, www.taipeitimes.com/News/taiwan /archives/2021/12/19/2003769850; US Trade Representative, *2021 National Trade Estimate Report on Foreign Trade Barriers* (Washington, DC: Executive Office of the President, 2021), https://ustr.gov/sites/default/files/files/reports/2021/2021NTE.pdf.

28. Eric Cheung, "Taiwan's President Billed Midterms as All About China. Now She's Resigning as Party Chief," CNN, November 27, 2022, www.cnn.com/2022/11/27/asia /taiwan-election-analysis-intl-hnk/index.html.

29. "Ex-president Ma: 2024 Vote a Choice of War or Peace," *Focus Taiwan*, January 1, 2023, https://focustaiwan.tw/politics/202301010007.

30. "Three Mini Links Resume Services Between Taiwan and China," *Taiwan Today*, January 9, 2023, https://taiwantoday.tw/news.php?unit=10&post=231345; Office of the President Republic of China (Taiwan), "President Tsai Delivers 2023 New Year's Address," news release, January 1, 2023, https://english.president.gov.tw/NEWS/6421.

31. Nicoco Chan, "'We Are All Chinese,' Former Taiwan President Says While Visiting China," Reuters, March 28, 2023, www.reuters.com/world/asia-pacific/we-are-all-chinese -former-taiwan-president-says-while-visiting-china-2023-03-28/; AP, "Ma Ying-jeou Visits Sun Yat-sen Site in Nanjing," *Taipei Times*, March 29, 2023, www.taipeitimes.com/News /taiwan/archives/2023/03/29/2003796927; Chung Li-hua, "Ma Ying-jeou Belittled on China Trip, Academics Say," *Taipei Times*, April 9, 2023, www.taipeitimes.com/News/taiwan/ archives/2023/04/09/2003797596.

32. Office of the President Republic of China (Taiwan), "President Tsai Meets US House Speaker Kevin McCarthy and Bipartisan Group of Congress Members in California," news release, April 6, 2023, https://english.president.gov.tw/NEWS/6487; Anthony Adragna, "McCarthy, Taiwan's Leader Meet in California Despite Threats from China," *Politico*, April 5, 2023, www.politico.com/news/2023/04/05/mccarthy-taiwan-leader-his toric-meeting-00090639; "China Holds Second Day of Military Drills After Taiwan President Tsai Ing-wen's US Trip," *Financial Times*, April 9, 2023, www.ft.com/content/e25807de

-16ed-4548-a457-00664d49c366; "China Escalates Military Drills Near Taiwan and Japan," *Financial Times*, April 10, 2023, www.ft.com/content/d506eb6b-750a-47bc-bc42-81b1c2e35cba.

33. Charlie Campbell, "China Plays Long Game with Softer Response to Taiwan President Visiting U.S.," *Time*, April 6, 2023, https://time.com/6269158/tsai-ingwen-kevin-mccar thy-meeting-analysis/; "US and Philippines Launch Largest Joint Military Exercise in Decades," *Financial Times*, April 11, 2023, www.ft.com/content/893aac2b-dcc0-41b5-83b3-f192 f3fd5146. On World War I, my thoughts have been shaped in particular by Barbara Tuchman, *The Guns of August* (New York: Macmillan, 1962), and Christopher Clark, *The Sleepwalkers: How Europe Went to War in 1914* (New York: Penguin, 2012). I came to the "edge of chaos" by way of Ian Malcolm in Michael Crichton, *The Lost World* (New York: Knopf, 1995).

34. Office of the President Republic of China (Taiwan), "President Tsai Meets Delegation Led by Japanese House of Councillors Member Seko Hiroshige," news release, December 28, 2022, https://english.president.gov.tw/News/6418; Sarah Wu and Yimou Lee, "Taiwan Welcomes First Official European Parliament Delegation," Reuters, November 3, 2021, www.reuters.com/business/cop/taiwan-welcomes-first-official-european -parliament-delegation-2021-11-03/; "In Taiwan, Former UK PM Truss Warns Against Appeasing China," Reuters, May 17, 2023, www.reuters.com/world/taiwan-former-uk -pm-truss-warns-against-appeasing-china-2023-05-16/; "China Protests 'Vile' Taiwan Visit by German Minister," Reuters, March 21, 2023, www.reuters.com/world/german -minister-says-honoured-be-esteemed-partner-taiwan-2023-03-21/; Yew Lun Tian and Eduardo Baptista, "China Raps Czech President-Elect Over Taiwan Call," Reuters, January 31, 2023, www.reuters.com/world/china-slams-czech-president-elect-over-phone-call -with-taiwan-president-2023-01-31/; Office of the President Republic of China (Taiwan), "President Tsai Meets Parliamentarians from Ukraine and Lithuania," news release, October 27, 2022, https://english.president.gov.tw/NEWS/6365.

35. Elbridge Colby, "If You Want Peace, Prepare for Nuclear War," *Foreign Affairs* 97, no. 6 (2018): 25–34. See also Hal Brands and Michael Beckley, *Danger Zone: The Coming Conflict with China* (New York: W. W. Norton, 2022).

36. "US and China Hold More Trade Talks Despite Strained Ties," *Financial Times*, May 27, 2023, www.ft.com/content/5ae755b3-8d21-48ac-ab37-d9ebd654a5e2; "Secretary Antony J. Blinken and People's Republic of China President Xi Jinping Before Their Meeting," US Department of State, June 19, 2023, www.state.gov/secretary-antony-j-blinken -and-peoples-republic-of-china-president-xi-jinping-before-their-meeting/; Office of the Spokesperson, "Secretary Blinken's Visit to the People's Republic of China (PRC)," US Department of State, June 19, 2023, www.state.gov/secretary-blinkens-visit-to-the-peoples -republic-of-china-prc/; Demetri Sevastopulo and Joe Leahy, "US Controls on Investment Will Not Harm China, Yellen Tells Beijing," *Financial Times*, July 9, 2023, www.ft.com .content/29fc010c-13db-4489-8101-259fc69955c9.

37. Rupert Wingfield-Hayes, "Has Janet Yellen's Trip to Beijing Improved US-China Relations?," BBC, July 9, 2023, www.bbc.com/news/world-asia-66146889; "China's Metal Export Curbs a 'Warning' to US and Its Allies, Global Times Reports," Reuters, July 5, 2023, www.reuters.com/world/china/chinas-metal-export-curbs-warning-us-its-allies-global-times -2023-07-05/; Shigeru Seno and Mitsuru Obe, "Ron DeSantis Says Deterrence Key to

Preventing Taiwan Conflict," Nikkei, April 25, 2023, https://asia.nikkei.com/Editor-s-Picks
/Interview/Ron-DeSantis-says-deterrence-key-to-preventing-Taiwan-conflict; Robin Opsahl,
"Presidential Candidate Nikki Haley: Hold China Accountable for COVID-19," *Iowa
Capital Dispatch*, March 10, 2023, https://iowacapitaldispatch.com/2023/03/10/presiden
tial-candidate-nikki-haley-hold-china-accountable-for-covid-19/; Nicolas Camut, "Macron
Was 'Kissing Xi's Ass' in China, Trump Says," *Politico*, April 12, 2023, www.politico.eu
/article/donald-trump-emmanuel-macron-was-kissing-xi-jinping-ass-in-recent-china
-visit/. On chips, see Chris Miller, *Chip War: The Fight for the World's Most Critical Technology* (New York: Scribner, 2022).

38. Chen Yun and Jonathan Chin, "Taiwan Already Independent, Lai Says," *Taipei
Times*, January 19, 2023, www.taipeitimes.com/Newfront/archives/2023/01/19/2003792832;
Demetri Sevastopulo and Kathrin Hille, "Washington Presses Taiwan Presidential Frontrun-
ner on White House Comments," *Financial Times*, July 19, 2023.

39. Rebecca Lin, "The Cop Who Became Taiwan's Top-Rated Mayor," *CommonWealth
Magazine*, September 21, 2020, https://english.cw.com.tw/article/article.action?id=2802;
Wang Hung-kuo, Yeh Su-ping, and Frances Huang, "KMT Presidential Hopeful Opposes
'One Country, Two Systems,' Taiwan Independence," *Focus Taiwan*, May 9, 2023, https://
focustaiwan.tw/cross-strait/202305090017.

40. "Fireside Chat with Dr. Ko Wen-je, Chairman of the Taiwan People's Party and Former Mayor of Taipei," Center for Strategic and International Studies, April 20, 2023, transcript,
https://csis-website-prod.s3.amazonaws.com/s3fs-public/2023-04/230421_Wen-je_Fireside
_Chat.pdf; Yang Ming-chu and Matthew Mazzetta, "China Should Clarify Its Definition
of '1992 Consensus': Ko Wen-je," *Focus Taiwan*, June 8, 2023, https://focustaiwan.tw/cross
-strait/202306080009; Chen Chien-chih and Lo Hsin-chen, "Lai, Ko Ratcheting Up
Campaign," *Taipei Times*, July 24, 2023, https://www.taipeitimes.com/News/taiwan/arch
ives/2023/07/24/2003803659; Helen Davidson, "Foxconn Founder Terry Gou Announces
Run for Taiwan Presidency, Pledging to Fix China Ties," *Guardian*, August 28, 2023, www
.theguardian.com/world/2023/aug/28/terry-gou-foxconn-founder-taiwan-presidency
-china-ties; Brian Hioe, "Invoking Mazu, Terry Gou Declares Run for President," *New
Bloom*, April 17, 2019, https://newbloommag.net/2019/04/17/terry-guo-presidential-run/.

41. Information in the above paragraphs from author's observations; Ben Blanchard,
"Ignoring Taiwan's Complaints, More Chinese Balloons Spotted Over Strait," *Reuters*, January 7, 2024, https://www.reuters.com/world/asia-pacific/ignoring-taiwans-complaints
-more-chinese-balloons-spotted-over-strait-2024-01-08/#:~:text=China%20views%20
the%20island%20as,island%20near%20major%20air%20bases; Yimou Lee and Sarah
Wu, "China Satellite Launch Causes Pre-election Political Storm in Taiwan," *Reuters*,
January 10, 2024, https://www.reuters.com/world/asia-pacific/taiwan-does-not-consider
-china-satellite-launch-election-interference-2024-01-09/; Kathrin Hille, "China's Military Warns Against Taiwan 'Independence' Plots Ahead of Election," January 12, 2024,
https://www.ft.com/content/0dad2e92-3b0e-4e07-ba4e-b13daa06acf3; Kathrin Hille,
"Taiwan's Ruling Party Secures Presidency as Voters Defy China," January 13, 2024,
https://www.ft.com/content/bc1b9521-8381-4fb8-aebd-80846a18085d; Shelley Shan, "Ma

Not Invited to KMT Rally Following Remarks," *Taipei Times*, January 12, 2024, https://www.taipeitimes.com/News/front/archives/2024/01/12/2003811980.

EPILOGUE

1. For comparisons with World War I, see Henry Kissinger, *On China* (New York: Penguin, 2011), Brands and Beckley, *Danger Zone*, and Graham Allison, *Destined for War?: Can America and China Escape Thucydides's Trap?* (New York: Houghton Mifflin Harcourt, 2017). For a much more satisfactory account of World War I—the emphasis on agency in it has informed my own thinking here—see Clark, *Sleepwalkers*.

2. On PRC conduct in territorial disputes, see M. Taylor Fravel, *Strong Borders, Secure Nation: Cooperation and Conflict in China's Territorial Disputes* (Princeton, NJ: Princeton University Press, 2008).

3. The concept of imperial overstretch is from Kennedy, *Rise and Fall*. On Deng's ideas about security, see Khan, *Haunted by Chaos*.

4. This is a rather extreme variant of what Kevin Rudd, *The Avoidable War: The Dangers of a Catastrophic Conflict Between the US and Xi Jinping's China* (New York: PublicAffairs, 2022), calls "managed strategic competition." Much as I agree with his assessment that the alternative is not to be borne, I just cannot see American politicians agreeing to this in this climate.

5. For an assessment of the consequences of a milder version of this policy, see Robert Blackwill and Philip Zelikow, *The United States, China, and Taiwan: A Strategy to Prevent War* (New York: Council on Foreign Relations, 2021).

6. Rosella Cappella Zielinski and Samuel Gerstle, "Paying the Defense Bill: Financing American and Chinese Geostrategic Competition," *Texas National Security Review* 6, no. 2 (Spring 2023), https://tnsr.org/2023/04/paying-the-defense-bill-financing-american-and-chinese-geostrategic-competition/.

7. Taiwan Incursion Updates, Missile Defense Advocacy Alliance, November 27, 2023, https://missiledefenseadvocacy.org/missile-threat-and-proliferation/todays-missile-threat/taiwan-missile-updates/; Haley Britzky and Brad Lendon, "Taiwan War Would Be 'Devastating,' Warns US Defense Secretary Lloyd Austin as He Criticizes China at Shangri-La Security Summit," CNN, June 3, 2023, www.cnn.com/2023/06/02/asia/austin-shangri-law-dialogue-speech-taiwan-intl-hnk/index.html.

INDEX

Huang Chen, 123
Huang Hsin-jie, 145
Huang Hua, 132
Huawei, 193–194
Hu Jintao, 166, 179, 186
Hung Hsiu-chu, 187
Hu Qiuyuan, 146
Hurley, Patrick, 28–29, 35
Hu Xijin, 3, 221

identity, 30, 183, 251
indemnity, 22
independence
  Biden on, 219
  Chen Shui-bian on, 173–177
  future for, 251
  Hou position on, 243
  lack of Bush administration support
    for, 175
  Lai stance on, 242
  Mao on, 31, 249
  movement in Taiwan, 39
  threat of referendum on, 170, 174–177,
    198, 204
India
  Dalai Lama's flight to, 141
  disputed territories, 113
  as market for Taiwan, 199
  Quad, 217
  UN seat for PRC, 60
  war with China (1962), 99
indigenous peoples, 154, 201

Japan
  in Cairo Declaration, 12
  consular relations in Taiwan, 120
  leery of China, 255
  Nonproliferation Treaty, 138
  nuclear arms, 255
  parliamentary delegation visit to
    Taiwan, 238
  PRC relations, 122, 223
  Quad, 217
  recognition of Republic of China, 17

surrender (1945), 32–33
  in Taiwan, 29–32
  Taiwan ceded by Qing empire, 16
  trade with China, 23
  Treaty of San Francisco, 65
  war with China, 20–21, 23–26
  war with Qing Dynasty, 16
Jiang Qing, 123
Jiangxi soviet, 19, 49
Jiang Zemin, 186
  Clinton and, 166, 168–169
  Lee Teng-hui and, 156–157, 159
  unification, 156
jingoism, 239, 241, 254
Johnson, Lyndon, 87, 96

Kangxi, 14–15
Kaohsiung, 145
Kennan, George, 34, 42–44, 52, 55, 57, 66
Kennedy, John F., 96
Kerr, George, 40
Kerry, John, 180
Khrushchev, Nikita, 105
Kim Il-sung, 58–59, 79
Kinmen Island, 51, 69, 81–83, 86–93, 97,
    102, 105, 180, 235
Kissinger, Henry
  on basic evolution, 71, 113
  Cyrus Vance, 128–129
  on Korean War and Taiwan's fate,
    106, 108
  normalization with PRC, 120–121,
    124
  on "paralyzed President," 122
  rapprochement, US-China, 104–106,
    112, 117
  on Republican platform, 128
  on Taiwan independence
    movement, 112
  Vietnam War, 106
  visit to China (1973), 121–124
  visit to China (1974), 124–126
KMT. See Kuomintang
Koo, Wellington, 80

Credit: Anna Beth Keim

Sulmaan Wasif Khan is the Denison Chair in History and International Relations at the Fletcher School, Tufts University. He is the author of *Haunted by Chaos* and *Muslim, Trader, Nomad, Spy*. His writing has appeared in the *Economist*, *Foreign Affairs*, and *Foreign Policy*.